LUCKIEST
ENGINEER
From Farm Boy to Skunk Works
and Beyond

Robert A. Retsch

ISBN 978-1-70540-069-2 eBook 978-1-09830-417-1

ACKNOWLEDGEMENT

Writing this memoir took fourteen months of hard work, burning over 1,500 hours of evenings and weekends. It was indeed more than I had estimated but, as an engineer, I'm used to projects taking more time than initially scoped.

Getting this memoir to print reminded me of visiting the Uffizi Museum in Florence. While admiring the antiquities, especially the exquisite marble statues, I contemplated the amount of work it took to complete each of them. Someone had to sever the blocks of stone from the quarry. Sculptors removed the excess material before carving the larger features, followed by all the intricacies. Finally, hours upon countless hours were spent polishing every curve and facet. They produced amazing works of art, but I would rather write a book.

Those sculptors had teams of helpers, and like them, I had a small team that assisted me. I'd like to recognize some of the members of my team.

First, my appreciation goes to several friends and colleagues for the many hours spent providing me with valuable critiques and suggestions.

Turning to editing, I am lucky to have had three special people who offered their valuable and professional assistance. One of my few lifelong friends, John W. Marshall, helped me with the initial development, editing, publishing, and marketing. He, like those who removed excess marble from the slab, helped me reveal and convert my stream-of-consciousness-splattered draft into a framed manuscript.

Krista Haraway, a local up-and-coming freelance editor, provided line and copy editing that helped me with the chiseling of the rough and fine details, as well as providing insight from a younger reader's perspective.

Dona Pratt, with a diverse career in software design, project management, and marketing, graciously took on this novice's first-time work and contributed hundreds of hours to execute the sorely needed final polishing that elevated my mid-level grammar "engineering" draft into a professional work worthy of publishing.

Without John, Krista, and Dona, it would have been impossible to arrive at market. Thank you all.

Finally, utmost appreciation is extended to my wife Judy, who, for the past year, put up with my self-imposed confinement in our home office.

DEDICATION

Any one person's life is affected to various degrees by loved ones, friends, family, bosses, and peers. My life is no different. Many people have made an impact on me by redirecting my goals, saving my butt in troubled times, teaching me valuable lessons in life, providing opportunities along the way, and giving critical advice in times of need.

Starting with my formative years, my father, Howard, was my first influence, and he continued to be a positive one until he died. My brother Fritz's mentorship was a presence from age 8 or so until I moved to California. My mother's brother, Richard (Duane) King II, used his technical and practical knowledge to inspire and coach me.

The women in my life—my mother, two grandmothers and maternal great-grandmother—exemplified the more subtle, but important, behavior and characteristics that can't be described using an engineering vocabulary. Their contributions to my life, while not appreciated at the time, have been very much valued as an adult.

Tom Bridgen, whom we sadly lost last year, gave me employment opportunities and challenges that expanded my mechanical abilities and taught me about the broader world existing outside the farm.

From my professional career, I would say that Arnie Gunderson had the most substantive and consistent influence on my growth as an engineer.

Credit also goes to my first engineering boss, George Rogers, from Pratt & Whitney and my Lockheed boss Gary Wendt, who saw talents in me that I had not recognized.

In addition, I'd like to express my admiration for my lifelong friend, John W. Marshall; my former roommate, John Kenney; and a dear friend, Therise Doolin.

There were so many engineers that I had the great honor and privilege to know and work with during my career. Some I tried to emulate, some I looked upon in awe, many were significant contributors to our design efforts, and several are good friends. A few include a fantastic test engineer and calming force, Robert Ivanco; the absolutely brilliant engineers John Kalisz and Al Gegaregian; a wise and talented boss, Chris Fylling; an engineer's engineer, Mark O. Wise; the best stress engineer I have worked with and close friend, Tauno Kartiala; a really talented engineer who unfortunately passed way before his time, Carl Glahn; a longtime friend, Dennis Failoni; and another talented stress engineer, Steve Norman.

I have been so blessed to know and work with all of these people. I have admired their talents and tried to learn from the best of their characteristics, their tutelage, and their leadership along the way.

To all these people that I've mentioned and many more who helped me along the way, I dedicate this work.

Contents

Part 3—177

MUSINGS FROM A B-737

The vision for this memoir began one fall morning in 1983 on a company-chartered Boeing 737. It was 08:15 and I was commuting to work, sitting in a starboard side window seat. My fellow employees called the plane the "Red and White." We had just taken off from the Burbank Airport and were climbing out northbound at around 6,000 feet, crossing over the peaks of the San Gabriel Mountains. The plane was headed for the not-to-be-disclosed classified test site somewhere in the state of Nevada. It is now known as Area 51.

Reading page two of that morning's *USA TODAY,* I had just taken a sip of hot coffee handed to me by the flight attendant and placed it on the tray table of the empty middle seat. That day there were thirty-five to forty other employees on board: engineers, mechanics, analysts, and support personnel spread throughout the hundred or so available seats. Since it was early morning, the sun was just breaking over the eastern horizon and spreading warm yellow-orange rays of light through the window and across my right leg, illuminating the newspaper in my lap.

At that moment, and for some unknown reason, I paused my reading and reflected on how great life was for me!

Graduating from college at the delayed age of 29 with a mechanical engineering degree, I had been lucky enough to land a job at Lockheed

Aircraft Company in Burbank, California in their Advanced Development Projects (ADP) department, also known as the Skunk Works. The program that I was assigned to was the highly classified F-117 Stealth Tactical Fighter, later to be named Nighthawk. I was earning more money than I had ever made, in a job that I loved beyond belief, working at one of the most innovative aircraft companies in the world. I was living in a beautiful house in the central portion of the San Fernando Valley with only a twenty-minute commute to work. Working on the F-117 Program, I was surrounded by the greatest aircraft design engineers in history. Although Kelly Johnson, the founder of the Skunk Works, had retired nine years earlier, he could be seen occasionally in the halls or parking lot. Ben Rich had taken over from Mr. Johnson at ADP and was my top boss. Sometimes it felt like I was living in a history book.

I thought, *How many recent engineering grads—or any other engineers for that matter—have it this good? How many of them commute to work in a company-chartered Boeing-737? Who else has this amount of responsibility with such short tenure? Damn, I am one lucky engineer!*

It took about fifteen seconds to process all these thoughts and then it was back to my newspaper. But those thoughts stuck in my mind and I revisited that moment often throughout my career.

Fast forward a few years to a different B-737 that I boarded in 1989. This time it was a commercial airline departing from El Paso, Texas. I was on a return leg from a business meeting at White Sands Missile Test Range in New Mexico in support of the YF-22 Program. Shortly after settling into my window seat, an older dark-haired, slightly graying gentleman sat down next to me in the aisle seat. Small talk led us to our commonality in the aerospace industry. The memory of ancillary details has mostly faded, and unfortunately, I lost his business card, but I believe he worked at Honeywell. I remember him saying that he had retired twice and was on his third career. I made some small talk, not able to say anything about my work because it was classified.

What I will never forget was the wisdom he shared, embedded in words from his father. He said that when he was just 14 years old, he lost his father to cancer. His father's last words were, "Son, it looks like I cannot be there for you as you get older, but I want you to remember one important thing. He who works the hardest is the luckiest."

My fellow passenger told me that he tried to live up to the goal his father had set for him and that now, as he neared the end of his final career, he found his father's words to be true. Feeling this conversation was meaningful enough, I jotted down his words in my notebook when I got home.

After this interaction, I often thought about that day. *How did this particular personal conversation occur? I could have easily ignored his presence and read my book or magazine. Why was it so impressionable to me that I wrote it down and saved it?* At the time, these questions were unanswered. As time went on, it became clear that this encounter happened for a reason.

Most of my remaining career was spent on many development programs that contained frequent moves. Each time I transferred to a new and exciting program over the next thirty years at Lockheed, later Lockheed Martin, these two 737 events stuck with me. Each new experience was a reminder of how lucky I was.

Over time, and comparing my career to others, I felt more and more compelled to write about my experiences. But between working long hours, raising a family, building two additions on our homes in southern and northern California, completely remodeling our five-bedroom home in Pleasanton, starting a part-time business, and consulting work, I never found the time. In retrospect, time flew by like the scene in Star Wars when Hans Solo pushes the Millennium Falcon into light speed. Writing a memoir has always been on a list of things to do, but it was buried somewhere in the back of my mind's overflowing file cabinet. I never found the time nor made it a priority.

After failing my 2014 retirement, I landed a job as a Subject Matter Expert (SME) at the Missile Defenses Agency (MDA). I found myself on a business trip that finally motivated me to start writing. Ironically it was on another B-737 traveling to Chandler, Arizona. As I was settling into my seat, trying to store my book, get out my noise-canceling headphones and finesse my water bottle into in the overly small seatback pocket, I overheard a conversation in the row behind me. A gentleman asked the woman seated next to him why she was traveling. "Business," was her abrupt response before she added that she was a ghost writer. I immediately thought, *Now is the time! What was I waiting for?*

But even with the motivation to write about all the experiences under my belt, I had to ask myself, *Why Bob Retsch? Who the hell is he? What did he do to warrant a memoir?* The first, and somewhat discouraging reply to myself in this mental conversation, zeroed in on what Bob Retsch wasn't: *He ain't no Kelly Johnson, Donald Douglas or William Boeing, that's for sure!*

I definitely wasn't like any of those people. I felt like I had lived an average life from humble beginnings. I was a middle-class, Western Pennsylvania steel town guy who, with harnessed determination, a hard work ethic, and a hell-of-a-lotta "luck," was able to achieve above average goals.

However, I'm unaware of anyone fortunate enough to have worked on such a variety of programs including the J-58 Engine that powered the SR-71; the F-117 Nighthawk; the YF-22A Advanced Tactical Fighter; a stealth cruise missile; Airborne Laser; the Orion Space Capsule; SBIRS and other satellites; various missile-powered targets; reentry vehicles; the D-5 Missile; and several other lesser-known or never-to-be-revealed programs that are still classified to this day.

I was lucky to have traveled to over 160 cities and towns, seeing and having many out-of-the-ordinary experiences. And, most amazingly, I was part of creating engineering hardware and subsystems that never before existed and pushed the envelope of current technology.

Perhaps it is my ego talking, but there is this feeling that my lucky life was different from that of the average engineer, and certainly different from where it started back on the farm. Perhaps deep down inside, we all feel this way. Who knows? But for me, I am writing this memoir for different reasons and to various audiences. You, as the reader, can pass judgment on the ego part.

I have learned that individuals within any given group will experience the same event through very different lenses, depending on where they fall in a given hierarchy. Much like the levels on a hillside-terraced garden, their perceptions are pieces that together make up the whole. My best example can be found in the book *Band of Brothers* by Stephen Ambrose. His work spawned the popular and critically acclaimed HBO television series of the same name. With the fame it brought, several surviving members of Easy Company subsequently wrote books sharing their own experiences.

Ambrose's book was written from a higher-level point of view with a more strategic context. The HBO series that followed brought to life on screen this story and the characters of the period. Major Winters went on to write a book from his point of view, the leadership role perspective. Works by Don Malarkey, William Guarnere, and Edward Heffron followed, describing the same events from lower leadership positions (e.g. sergeants), as well as accounts from those who experienced the same period from the lowest ranks (private, corporal, etc.). All had an accurate perspective of the same historical event(s), yet from different angles and with different stories to tell.

My thirty-eight years as an engineer consisted of ten at the Skunk Works in Burbank, nineteen at Lockheed Martin in Sunnyvale, almost five years in Huntsville, and four-plus years as an SME at MDA. Most of those years coincided with the era of celebrated aerospace leaders like Kelly Johnson, Ben Rich, and many others. My experiences during that time of historic aerospace events were viewed through a different set of eyes than those dominating the news articles, countless books and other personal stories. This memoir is written from the trenches, much like the stories in *Band of Brothers*. Consider my musings as similar to the accounts from the lower ranks—the sergeants and corporals.

To my various readers, I have recorded these stories hoping to provide additional perspectives from this time period. Also, it is my hope that all may learn from this memoir in such a way that it will help avoid the land-mines that life inevitably plants in our paths and prevent needless loss of time, money and opportunities. More importantly, I hope others will gain a better understanding and a fuller meaning of life itself.

To young engineering students or recent graduates, I hope these writings will encourage you to work hard and become productive members of whatever program in whatever company you join. With hard work and dedication—and yes, some luck, however you define it—I know you will achieve the financial benefits we all seek as well as the biggest reward, that of personal satisfaction.

To other young readers, regardless of the profession you may seek, I hope this book will be of benefit as an inspiration to take full advantage of your known and soon-to-be-discovered abilities. To seek out your hidden talents and prosper. To assure those who doubt themselves or are reluctant to take chances in life. Failure is not what most people assume it is. Failure is an opportunity to learn and blossom.

To older readers, especially my colleagues, I've included some of the more amusing stories to produce a laugh or two as well as trigger some heart-felt reminiscing.

To my children, this is a history of how your father became who he is and how his events and experiences have shaped his life.

And to my grandchildren and others who will travel into the future, a place where I'm forbidden to go, it is my wish that you will realize the potential of what you can become by learning who I was and the life I lived. Hopefully it will challenge you to seek a career you will love and achieve what you were born to be.

Another important goal of these words is to shed light on thousands of people who humbly contributed to the amazing and historical products that Lockheed produced. Most of these professionals lived outside the limelight or within the shadows of their leaders with the silent and personal satisfaction knowing that they, collectively, were the real reason all of it was possible.

One final thought: No great work of literature will be found in these pages—no thriller—no bestseller like *The Hunt for Red October*—but the story of an engineer with a Type A personality and blessed with a tenacious work ethic, which fortunately stayed with him throughout his life. A farm boy with a natural curiosity that enticed him down many roads that opened several doors to a wealth of life experiences. A fan of the well-executed prank, often the perpetrator but gullible enough to be many times the subject.

A hard-working engineer who was damn lucky.

PART 1

Farm Boy

1

On the Farm

March 1952 is when my story began, in a small town some sixteen miles down the Ohio River from the steel city of Pittsburgh. Leetsdale is one of many towns and small cities that made up the large, industrial steel complex of Western Pennsylvania. Nineteen fifty-two was a short seven years after the end of World War II and right in the middle of the Korean War. President Truman was in the last year of his second term and Dwight D. Eisenhower was about to be elected in November.

The economy was improving, following a post-war inflationary period, and 1950 to 1960 turned out to be a prosperous time with an economic growth of 37 percent. My father, Howard Arthur Retsch, worked at Spang-Chalfant (later bought by Armco Steel), a steel plant in Ambridge, Pennsylvania, that manufactured seamless tube drill pipe. Ambridge was a thriving town a little further down the Ohio River from Leetsdale. He held various positions during his thirty-five years there before retiring as a foreman.

I arrived two years into Howard's second marriage. At my birth he was 38 and married to my mother Dolores (nee King), a much younger 22-year-old woman. My 12-year-old half-brother from my father's previous marriage,

Fritz, lived with us. A sister, Bonnie, came along two years later and a brother, Tad, one year after her. My mother must have had a significant life-changing adjustment when she married my father—a city girl two years out of high school working as a clerk in various offices, marrying a middle-aged hard-nosed man and inheriting a somewhat wild 12-year-old boy. A couple of years later, she was dragged off to the country to live on a working farm. But, being a tougher woman than I gave her credit for in my youth, she handled those changes quite well.

Mother, Dad, Fritz and me at 2 years old

When I was an infant, we lived in Leetsdale for a short period of time while my father almost single-handedly built a new house in a town called Baden, just downstream from Ambridge. We moved when I was about two and lived in this new house a short time until the Northern Lights Shopping Center was built right next door to our property. Angry that this quiet, small residential area had been invaded by a noisy multi-store shopping center (a precursor to malls) that included a twenty-five-foot steeply excavated hillside, he looked for an area more conducive to raising his small children.

When I was four, my father bought a small, fourteen-acre farm five miles due east of Ambridge. The farm was on the northern edge of the Sewickley post office region, but in the southern jurisdiction of the North Allegheny School district where I attended school until the ninth grade. Looking back, I realized how much that move to the farm shaped who I became.

The upper half of his farm was on a gently sloping hill that dropped off more steeply in the lower half. The house and barn, along with several ancillary buildings, were surrounded by a large yard in the middle of the property and hidden from the main road. Dad fenced in the upper half of the property with its many fruit trees and turned it into a pasture. He did the same with the lower half but, due to the terrain, it had limited use as a pasture. In addition to the apple, pear, peach and cherry trees, he planted a large vegetable garden, grapevines, berry bushes, and strawberry patches in the land surrounding the farmhouse. Each fall, my mother and Dad's mother would can all kinds of harvested foods for our winter consumption.

Our farm house in the early 1960s

In addition to farming, Dad worked what was called a rotating shift at the mill—first week was daylight shift (7:00 a.m.-3:00 p.m.), next week swing shift (also called 3-to-11), and the third week "night turn" (11:00 p.m.-7:00 a.m.). The fourth week then rotated back to the daylight shift. He did this for a little over thirty-four years.

He, as well as his father Fred, were typical hard-working German folks. Their work ethic was something that seemed to be passed down to their off-spring. Illustrating this trait, Dad, after working eight hard hours in the mill, would come home and tend to the many chores that a small working farm required. Those chores included plowing fields in the spring, harvesting hay in the summer and fall, planting feed corn, and raising beef cattle, chickens, and pigs. He grew a large vegetable garden every year, maintained the fruit trees, performed never-ending maintenance on farm equipment and tended to many other weekly farm chores. I admired how my father was a self-taught man who learned how to caponize chickens, butcher pigs and steers, overhaul tractors, make and smoke sausages, and weld and braze metals. And those were just a few of many skills he learned over the years.

Strangely enough, when I was almost the same age as my father, I was in a similar situation. Both my wife and I were in our second marriage, raising her four children plus one of ours. Although we were blessed with having a higher relative income than my father, affording us a more comfortable life-style, it was still tough. I understood and appreciated how hard my mother and father worked to raise our family and run a small farm.

I loved living on the farm, and to this day I harbor the fondest memories of my childhood. My sister and brother also enjoyed the outdoors both summer and winter, spending as much time outside as possible. My brother Fritz was in high school and was off pursuing other interests typical for his age. The three of us would leave the house after breakfast and not return until we were hungry. After refueling, we would go back out until dinner or dark, unless it was raining. When the cherries, peaches, apples or grapes were ripe, we were able to stay out longer, feeding off the orchards. We played neighborhood pick-up games like baseball, football and hide-n-seek, rode our two ponies, played cops and robbers, and explored wooded areas as far as three or four miles away. Another fun excursion was to walk down to the creek that ran through the lower pasture and build dams for swimming. It was simple stuff, but it was downright fun back then.

For a young kid, the farm was a wonderland with exciting new and different things happening. I loved it that every weekend, Dad had a chore, or a goal that he had set for himself, which meant there was something new to watch or help with. When extra hands were needed, friends and relatives traveled out from town to assist.

One chore, shortly after we moved to the farm, was clearing some apple tree stumps in a newly converted pasture. For this effort, instead of digging around the stumps and chopping the attached roots, Dad chose a more efficient—and more exciting for us—method. Digging a small hole under the main part of the trunk near the tap root, he stuck some dynamite in it, attached a blasting cap, and ran the wires a safe distance away to the tractor. (Back then, anyone could buy dynamite or nitroglycerin.) We all crouched down behind the tractor, and he set off the dynamite by touching the wires to the tractor battery terminals. It was literally a blast to witness those stumps and tree trunks blow up into the air. Plus, it saved a ton of labor and was better than any vacation or excursion to the city. One time he put a little too much charge in the hole, and the next-door neighbor swore it broke a couple of windows in his garage.

Another explosive time that always makes me smile when I think of it occurred late one fall when Dad was finishing off the steers he had bought the previous spring. "Finishing off" refers to feeding them a mixture of grain, corn, and molasses to fatten them up for better quality marbled meat. The steers were all in the cow barn, a long narrow building about 20-feet wide, with a feed trough along its length. Nine gorging steers lined up in a row twice each day to happily eat that sweet feed.

For some long-forgotten reason they got sick, perhaps eating too many apples or contracting some type of field bacteria. I do remember that the vet placed them on an antibiotic, causing every one of them to have explosive diarrhea. Whenever it happened, cow shit would shoot out of their rear ends like a bazooka! I'm talking high-velocity with a horizontal trajectory that traveled for a good eight feet.

So, while they started to feed, Dad made the dumb mistake of walking behind them to do something against the back wall. Just as he reached the middle of the pack, several of the steers curled their tails back and started to cut loose. Seeing the tails go up and realizing that he was trapped, he tried to make a run for it. Being on the safe side of the feeding trough, I nearly wet my pants from laughter watching him dart back and forth trying not to get nailed. I had to give him credit though—he was better on his feet than they were with their aim.

Barn fun aside, there was one aspect that really stuck out to me as a child, almost like an addiction: machinery. Lawn mower engines, tractors, our truck, hay bailers, hit-n-miss one-lungers—just about anything mechanical captured my attention. I especially loved to drive our tractors once my legs were long enough to reach the pedals. I used to bug the hell out of my father to let me drive his truck while we collected hay for the barn, or brother Fritz to let me drive his old jalopy.

I have memories clear as a bell of hanging around Dad when he overhauled the engine of his tractor, an International Harvester Super-A. Whenever he needed one or two extra hands, I eagerly assisted, knowing that he would explain how it operated. I sucked up everything he said, and for some reason those details seemed effortless to grasp.

Another memorable farm experience was the time when the apple orchard was infested with what we called Tent Caterpillars (*Malacosoma americanum*), which were extremely destructive to our apple crop. To eradicate them, Dad mixed up a batch of DDT in a large two-wheeled wooden tank/sprayer trailer. He hitched it up to the tractor's tow bar with its pump operated by the tractor's Power Take-Off (PTO) system. I was about eight years old when I began to drive the tractor through the field as he walked behind the trailer, dragging the hose and spray nozzle with him. As we moved through the orchard, he whistled when he wanted me to stop, and I would lock the brakes and engage the PTO. He would spray the surrounding trees, and when finished with an area, whistle again so I knew to disengage the

PTO and drive on to the next cluster. I was so short that I had to stand and hold on to the wheel just to depress the clutch. It may seem like nothing reading this today, but back then, boy, it made my day! I always liked working with my father, but driving that tractor really got my juices flowing.

In 1965 when I was thirteen, my older brother Fritz returned home from Germany, where he was teaching elementary school on an army base in Schweinfurt, and moved back in with us on the farm. We all looked up to him, so it was great that he was back home. But the best part of his return was that he shipped back a brand-new white convertible 356c Porsche from the factory in Stuttgart. And he let me drive it! Sitting on a pillow so that I could see over the dashboard, I would drive it to the bottom of the hill a mile away, and he would drop me off and continue on to his date or wherever he was going. It was a long walk back up the hill by myself but worth the added stick time.

Fritz's Porsche with my brother Tad standing behind

Fritz had a big influence on me as a child and well into my college years. He always treated his younger siblings with kindness, similar to the way he treated his favorite students. He let us go outside the limits of where our parents would have drawn the line. These benefits always had a hitch.

On Saturday afternoons, he would pile us into his car and take us for ice cream or a pop (Pittsburgh for soda) at a local grocery store, but only after we helped wash his car. When I was six, he showed me how a manual gear shift worked on his 1951 Chevy and let me do all the shifting as he drove along. These were simple acts of kindness from an older brother, but to a kid it was pure excitement.

Later on, when I was in high school and had my driver's license, I would meet him for Sunday morning breakfast at Eat-n-Park in Ambridge. We usually talked for a couple of hours about school, work, a date one of us had the night before, and other subjects. It was during one of these Sunday morning conversations that he passed on some valuable insight about human behavior. He said that most people like to talk about themselves, be it about jobs, family, children, hobbies, or whatever. It's easy to start a conversation with almost anyone when it's about that person and, with little effort, delve to any depth. You have to be sincere in showing interest—faking it doesn't work. Start with a simple question and then build the next set of questions based upon the previous answer. Amazingly, after a little time, most people will reveal some of the most intimate details of their lives. This wasn't that hard for me, since I had a natural curiosity and always found other lives and experiences more interesting than my own.

So, being the curious one, I tried this out at times with various people including a few girls whom I hoped to date. Sure enough, like magic, it worked more often than not. This little pebble of human behavior served me well throughout my life—powerful stuff mined from a Sunday morning brother-to-brother breakfast chat.

Of the many role models I looked up to in my youth, my mother's brother Duane was a special one whom I admired and respected. He would come help my father with the farm or join in with other family members for Sunday dinners and Fourth of July celebrations. My earliest memory of him was the time he brought out some weapons he had acquired from his time in the U.S. Army while stationed in Germany, among them an M1 Carbine and

German 9mm Luger. All the guys and my younger sister went down to the lower pasture for some target practice. That's when I fell in love with target shooting and especially those particular firearms.

Every Fourth of July, Duane brought out loads of fireworks. I will always remember the first time he drove up in his 1962 green four-door Chevy Bel-Air to reveal a trunk filled to the brim with all kinds of fireworks and bottle rockets. Most he had purchased; others he fabricated in his basement. I loved fireworks, so I always hung around as he showed us his cherry bombs, ash cans, bottle rockets, black snakes, and helicopters, to name a few. When I say hung around, that barely describes it. It was more like I was glued to his leg, wanting to see and experience everything he was about to do. Was it that he took me under his wing, or that I just never let go? Sadly, anyone who could answer that question is long gone.

On one visit, Duane wanted to show me that cherry bombs were waterproof, so he told me to fetch a bucket of water. I came back with my father's best galvanized bucket half-filled with water. He lit one and dropped it into the bucket and we both took off. KA-BOOM! We ran back to see a nicely punched 2-inch hole halfway up the side of the bucket, rendering it completely useless. Needless to say, Dad was not a happy camper with a bucket only half as good as it used to be. A week later, Duane arrived on the farm with a new, heavier bucket that my father kept and used for the next twenty years.

He also introduced me to building control-line-flying model airplanes. I built some from kits and designed a couple myself. On several occasions I visited him overnight at his house in Zelienople, another Western Pennsylvania town nearby, and flew combat with him and his two buddies using the model airplanes we all built. Each airplane had a ribbon attached to the tail with different marks on it. The goal was to fly up on your opponent and slice his trailing ribbon off with your propeller for either a hit or a kill. I wasn't worth a damn in the competition and spent most of my time helping others start and launch their planes. I guess you could say that to me, Uncle Duane was a combination of father, big brother, admiring uncle, and later a friend. At the very least, he had a great influence on what I became.

Around this same time, Duane had loaned me *The Flying Fortress* by Edward Jablonski, the first adult-level book I read. It was about a famous WWII bomber, the Boeing B-17. It introduced me to the world of history and aviation, particularly the second world war in Europe. My preoccupation with this time period was almost like an obsession, so much so that I wondered if I was a reincarnated aviator whose previous life was prematurely terminated during that war.

In my early teens, I began to venture farther away from the farm. To facilitate this wider travel radius, I saved my grass-cutting wages and bought my first bicycle, a Sears 26-inch three-speed for $48! As distances grew, my next mode of transportation was thumbing a ride, otherwise known as hitch-hiking. The practice was quite popular and more frequently adopted then, probably because it was a much safer world. To those who may not know this method of travel, you simply start to walk in the direction you need to go. As cars approach, you turn around and make eye contact with the driver, use your right hand to make a fist, hold it out, and extend your thumb. About half the time, a driver will stop to give you a free ride as far as both directions coincide. If dropped off before your destination, the process is repeated. This was the way a lot of us got around before we were old enough to get a license or whenever our parents wouldn't let us have the family car.

In early 1967, Dad put the farm up for sale, having decided to move closer to town. He never told me, but at 53, he seemed to be feeling his age and was getting a little burned out from working two jobs all those years. My mother also wanted to get back closer to civilization. My siblings and I were in our teens, losing interest in farm life, and Fritz had already moved to a duplex in Ambridge the previous year.

The sale happened quickly. Before school started in the fall, we moved to Quaker Heights, a new Ryan Home tract development just a mile up

Camp Meeting Road from Leetsdale, the town where our paternal grandparents lived and where Mom and Dad had started their married life.

2

Rearview Mirror

Looking back over the bigger picture, my sixty-plus years on this rotating ball, I have collected an abundance of observations, learned many lessons, and drawn several conclusions about life. This is a good time to briefly pause and share a few that will reappear on the radar as we move on.

More to the point, hindsight is a wonderful thing, lifting the fog of the past and thereby creating a more acute perspective. Over time, I became aware of scenarios, events, and circumstances that happened over and over until I was compelled to take notice and evaluate their meaning. As I started to make sense out of these events, I was able to separate my observations into three categories about life.

Life is a series of circles

There are no straight lines found in nature. If you see a straight line, you can bet it was created by man. Most of our universe is made up of circles. The phases of the moon, the tides of the oceans, the orbit of the earth around the sun, and the rotation of stars in the galaxies all move in circular patterns.

The tree demonstrates one of those circles in life. It starts from a seed, grows until it is tall and strong, dies, and falls to the ground and rots. In that process, the tree returns its nutrients back to the soil to support any seeds that dropped, starting the cycle anew. You cannot stand among the giant redwoods trees in California without realizing that this cycle has been churning away for thousands of years.

We've all had experiences that take us back to another time in our lives. It could be the unexpected reappearance of a person we hadn't seen or heard about for many years, a random occurrence that doesn't feel altogether random, or the sudden rise to importance of something insignificant from the past. Some feel like déjà vu and we move on; others have more impact on our lives. I think of them as "life circles," life circling back to an earlier episode and either completing that circle or getting it closer to completion.

One series of circles in my life started while I still lived on the farm. It was a seemingly small event at first, but it turned out to be pretty significant. Across the street from our upper pasture was a small house that several families had rented over the years. In the mid-1960s, a family with a young daughter, Betty, moved into this house. They were friends of another family, the McCulloughs, and Judy McCullough was Betty's friend. I don't remember Judy specifically, but we played often with Betty, her sister, and their friends for the short time they lived there. Although Judy and I were proverbial ships passing in the night, this was the first of four times that Judy circled in (and three times out) of my life.

Life is a collection of knowledge and experience

As we walk along various roads in life, we acquire pebbles of knowledge along the way that we collect and store to use in the future. The more we pay attention on our walk, the more pebbles we collect.

Each period in our lives can be equated to one of the many roads along that journey: childhood, education, married life, parenting, career paths, retirement, grandparenting.

There are only so many pebbles we can find and pick up on each road, and the quantity diminishes the longer we stay on the same path. To continue learning and enjoying new experiences, we need to switch to another road and resume collecting. If we were to continue high school after four years, for example, the experience would yield less in terms of educational benefits. Moving on to higher education starts the process anew.

Throughout my lifetime, I was on an addictive quest for knowledge and new experiences, always eager to add more pebbles. The farm was my first road. When Dad sold the farm, we all were ready to move on, having collected most of the knowledge and experience it had to offer, relative to our ages.

I could not ignore spirituality

This third observation is about a premise that I rejected many times before finally realizing its value, and my story wouldn't be complete without it. Starting in early adolescence, I struggled for a long time with the notion of spirituality and the existence of God.

My parents raised us in the Lutheran Church. At my Confirmation ceremony, along with my fellow students, I had to recite the Nicene Creed, a declaration of belief in God and Jesus Christ. When it came time for the Creed, I lied. From my young mind's perspective, the Bible was a bunch of stories that that seemed to conflict with each other; they just didn't make sense to me. How could they justify killing in one book of the Old Testament, but preach *Thou Shalt Not Kill* in another? I didn't dare admit my disbelief in front of my pastor, my father who sponsored me, or my family, let alone the entire congregation.

That lie bothered me for the next eighteen years. While this a story about engineers and aerospace, I would be remiss if I didn't touch on the few memorable instances leading up to my realization that spirituality could no longer be ignored.

3

Quaker Heights and Station Stories

Our new house was completed just in time for the start of the new school year. It was the second home built in our subdivision. Over the next twenty years we watched Quaker Heights grow to just short of one hundred homes, containing a variety of middle-class white-collar professionals as well as blue-collar steel workers from plants up and down the Ohio River Valley. Life for us and our friends in that subdivision was, generally speaking, very good. The economy was humming along, unemployment was below 4 percent, the space program was advancing at a rapid pace, and our country was racing to land a man on the moon before 1970.

In the Pittsburgh area at that time, wages were decent for blue-collar workers. When I graduated high school in the spring of 1970, few high school graduates from that area went on to college because the financial incentives were not all that great. A high school graduate could make almost as much, or more with a little overtime, in the mills or trades as a college graduate with a bachelor's degree. The U.S. Federal Minimum Wage when I finished high school was $1.45/hour. The median hourly rates for that year in Pittsburgh (Bulletin of the United States Bureau of Labor Statistics, No. 1660-60) were:

Non-skilled laborers	$3.00 to $3.25/hr.
Heavy haul truck drivers	$3.50 to $4.00/hr.
Machine tool operators	$4.00 to $4.25/hr.
Draftsman	$3.50 to $4.25/hr.
Computer programmers	$4.10 to $4.80/hr.
Engineers	$5.00 to $5.25/hr.

Considering four years of lost wages while attending college, it would take ten to twelve years to break even in bottom-line gross pay, not including tuition costs.

High schools in the area offered four types of curricula to support the community: fast academic, academic, commercial, and vocational. Fast academic students finished their senior year having taken upper-level pre-calculus math and physics courses. Academic stopped at plane geometry and trigonometry with equivalent levels in physics and chemistry. Commercial curriculum included mostly young women preparing for secretarial, administrative, or clerical work. Vocational students took basic math but concentrated heavily in trade-type courses; some junior and senior vocational students spent the mornings in class and worked at various businesses in the afternoons.

I transferred and entered the Quaker Valley school district as a sophomore with average grades and was placed in the curriculum track labeled academic. To my knowledge, there was no discussion nor a formal decision about my placement in the academic curriculum. I think it just happened that way. Luckily, taking the academic curriculum route turned out to be the trigger for a life-changing career event down the road.

One decision I did make was to take typing. I was one of two male students in a class of about twenty-five. It paid off big time in college, and especially when personal computers (PCs) became prevalent in the workplace.

And no, being surrounded by young ladies was not the motivation. If anything, it was quite intimidating. Teenage girls must have better fine motor skills than boys, because they typed circles around both of us!

Socially, living in town was understandably different and much more active than living on the farm, with parties, dances, dates, and a variety of other social events for my entire family to enjoy. Our subdivision even had a rock band made up of four of my classmates.

Observations about generations and the times

Living such a comfortable life and in that location was a gift from our parents and their peers, later identified as "The Greatest Generation." We were immersed in the lifestyle created for us by many self-sacrificing wonderful people who fought and contributed to the World War II effort. Like coins in any currency, there are two sides to everything, and there was a downside to their generosity. Those who served overseas witnessed horrible sights, and those who were fortunate enough to come home wanted to create a life for their children that was far better than their own. We, as beneficiaries, sacrificed very little or nothing. On the other side of the proverbial coin, I believe this gift of love, well-intentioned as it was, created the foundation for the "me generation." Many members of my generation and the subsequent ones developed an air of entitlement: "It's all about me." In my humble opinion, this foundation grew into a cultural divide some forty years later, and we are seeing the worst of it now.

To be honest, those times were not all days of wine and roses, and we certainly had our share of strife, tensions, and civil unrest. Events like the assassinations of President John F. Kennedy, Dr. Martin Luther King, and candidate Bobby Kennedy hang grimly over those years. The Vietnam War protests ramped up in the late sixties and the Civil Rights riots broke out in 1967.

These protests and riots were scattered all around us, but none erupted in our community nor in our high school. We seemed to be isolated from it all. For much of this isolation I give credit to our strong high school principal, Dr. Robert McNamara. He foresaw the inevitable racial tension which could have infiltrated our school, and he took preemptive measures rather than reacting later from a defensive posture. As a result, we had little or no trouble despite other integrated schools like ours in the area faring much worse: Ambridge and Aliquippa districts, for example. Hindsight reveals that Dr. Mac was my first example of great leadership by a societal authority figure.

License? What license?

During the summer of 1967, as our Quaker Heights home was being finished and the farm was in escrow, my brother Fritz lived in a rented duplex in Ambridge. The duplex's other half housed a tenant, Tom Bridgen, who owned and operated a large Sunoco service station on the Ohio River Boulevard in Leetsdale and a smaller one in Sewickley. Fritz knew that Tom needed some help, and with my farm-honed mechanical skills, he felt it would be a good match. When he suggested to Tom that he hire me, Tom asked him if I could drive. Fritz replied that I did, which was technically the truth. What he didn't tell him was that I was only fifteen and did not have a driver's license. Tom hired me, and I started at the Leetsdale station right away. But just a couple of days after I started, that slight omission became an issue.

Part of the job description included road service calls—jumping dead batteries, changing flats, going to the parts store and delivering parts to his other Sunoco station. One day shortly after being hired, he and I were the only two people working and he needed a part delivered. Tom could not leave to take it himself, so he asked me to do it. I said yes, but mentioned that I didn't have a driver's license. He was a little upset, but being in a bind, he reluctantly gave me the keys to his 1965 Dodge Power Wagon (four-on-the-floor manual transmission). Just like that, I headed out to deliver the part to his Sewickley station about five miles down the boulevard. Now mind you, I had never driven unsupervised on public roads, let alone a busy four-lane divided highway. A short time later and without incident, my mission was accomplished—an unbelievable and exciting milestone for a teenager! To this day, I can recall almost every detail of that drive. Fortunately, he stuck it out with me and I didn't get fired. He had me run errands other times over the next eight months until I got my license. Looking back, I was damn lucky that I didn't get into an accident. It helped that I had the experience of driving various farm equipment and my brother's car, which gave me the confidence I needed to take Tom's truck on a fast-moving boulevard.

Tom's Sunoco station in Leetsdale

At the Sunoco station I was a quick study and learned how to pump gas, run the cash register, provide good service (with a smile), check fluids on a huge variety of cars and, more importantly, rapidly diagnose problems on customer's vehicles. Back then a $2.00 gas purchase (roughly six gallons) also got your front windshield and back window washed and engine fluids checked, if requested. Tom recognized my general mechanical capability and over time he gave me increasing responsibilities. Within a year my tasks included service work in the bays: changing and balancing tires, doing oil and filter changes, lube and brake jobs, tune-ups, exhaust system replacement and the like. As a sixteen-year-old, I could do every service he offered. Pennsylvania had a mandatory semi-annual vehicle inspection requirement for all passenger cars and trucks. It was quite extensive, and I quickly picked up that skill as well. As time went on, I became more efficient with various jobs and even built up a clientele of my own. Customers liked the quality of my work and trusted me.

One day, Max Barr, a businessman who owned a wholesale distributorship up the street, pulled in saying that he was having trouble starting his Cadillac. I waited on him and diagnosed the problem as dirty battery terminals instead of a dead battery, a less expensive fix which initially made him happy. I got every tool that I needed from inside the bay including a fender cover. Apparently, Mr. Barr got a little frustrated because I wasn't out there fast enough to start the job. But when I got there, I had all the tools and supplies needed to complete the job quickly and efficiently without making repeated trips back to the service bay, and he was happy again. He never said anything to me personally, but he knew my father and mentioned how impressed he was with the quality of my work and my planning. He even asked my father if I might be interested in coming to work for him! I didn't take his offer, but it confirmed that I was working effectively and that other people noticed. At the time I felt lucky; however, it would be several years until a man on an airplane explained the relationship between working hard and being lucky.

Tom was open seven days a week from 8 a.m. to 11 p.m., Monday through Saturday, and 9 a.m. to 9 p.m. on Sundays. A year later I was given the responsibility of closing, which meant I was the one in charge until 11 p.m., a responsibility usually reserved for adult employees.

It wasn't just pumping gas

I loved working there, making money, and getting to know older colleagues and our many customers. Tom and I became very close and stayed that way until he passed in 2017. He owned a cabin and ski boat on Lake Latonka in northern Pennsylvania, near the town of Mercer. I was invited up many times, and I learned how to water ski and drive his boat. I enjoyed spending time with the older men at the station, and working there made my classmates seem so much less mature. I became one of the guys in that little circle and didn't mind the pranks they played on me as the young kid.

Tom playing ping pong in his basement

It wasn't often that I could turn the tables on them. However, one afternoon, Tom was standing at the workbench with his back to the service bay door, heating an upper-control arm in the vise with an Ox-Acetylene torch, preparing to remove a pressed-in bushing. Now, working around many flammables in a gas station, the chance of an explosion is always present in the back of one's mind. Seeing my opportunity to have some fun, I lit one of the firecrackers I had in my toolbox and tossed it under the car up on the lift in the first bay, the one Tom was working in. It landed perfectly, right behind his heels. I bent low to observe his reaction, and was not disappointed. From my view, I could only see his feet, and as soon as I heard the bang they disappeared. He seemed to levitate for a second or two, issuing a stream of profanity once his feet returned to the concrete.

As much as I had fun and enjoyed earning money, working at the station became a liability when it came to my schoolwork. In my mind, work came first, and consequently, my grades suffered. While I was smart enough to get A's, I never applied myself and got B's, C's and a couple of D's, contributing to a sense of academic insecurity that took fifteen years to shed.

From a personal standpoint I learned a lot about people through dealing with the public. Like food, gasoline is something everyone needs, and we had a diverse cross section of society as clientele. Sewickley and Edgeworth were quite affluent towns, while Leetsdale and Ambridge were considered middle and lower middle-class areas. Being in the center of those four towns, Tom's station drew business from this mixture as well as out-of-towners, including the occasional huckster. We had all kinds of customers—a wealthy, eccentric elderly woman who raised goats; a 70-year- old industrial park guard who lived on the park's property in a one-room shack without heat or running water; and celebrities like Lou Christie, a well-known rock singer of that era. Christie had grown up across the river from our station, and he often stopped in to fill up his Jaguar when he was in town. In addition to these colorful personalities, we had every type of customer in-between.

The guard had two German Shepherds that slept with him to keep him warm in the winter. That's when I learned how the rock band Three Dog Night got its name. (An Australian expression, it means, the colder the night, the more dogs one needs to keep warm.) Goat lady's 1965 white Dodge van and the two-dog-night guard's 1962 green Chevy pick-up both reeked, one of goat manure and the other of dog shit. We really hated to deliver their cars after servicing them, and once we all flat-out refused to do it, Tom got stuck with this olfactory-offensive task.

After waiting on thousands of customers, I developed the street smarts to quickly determine what type of person I was dealing with. It was something that has served me well throughout my life. Many years later when I read several books about body language, I learned the science and context that explained it.

Generally, we had nice customers, but we also had some real low-life types who rarely paid their bills and stuck Tom with their debts, which added up over time. All, regardless of their behavior, had to be treated kindly and with an attitude demonstrating that "the customer is always right."

Later, Tom purchased a used tow truck and we became a AAA Road Service Dealer, which meant more business for jump starts, flat tires, and towing. Because he had the only tow truck in the area, the Leetsdale Police exclusively called us when wrecked cars needed to be removed. And there were quite a few, especially in bad weather or on weekend nights.

Going on those calls was both exciting and challenging. Each one offered a different problem to solve. Driving up to the scene, we had to quickly assess the situation and determine how to separate the cars, roll over the vehicles that had flipped, hook the disabled ones up to the truck, and help the police get traffic flowing again as quickly as possible. As a bonus, accidents put a temporary halt on the normal routine at the station and gave us the opportunity to drive somewhere new. The only downsides were rain in summer, bitter cold in winter and being called out in the middle of the night.

An observation I made from picking up accident vehicles over the years was that drunk drivers seldom seemed to get seriously hurt. We saw unbelievable crashes with terrible damage to the cars involved—ones where you would swear the driver could not possibly have survived—but most of the time they walked away with a couple of minor cuts and bruises. My speculation, for what it is worth, is that the alcohol must have delayed their reaction time, so their bodies were more relaxed during impact.

I remember a head-on collision involving a 1957 Cadillac with three teenagers in the car. They weren't wearing seatbelts and the front seat passenger, who happened to be from my school, flew forward with his forehead going partially through the windshield. As he fell back again, the glass had sheared off about a 3- to 4-inch hunk of skin right down to his skull. We towed the car back to the station with his skin still clinging to the outside of the windshield. It was a gruesome sight. About twenty minutes later, the ambulance rushed back, carefully removed the severed portion of skin, wrapped it up, and took it back to the hospital for a successful reattachment. From that day on, I never drove or rode in any vehicle without being belted in.

Being an authorized AAA towing service station also offered an advantage for me personally. One Saturday afternoon, three teenage girls came coasting into the station after their car's engine had quit just a hundred yards up the road. The girl who was driving the car was gorgeous—dark complexion, jet black hair and well-dressed. She called her father, and we were instructed not to diagnose the problem but to tow her car back to the North Side of Pittsburgh. I luckily got the job and, for obvious reasons, cherished the assignment. I hooked her car up to the tow truck and the four of us squeezed into the cab. On the forty-minute drive to her home, I talked her up and got her number with the intention of asking her out.

She said yes, and the next weekend, with high hopes, I was on my way to pick her up. It was an affluent part of town, and it was evident that her family had money. The excitement started to build as I walked up to the front door of a large Victorian three-story home.

She answered the door, greeted me pleasantly, then told me that I had to come in and meet her father before we left. "Sure, no problem, we have time before the movie."

I had no idea what was waiting for me. We walked from the foyer into her father's large study, stuffed bookcases lining two of the four walls. A large, wooden, antique desk sat in front of the bookcases, and the whole room was decorated with a traditional Victorian flare. In front of the desk stood a tall, well-built man with an Italian appearance that matched his last name and a dark complexion and hair like his daughter. He was dressed in a finely tailored dark brown pin-striped vest, dress pants, a white shirt with expensive looking gold cuff links, and a silk tie. Halfway through a large ring gauge cigar, this gentleman spoke and carried himself with an air of easily recognizable dominating authority. I have to admit, being in his presence made me a little uneasy.

After a brief conversation we were off to the movies in downtown Pittsburgh. On the way there, and being a little curious, I nonchalantly directed my conversation to her family and gingerly worked around to asking what her father did for a living.

"Oh, he's in business," was her equally nonchalant but vague, almost evasive reply.

"What kind of business?"

"Different, uh, merchandise-type things." She seemed to be dancing around trying to avoid a direct answer. "He has some business partners in New York City."

My overly dramatic adolescent mind immediately thought, *HOLY SHIT! He's in the Mafia.* And then, *Oh crap. I don't want to make this girl unhappy or I'll end up in the Ohio river with concrete ankle bracelets.*

I had seen too many gangster movies, and sleeping with the fishes was all I could think about. Needless to say, I remained on my best behavior the rest of the evening but was too afraid to ask her out again.

Speaking of dating, it was shortly after this brief encounter that I began my first serious relationship. Judy and I met in the middle of my junior year—and it turned out to be the same Judy who was friends with Betty during my time on the farm. She was a year older, a senior at Quaker Valley High School. We dated for six months up until the time she graduated and broke it off. We didn't know it at the time, but our paths would cross again.

My first exposure to politics—corrupt, that is—came from working at the station. As mentioned, Tom had an exclusive verbal contract to do all towing from any accidents that occurred in Leetsdale. This agreement had been made with the Leetsdale Chief of Police, Lou Perry, an honest man whom I admired. It was a good deal for the police because Tom, who had the only tow truck in town, was able to clear wrecked cars and quickly get traffic flowing again.

Upon retirement, Chief Perry was replaced with a new chief who wanted to renegotiate the contract with Tom. In fact, he wanted a kickback from Tom for each wreck that he towed. Tom, being an honest man, refused to pay him the bribe. From that time on, we never got another call for accident towing. A gas station several miles away in Sewickley got the business. I wondered how much was donated by this owner, as it didn't seem like a very efficient way to clear a busy highway. A short time later, an accident happened within a hundred yards of our gas station, and it took some fifteen minutes after the police arrived to get the tow truck from Sewickley on scene to clear the wreck. We could have been there in two. I thought to myself at the time, *If bribery and payoffs exist at this level, the lowest form of government, just think what must exist at the state and federal levels!*

About two years after I started, Tom acquired a contract to plow and salt the roads in Leet Township, which was adjacent to Leetsdale and included the housing plan where we lived. He used his half-ton 1965 Dodge Power Wagon with a snowplow attachment. He bought a salt spreader and I designed and fabricated a steel weldment, bolting it to the back end of the truck bed. (Welding was one of the skills I picked up from helping my father on the farm. In fact, I may have used his welder to do the job.) Tom's older brother, Kenny, built a large wooden shoot/hopper above the spreader on top of the truck bed. The hopper could hold several 100-pound bags of rock salt.

Whenever the Leet Township police officer on duty determined that the snow or ice accumulation was at a dangerous level, we would get a call to clear and salt the roads. It was exciting for two reasons. It paid $7.50 an hour—three times what we usually made—and plowing and salting were fun. We had the personal satisfaction of making the roads safer for travel. As mentioned, Quaker Heights, where my family lived, was in Leet Township, so when I was on duty, I got to take care of the roads in my neighborhood as well as the rest of the township. Sometimes I would pull into our driveway and those of some friends and remove the snow at no charge.

The salt bags we used were stored in a barn two miles outside the Township; it was out of our way, and I didn't like making those long trips to load up. One time I went out to the barn and loaded more than twenty bags in the chute and truck bed, which meant I had over a ton of payload in a half-ton truck. With the additional weight of the salt spreader, chute, and plow, I was way over the gross vehicle payload weight limit of a half-ton. This caused a reduction in weight over the front tires, resulting in a lack of steering control. On that trip back I lost control in the middle of a descending sharp turn and almost crashed into a huge tree. Man, the stupid things we do at a young age, but I luckily managed to avoid a catastrophic event, and it was a good lesson learned.

The entrance road to Quaker Heights was just to the left of a decent grass-covered, sloping hill where, in winter, neighborhood kids would go sled and toboggan riding. One early night, it was my friend Dennis Hencher's turn to plow the entrance and neighborhood. A bunch of kids had erected two shoulder-high snow forts in the middle of the hill just adjacent to the road. The fresh, heavy snow was still falling when Dennis started plowing the entrance, and the kids were in the middle of a giant snowball fight. The red truck with its flashing yellow light, slowly plowing its way up the road, made an irresistible target for kids on both sides of the battle. Sticking his head out the window to view the edge of the plow, Dennis occasionally took a couple of direct hits to his noggin.

So, after clearing all the roads in the development, he had revenge on his mind. On his way out, he took a detour, swerving to the left and driving up over the curb, heading straight for the two forts. As he approached, he dropped the plow, aligned his sights on them like a fighter plane coming in for a strafing run, and, bearing down, obliterated both forts. He later told me that he never saw kids scatter so fast.

4

Communism and a Wake-up Call

In January of 1968, Fritz approached my parents with an opportunity for me to travel to Germany on a ten-day student tour with the German language teacher from his junior high school. She was taking several students from her classes in association with the National Carl Schwartz Society. I remember that the cost was $410, and, to my amazement, they agreed. We went in March, flying out of Philadelphia on Lufthansa Airlines along with fifty students from various places on the East Coast. Landing in Köln, Germany, we boarded buses to visit West Berlin, Rotenburg ob Der Tauber, Nuremberg, Munich, (or München, as Germans call it) and the Dachau concentration camp.

The biggest eye-opener with the most impact on my young, impressionable mind was our tour of East Berlin. In 1961, the Soviets built ninety-six miles of wall, which we knew as the Berlin Wall, that completely encompassed West Berlin to stop the citizens of East Germany from escaping to the west. Postwar West Berlin contained French, British, and American sectors which could have provided a gateway to freedom. One could go to East Berlin, controlled by the Soviets, but they had to go through certain checkpoints.

Our bus entered through well-known Checkpoint Charlie. We were made to stop just across the demarcation line and surrender our passports to East German guards. Our West German tour guide was then taken off the bus and replaced with an East German guide. Two East German soldiers came on board with rifles over their shoulders and our passports in hand. To us, they looked mean and scary—no welcoming smiles or friendly chitchat. The two slowly and methodically matched each passport photo with its owner's face before handing them back. Then several guards meticulously searched the luggage compartment and even had large rolling mirrors for checking under the bus. Finally, we were permitted to proceed to East Berlin.

We subsequently were taken to some sections of the city that included government buildings, monuments, a school, and what was left of Hitler's Bunker. As soon as we left Checkpoint Charlie it was shockingly and sadly obvious that East Berlin was the total antithesis of West Berlin. East Berlin streets, street cars, roads, and lamp posts were vintage 1940. Almost nothing had changed since the war ended—it was like stepping back twenty-eight years. Many of the buildings still had WWII bullet and shrapnel holes pock-marking their facades. It was apparent that only a minimum amount of rebuilding had been undertaken, just enough to get the city operational. All the while our East Berlin guide espoused the greatness of communism and talked about the wonderful lives the citizens had with free education and health care (sound familiar today?). She neglected to tell us that the state, and not the individual, determined, for example, whether a student could continue their education beyond Hoch Schule (high school). In other words, the government decided what a person would become later in life, and the individual had no say in the matter. What I was hearing and seeing was so disturbing that all I could think was, *This is pure propaganda bull shit!* (Yes, working at the gas station, I learned a few words of profanity for times like this.)

At one monument we were permitted to step off the bus and walk around. My roommate Mark took a photo of the monument that happened to have two East German soldiers in the foreground. They bolted over, yanked the camera out of Mark's hand and stripped the film out of his camera—essentially ruining every shot on that roll—all the while yelling at him in German. Shocked, we both stood there and said nothing. In that single moment, I became a political conservative, a confirmed capitalist, and an American patriot. If what I saw in those few hours was communism, I wanted no part of it for me, nor for my country. Going back through Checkpoint Charlie to West Berlin, the scrutiny and searches were even worse, further strengthening my resolve.

We had many memorable experiences, traveling through the country I had read so much about in the context of WWII. I enjoyed seeing differences between what I was used to from home and the idiosyncrasies of this unfamiliar culture.

For example, we stayed in what were considered full-service hotels, but the rooms didn't have showers or toilets. We had to use the community toilet on each floor and were told that there was a bathtub somewhere, but we never found it. We resorted to sponge baths for most of the trip.

Switchblade knives were popular, available everywhere we went in Germany, but were outlawed back home. Mark and I bought as many as we could and hid them on the flight home, intending to sell them for a profit. Sitting on the long plane ride with four switchblades in my underwear was more than a little uncomfortable. Plus, we were terrified of being caught going through U.S. Customs and subjected to unknown consequences. Little did I think then of the more realistic consequence of moving the wrong way and accidentally pushing one of the buttons that opened the blade. On the other hand, it would have also opened a whole new career as an opera tenor.

With all my excitement over that trip and the fun I was having in my job, it wasn't until late fall of my senior year that I was hit with a stark reality. I was spending the evening at Jackie's house, a longtime friend, and we were talking on her front porch when she excitedly told me about her acceptance letter to nursing school. It was at that moment I realized I had totally and foolishly neglected my future. I thought with embarrassment and shock, *Holy Crap! What the hell am I going to do for the rest of my life? Man, what was I thinking?*

After some panicked consideration, I applied to and was accepted at Pittsburgh Institute of Aeronautics (PIA). It was a technical school for airframe and powerplant mechanics located at the West Mifflin Airport, about ten miles south of Pittsburgh. After taking the coursework and successfully passing some federally regulated tests, graduates received a license to perform maintenance on aircraft.

This three-year period in my life, high school and my job at the service station, had opened the door to a new world very different from my previous and somewhat secluded farm life. New experiences, new people, new places—I loved exploring them all and satisfying a curiosity I didn't even know I had three years earlier. New skills, more pebbles. While I wasn't drawn to college yet, this period did build my confidence in other abilities, especially with respect to mechanical skills.

Looking back, I chose technical school over college because I simply did not think I was smart enough to tackle college academics. Perhaps it was my grades, or maybe a lack of interest—who knows for sure?—but I was a natural when it came to mechanics, and it was a curriculum I thought I could easily manage. I was happy with the decision I made to pursue my interest in aviation.

So, in the beginning of August 1970, I was off to my next adventure.

5

Tech School

It was a short summer after high school graduation before reporting to technical school the first of August, but I was eager to start. PIA was established in 1929 and is still operating today. After completing the twenty-one-month curriculum and passing the FAA written and practical exams, I would get an Airframe and Powerplant (A&P) license and an associate's degree in Specialized Technology. It took me twenty-four months; halfway through the program I had to drop out for a quarter due to contracting mononucleosis.

At first, I commuted to school every day, and although it was only forty miles from home, it took between fifty to eighty minutes each way. That got old fast, and after the first quarter I rented a room in a house in nearby Clairton for a couple of months. Ironically, the landlady had known my great-grandmother and she immediately took a liking to me. The bad thing was that there was only one bathroom and several other boarders, which quickly became an issue. About that time, I befriended an older guy from Fairmont, West Virginia, M. L. Sprigg III, a laid-back slow-talking "hoopie" (one of several derogatory but, in most cases, affectionate nicknames given by Pittsburghers to West Virginians). He was heavy into Harley

Davidson motorcycles and his preferred evening entertainment was going to strip clubs and drinking beer. I was invited, but after going a couple of times, I went with him only every few months. M. L. and I became roommates in a one-bedroom one-bath apartment in an older three-story apartment building in Wilson, another small town near our school. Rent was a mere eighty dollars a month which we split, an unbelievable amount by today's cost of living. M. L. called me Slick for some unknown reason and, other than the drinking, we got along great. I kept in touch with him for the next ten years, but the relationship faded when I moved to California.

School was great! I relished both the classes and the practical work in the shop. After the first quarter we spent a half day in each. The curriculum covered many areas and provided an excellent, well-rounded education in both theory and practical maintenance. We studied flight dynamics, weight and balance, and virtually everything about aircraft engines, both piston and turbine. We had sections on airframe structures including fabric-covered, wood, aluminum, and tubular steel, and we studied welding, hydraulics, electrical and electronics systems, and radio communication.

Well over half of my classmates were veterans, most of them coming back from tours of duty in Vietnam. Quite a few had seen action overseas. As a mix of recent high school graduates and war veterans, we got along tremendously and became good friends. Although they were only three to four years older than us, they seemed so much more mature. Some were married and even had children. During lunch and after school at the airport coffee shop, I got to hear many stories about the war and what it was really like in Vietnam, including but not limited to the fine details of Southeast Asian prostitution.

An observation I made by watching the veterans interact with our instructors was that those guys didn't take any crap. All my life, I was taught that contradicting teachers led to unpleasant consequences. But at PIA, if the instructor wanted us to do something that was a waste of time or just busy work, the veterans pretty much told him where to go. It was where I first learned the term "chicken shit." I was surprised to see that most of the time the instructors backed down. I later concluded that the school generated over half their revenue from veterans and was not willing to jeopardize that income. Most of the instructors were veterans themselves, and deep down inside, they understood where these guys were coming from.

"True" crime story

The rest of the student body was made up of young kids like me, right out of high school. Most were from outside the Pittsburgh area and this was their first time living away from home. Similar to first-year college students, we indulged in our share of drinking and pranks. Some were simple pranks—like taking a ketchup-smeared rubber finger and placing it on the edge of the sheet metal shears. Others were more sophisticated pranks, the kind that could really get someone in trouble . . ..

As the story goes, one group of six or so fellas in my class lived together in an apartment building in the nearby river town of Glassport. They were pretty creative and, being a little bored late one weeknight evening, decided to have some fun. They created a live action play to be staged in front of a small convenience store directly across the street from their apartment building. The main actor, Randy P. (whom I later roomed with in Florida), and another roommate of his in the same building, Stoner, stood in front of the convenience store and waited for someone to come out.

A short time later, an older woman walked out of the store carrying two full paper grocery bags. As she approached Stoner and Randy, Randy pulled out a starter pistol, pointed it at Stoner, and yelled, "I told you I would kill you, you bastard!" Then, at point blank range, he shot Stoner in the chest, or at least it looked that way. For a more realistic effect, Stoner had some ketchup in a plastic bag and surreptitiously smashed it against his chest right before he fell to the sidewalk. The poor lady screamed, dropped her bags in the middle of the sidewalk, and ran back into the store, scared to death.

For Glassport, a sleepy low-crime town next to the Monongahela River, this apparent shooting was big time! Police from all the surrounding towns converged on the crime scene and attempted a coordinated response. They interviewed the witnesses, searched all the streets, and started going door-to-door asking questions.

Right after the woman ran back into the store, both Randy and Stoner panicked and ran like hell down the street a short distance, made a turn, and headed toward the river, a half-block away. They doubled back to the rear of their apartment building. Dave Rigau, another buddy of mine, and several other PIA students were watching it all from their upstairs windows.

Frightened of the sirens and the police descending on the scene, Randy and Stoner ran up the rear fire escape stairs and hid in the bathroom of Dave's apartment. His roommates took out their books and acted like they were studying when, a few minutes later, the police knocked on their door. The officer asked Dave if he knew anything about the shooting and Dave replied that they heard the shots and sirens, but didn't see anything because they were busy studying. Peering past Dave in the doorway and seeing the little angels with their heads buried in their books, the officers reluctantly moved on to other apartments.

Later that night, a boat with search lights was spotted out on the river looking for a dead body. Nobody was found and no one was arrested. Needless to say, we couldn't talk about anything else that week.

Learning from mistakes

A couple of school-related screw-ups are worth mentioning. The first was when the Powerplant class instructor fired up a gas turbine engine as a demonstration. Mind you that almost all engines in the shop were donated to the school and, as one would imagine, they were not the newest nor in the best running condition. This was a "high-time" jet engine, meaning it was at the end of its safe-to-operate limit and required overhaul, but was still a functional powerplant. Sadly, the instructor did not know how bad its condition really was. Once it was started, he wanted to impress us by running it up to full power. Unfortunately, it threw a couple of compressor blades out through the case and subsequently cobbed (stripped) the engine. Fortunately, no one was hurt. But that was the last jet engine run-up the school performed for students.

We also had an incident in Hydraulics class where the school had a fully functional hydraulic system mock-up of a D18 Beechcraft inside the classroom. Bill, one of the students in my class, was assigned the task of replacing a ¼-hydraulic line somewhere in the system. He took his wrenches to crack the first B-nut on the line, but didn't know that, earlier that day, someone had used the hand pump to pressurize the system. The accumulator held a lot of pressure and a significant volume of red hydraulic fluid, which subsequently drenched him from head to toe. The reaction was a trifecta of shock, panic, and embarrassment. When the pressure bled off, we all got a good laugh at what 1000 psi could do to an unsuspecting mechanic.

Moving on

The whole time I was at school, I went home each weekend and continued to work at the Sunoco station. The job provided me with spending money and kept my mechanical skills sharp.

Graduation rolled around in August of 1972, and the time came for me to land a permanent professional job. Unfortunately, all the choice jobs I had hoped for were with the major airlines, none of which were hiring due to a downturn in business. Only the five students who were people of color got jobs at a major airline. Since it was shortly after the Civil Rights Movement, industries were pressured or required, depending on how closely they were related to the Federal Government, to fill a minimum quota of minorities. But the flip side of not getting a job with the airlines was that a better opportunity opened elsewhere.

Our school's recruiting office was contacted by Pratt & Whitney Aircraft in West Palm Beach, Florida. They were looking for mechanics and technicians. Grumman Aircraft in Mobile, Alabama, that produced the Tiger aircraft, also reached out to the school about applicants. Several fellas went there for a year or two, but later on, most of them ended up at Pratt. After filling out an application for Pratt, I decided to drive to Florida and give it my best shot. I was interviewed by an engineering supervisor named Tom Weigel. He noticed that I had taken academic math classes in high school and asked if I was interested in becoming an engineering aide. I asked him what my duties would be and, after hearing his response and without much hesitation, said "Sure, I'll give it a try."

The offer was $3.90 an hour, almost double my wages at the station. I drove back home, filled out loads of security clearance paperwork, packed my '67 Buick Grand Sport, and headed back south to West Palm for my first professional job. Just like our family moving from the farm, PIA had provided me with a vehicle to another frontier.

It was not until much later—well into my career in California—that I pondered that transfer to Quaker Valley and my placement into the academic curriculum. A seemingly unimportant decision about curriculum, coupled with my future supervisor's observation years later and eleven hundred miles away, had eventually taken me down a road I never imagined.

I didn't appreciate it at the time, but that curriculum placement was the determining factor in changing the direction of my career and my life.

6

Pratt & Whitney

Although Tom Weigel had described the position and its associated responsibilities during my interview at Pratt & Whitney, I had no idea what my day-to-day responsibilities would be. At first, driving pencils and pens at a desk with my butt in a chair was completely foreign, especially coming from an active job at the service station, where I was on my feet all day.

Despite my initial hesitation, I hit the ground running with the goal of perfecting every task put in front of me. After the second month, I really began to like this engineering stuff.

I was being exposed to a whole new world completely separate from my previous environment of the farm, the gas station, and the culture of Western Pennsylvania. Everything was new, exciting, and fresh. I was sucking up experiences like a vacuum cleaner. On Saturday mornings, I'd wake up and realize I couldn't wait for Monday when I could go back to work. It was a feeling I had a couple of times later in my career, but never at the intensity as while working for Pratt. This was indeed a fresh new road to travel, loaded with lots of pebbles.

The J-58

I was assigned as an aide to three test engineers, George Rogers, Lyle Metz, and Dick Whiting, each responsible for testing his own experimental J-58 Gas Turbine Engine, the very same engine that powered the famous Lockheed SR-71. Talk about landing a job on a legendary aircraft! My first assignment was not only cutting-edge technology, it was my first classified program. The most exciting aircraft or engine I had ever touched up to that point was a vintage 1940s D-18 Beechcraft or a Lycoming IO-540 piston engine. How lucky can a 20-year-old grease monkey with an A&P license from Pittsburgh get?

Of the three test engineers, George was my favorite—smart, easy going, quick witted, with somewhat of a sharp tongue. George called me Kid, and I guess he took a liking to me. I liked working for him, perhaps because of the fatherly attitude he showed toward me. Later on, George and others urged me to go back to school and get my engineering degree. I guess he saw something in me that I did not see or realize at the time.

By 1972 virtually all the hard-core development work on the J-58 had been completed. The aircraft that these engines powered made its first flight in the latter part of 1963. The vehicle became operational later in 1966 and flew with the Strategic Air Command out of Beale Air Force Base in northern California and two overseas locations. By the time I was hired, Pratt was operating under a Sustaining Engineering Program (SEP) contract, an ongoing program that brought in $4-5 million/year.

At the time, the SEP contract was a decent-sized program that concentrated on improving the longevity (time between overhaul) and reliability of the many components and subsystems, such as hydraulic pumps, turbine blades, interior afterburner ceramic coatings, first stage blades, blade tip seals, gearbox bearings, and several other components I have long forgotten.

Staffing on the program consisted of a program manager, three secretaries, five mid-level managers, nine engineers and eight engineering assistants and their aides. There were usually fifteen to thirty mechanics working in the main plant shop floor on engine builds and teardowns, another fifteen to thirty in the test area, and an unknown number of technicians working in the component test area on what we called "rigs."

With the J-58 powering the SR-71 aircraft, it set flight records that still remain unchallenged today. The most notable was its sustained speed capabilities over *Mach 3*. Some NASA X-Planes could match it, but only for short periods of time, which was not suitable for reconnaissance. Aside from the airframe having made a quantum leap in aerodynamic, thermal, and RCS technologies, the technological enhancements to the engine raised the bar just as high. The J-58 was an engineering marvel that broke through many previously limited boundaries in gas turbine performance.

SR-71 aircraft

To mention a few, the engine was capable of running in continuous afterburner while others could operate no longer than fifteen minutes. The compressor air inlet temperature at cruise was 800°F, twice the temperature of then-current technology. Fuel temperature upstream of the fuel control was 300°F, and at the nozzles in the burner cans, the temperature was 600°F. Engine lubrication oil ran at 700°F when other oils in the market were rendered useless above 300°F. Turbine inlet temperature was five hundred degrees hotter than current temperatures of high-performance engines at 1500°F. The fuel that the engine burned served a dual role as hydraulic fluid that ran the actuators. If your eyes have not glazed over from all these statistics, it was also the first mass use of nickel-iron alloys (Waspoloy) and directionally solidified turbine blades.

All of these firsts took a tremendous amount of money and effort to develop and make operationally reliable. The whole program was highly secret from the late 1950s to the middle 1960s, with each employee working under Special Need to Know (SNTK) limitations.

In September of 1974, the SR-71 broke two airspeed records. The first was New York to London with an unprecedented time of 1-hour, 55-minutes, 32-seconds. The return trip, London to Los Angeles, set another record, coming in at 3-hours, 47-minutes,39-seconds. We were all proud to be one miniscule part of the much larger team responsible for these feats.

Test rigs and stands

In any development program, especially during that of the J-58 engine, many of the components were tested individually on test rigs and perfected before being installed and run on the assembled engine.

George Rogers told me about his experience, as a young engineer out of college in the 1960s, working on one of these components, the oil pump test rig. For several years he was not permitted to know anything about how this oil pump was being used. He was essentially working blind. Then one day in 1964, George was watching the evening news when President Johnson came on and announced the existence of the "SR-71." George realized then that the oil pump he had been working on was part of the powerplant for that aircraft. But there was one major glitch: President Johnson had screwed up its name. It was supposed to be the RS-71, with the RS standing for Reconnaissance Strike. He made a simple mistake on national television that could have easily been corrected, but it was less embarrassing to the White House for both Pratt and Lockheed to revise thousands of documents than to make a public statement. Just think of all the money it cost the government (better yet, the taxpayers) for that simple slip of the tongue.

We had two stands available to us for testing our engines. Both were five miles due west of the plant, farther into the Florida swamps. The area was teaming with alligators and water moccasins, new wildlife experiences for a kid from Pittsburgh. The majority of the testing was performed in the sea-level test stand called A-1, with some in the altitude chamber called C-5.

An early picture of A-1 Sea-Level Test Stand (without the Ejector)

The A-1 Stand had a dual purpose. It could run the engine at sea level or at simulated altitude. For simulated altitude tests, the facility had a J-75 non-afterburning turbojet engine plumbed to the front of the stand, with ducting and valves that dumped or rammed from 0 percent up to 100 percent of the J-75 exhaust gasses down the inlet of the test engine. The J-75 engine was used in the early days on the Boeing 707, Douglas DC-8, and Lockheed U-2. It was a highly reliable gas turbine. That year, a news article stated that this engine set a record in a TWA 707, running twenty-five thousand hours before being removed for overhaul.

One more piece of large equipment was needed to run the test engine at altitude. In the back of the J-58 test engine, the test stand crew attached an ejector that was sealed around the afterburner section of the J-58. It looked like a giant forty-foot-long megaphone that essentially drew a partial vacuum on the exhaust gasses as they exited the engine, thereby creating a lower ambient air pressure which resulted in simulating a higher altitude. All ducting for the ejector assembly was double walled with swamp water pumping through it for cooling. The test area was surrounded by swamps, so there was plenty of supply. This piece of equipment and configuration plays a part in a later story.

My memory recalls that the C-5 Stand was used only two or three times in the 2½ years I worked there. It was capable of simulating exact altitudes up to and in excess of 80,000 feet. High pressure steam was used to heat the air that was forced down the inlet, and huge pumps pulled a vacuum downstream of the afterburner. As one can imagine, it was extremely expensive to operate.

The engine testing process involved assembling the engines in the shop with development parts or experiments and attaching the required instrumentation—the build—then transporting the engine to the test area five miles down the road. The engine run time duration for each test was usually five hundred hours. If there were no failures or significant problems, the engine would go back to the shop, be torn down completely, and a 100 percent inspection on every component would be conducted, as well as an evaluation of the development parts. Then the process would start all over again with new or development parts slated for the next endurance testing.

My job was to assist the three test engineers with their ancillary duties. For example, they would send me running around the facility to chase down parts being modified, or coordinate with purchasing, which gave me an opportunity to interact with professionals throughout a wide range of departments. I was asked to convert raw data from tests and plot the results, putting my left brain to work and challenging me to see patterns and outliers. When the mechanics tore engines down into hundreds of parts, I was tasked with overseeing their work: reporting progress, helping with problems, communicating issues to management, and writing reports. Every day was different and NEVER boring—I did whatever the engineers needed me to do and I loved every minute of it.

J-58 engine running at night with AB section glowing red (see cover)

During my time working at A-1 Stand, we worked many long hours when the engine was running an endurance test. We ran two shifts and I sometimes had to support second shift operations the same as the other engineers in the group. During those times I heard many war stories of catastrophic engine failures—meaning they literally blew up. The engineers recounted stories of failed engines 300 to 400 yards away. Since I was responsible for pulling records, drawings and other historical paperwork from archives, I also had the ability to pull photos of engine failures, something pretty cool for a young kid who had grown up playing with fireworks and blowing things up.

COOLING WATER!

My most memorable engine build test was in the A-1 Stand for its first altitude run on George Roger's engine, called FX-120. We had just completed the sea-level check-out runs looking for leaks, system and instrumentation functionality, and engine thrust performance. After this successful series of runs and adjustments, the crew then plumbed the engine and test stand to run at altitude. They rigged the ducting from the J-75 to the inlet and installed the ejector with its afterburner encapsulating shroud. To keep the ejector cool, large diameter pipes were connected to the ejector and swamp water was pumped through the cavity between the inner and outer liners.

On the first run-up we went through idle checkout, and pushed the engine up to Military Power (meaning, no afterburner). After a minute or two, the A-1 Test Stand lead operator, Frank Hill, suddenly panicked. He remembered that the ejector cooling water was not turned on. Frank bolted out the door yelling "COOLING WATER" and ran to the stand to turn it on.

Well, the problem with Frank's reaction was that the ejector inner liner by then had gotten close to red hot from the exhaust gasses, and dumping cold water into its cavity would create a disaster. I vividly remember standing in the blockhouse just behind George, who was in front of the bullet-proof glass waving his arms frantically to get Frank's attention. George knew that the water hitting that hot liner would immediately create tremendous amounts of steam and unbelievable pressure that could not be vented fast enough, putting Frank in potential danger.

As soon as the cold water hit the hot cavity, the resulting pressure spike, as feared, separated one of the panels of the inner liner forcing it down into the engine exhaust airflow, halting the high-velocity exhaust gas. The next events happened in rapid succession. First, a pressure wave traveled back up through the afterburner into the turbine section failing some blades, resulting in slicing a circumferential hole right through the turbine case between eight and twelve o'clock, spewing hot flaming gasses out the side. At the same time, the ejector tie-downs failed and the inside pressure blasted the ejector twenty yards aft of the engine. When the slave engine operator in the blockhouse saw this happen, he reached over and shut down both engines, but it was too late to save the J-58. Miraculously, Frank wasn't injured by the blast or flying shrapnel.

No more than fifteen seconds had passed since Frank bolted out the blockhouse door. I have to admit that I was excited at the time to witness this rare event, and was about to say something like "That was really cool!" but fortunately I caught myself. The subsequent cost and schedule delays were huge, with George and Frank responsible for this catastrophic fiasco, so I kept my mouth shut.

A lesson about coffee

The biggest program in the plant was the F-100 engine program that powered the F-16 and F-15 fighter aircraft. It had the largest budget and the most work, with a correspondingly higher priority in the shop and on the test stands. The J-58 program was considered lower priority than the F-100, so we often had trouble getting jobs completed in the sheet metal and machine shops. During one of these holdups, I learned a good lesson from Hank Butler, an engineering assistant working on the afterburner. He took me along with him to the shop to check the status of a liner that was delaying the assembly of our engine build.

On our way down he said, "Let me show you a tip on how to get things done. Just keep your mouth shut and watch." This was something I always admired him for—the tips he gave me to get things done the easy way without pulling rank or playing the power role. On the way to the shop, Hank and I stopped at the cafeteria where he bought us each a coffee and picked up a third one to carry to the shop. He knew that the supervisor we were going to see liked coffee with one sugar and a little cream, exactly how the third cup was made.

As soon as we walked into the shop, he handed the supervisor the coffee. It was a small token and much appreciated since shop personnel were not permitted in the cafeteria during non-lunch hours. Hank started to chat about the previous weekend, asking the supervisor if he had gone fishing. Like many Florida natives, they were both fishermen. After a little while shooting the shit, Hank started to turn as if leaving for another location, but then paused and nonchalantly asked, "By the way, when do you think you can start the mods on our afterburner liner?"

The supervisor replied that he would put someone on it right after lunch and, sure enough, it was completed as promised and in time for the build. This taught me that you don't need to push your weight around to get things done. It also brought back my brother Fritz's words about the importance of taking an interest in people. And a little coffee doesn't hurt either.

7

Florida Life

O verall, I was having the greatest time of my life. I was completely self-sufficient and not dependent on my parents. The weather in Florida was beautiful almost year-round, especially compared to Pennsylvania. Quite the contrast to all those cloudy IFR Pittsburgh days. The beach was a five-minute drive with boating on both the inlet and open ocean. There was fishing, motorcycling, and sights to see: Disney World, Busch Gardens, the Florida Keys, and Daytona Race Track. Relatives from up north came down for their vacations, and I had fun entertaining them with all there was to do. Both Dennis Failoni, a fellow Pittsburgher, and Norm Jones, another program colleague, owned boats and we would scuba dive on the weekends. We explored shipwrecks and reefs or dove for lobster and fish for that evening's dinner. Dennis was an avid motorcyclist, and after I bought my own, we frequently went riding. We even took a bike trip one summer to Pennsylvania and back.

Dennis and Norm after flying

Both Dennis Failoni and a mechanic from World Aviation, Warren Sherwood, had their pilot licenses. I would occasionally go flying in rented planes with them. John Lillberg (aka Grinn Finn), who was partner in a two-place S-2A Pitts aerobatic biplane, also took me up. Rides with Dennis and Warren were more like pleasure cruises. But flying with John was a completely different story, especially considering that he loved aerobatics and later became a member of the U.S. National Aerobatics team. I would occasionally perform minor maintenance for John on his Pitts, and in exchange, he would give me short rides. He was never cheap in returning the favor; a brief few minutes of aerobatics was all it took before I was ready to blow lunch! On milder rides he taught me how to do loops and barrel rolls, but I never got the bug to do the aerobatic thing.

John Lillberg next to his Pitts

Me in the front seat before takeoff

At the controls at the top of a loop

John was an intelligent guy, but a bit quirky and obsessively frugal. There are many legends about John but I will only mention a few. He was extremely precise with scheduled maintenance on his vehicles. His commute car was a four-door Volvo, and he carpooled with some other engineers who shared a funny story with me. One day on the way home, with them still in the car, he noticed that the odometer had reached a certain milestone that, for any normal person, would trigger a mental note to change the oil in the near future. He immediately pulled over off the road, opened the trunk, and took out a jack, drain pan, wrench, and four quarts of oil. He then proceeded to change the oil right on the spot.

Another story he related to me himself. Since the oil for his Pitts was expensive, he would take the drained oil from his Pitts and use it in his wife's Mustang. When it came time for an oil change for her car, he then recycled that same oil in his lawn mower, and after that, he dumped it in his home-made fogger to rid mosquitos from his backyard. Did I mention that he was frugal? I swear that if one were to look up the word "cheap" in the dictionary, John's picture would be right next to the definition.

The last story ends on a note that I would almost call psychic. At lunch as many as eighteen of us would eat at one table, and every day we played the Coffee Game. Most of the time it was the highlight of the day because it involved a combination of plotting, trickery, conspiracy, and sometimes downright cheating in order NOT to win the game or to set up someone else to "win." The winner was obligated to buy coffee for and personally serve all the other players. I won't take the time to explain all the intricacies of the game, other than to say it involved each member writing down and concealing a number from one to thirty. We then took turns going around the table, starting with the first player, who called out a number which was then crossed off a master list kept by one of the players. The next player had the option of calling another number or claiming that his concealed number was the same as one previously called, which meant that he could go out. This process went on until only one person was left in the game, and he was the unfortunate winner.

Now, the winner had two options: accept his fate and fetch the coffee, or challenge the most likely liar by forcing him to show the actual number he held. If it turned out that the challenged person had, in fact, lied, then he was the one to go buy the coffee.

One day I was the victim of a well-planned conspiracy and ended up being the winner. With my one challenge I picked John Lillberg. He said, "Okay, if you know I lied, then what number do you think I really have?" I told him 17. Sure enough, he had 17, and indeed had lied by going out on another number. My chances of guessing 17 were one out of thirty, and John was intrigued by my luck.

After lunch, he wanted to investigate this a little further and we went back to our office with the intent of me trying to guess some more numbers. One at a time, he wrote down a number from 1 to 15 and challenged me to guess what he wrote. After writing each number, he would fold the paper and hold it up to his head while concentrating, reminding me of Johnny Carson playing "Carnac the Magnificent" on the *Tonight Show*. On the first six out of seven times, I guessed it correctly. What are the odds of guessing the number correctly six out of seven times? After that clairvoyant event, I began to believe that there must be unexplored types of communication aside from the traditional visual and verbal, and I continued to watch for those unexplainable coincidences.

I remained friends with John until he was tragically killed in July, 2000, near Boca Raton in a mid-air collision with a Lear Jet. I was devastated to see a good guy like John go so early in his life and in such a horrible way. He was and still is, to this day, greatly missed by many who knew and worked with him.

Another kind, mentoring figure to me was John Niro from New England, who spoke with a heavy Boston accent. Without exception, he always had a smile on his face and exhibited a positive attitude about everything. He walked with a bad limp, and for a long time I didn't ask him about it. But I did find out later that on the second day of the WWII Normandy Invasion, he took a hit from a German machine gun that almost severed his leg just below the hip. Many years later, while living in California, I made donations in honor of John and two other veterans to the WWII Memorial in Washington D.C., and there are bricks somewhere on the plaza with their names on them.

World Aviation

Because of my work ethic and the desire for more disposable income, I got a part-time evening job with World Aviation at the Palm Beach International Airport. They were a Fixed Base Operator (FBO) whose main business came from a contract with the U.S. Navy to supply their base in the Bahamas known as AUTEC (Atlantic Undersea Test and Evaluation Center). World used three DC-3s and a Fairchild Hiller F-227 to execute this service contract. I was hired as a cleaner (basically a janitor for the aircraft) and part-time mechanic on the F-227 assisting a supervisor, Bill Melvin, and two other mechanics, Art Jacobs, and Warren Sherwood. This aircraft was identical to the Fokker F-27 with two modifications: a six-foot stretch in the fuselage and a large cargo door on the port side between the cockpit and cabin.

Bill Melvin and Art Jacobs in front of the F-227

As an aircraft cleaner, I was responsible for other people's messes. It taught me to respect those who work in that type of service industry: building janitors, hotel maids, house cleaners, junk haulers, trash collectors, etc. Others might use the term "lower class" or, to borrow a phrase I picked up in Germany, "unter mench," but I learned that people with those jobs were just trying to earn a living like I was. Not that I was ever rude to anyone, but as a result of my experience at World Aviation, I began to empathize with those who have the unpleasant task of cleaning up after us and to treat them with more respect.

The World Aviation guys were a great bunch and my time there went quickly. Most of the employees and pilots at World Aviation had previously worked for Air America, a company owned and operated by the CIA during the Vietnam War. They were tight-lipped about their experiences, but occasionally would share some good war stories. They also said that working for Air America was extremely good money for all job classification levels.

My specific tasks included cleaning the aircraft interior after each day's flight and reconfiguring the cabin to accommodate passengers, cargo, or both. Sometimes the manifest required transporting a full-sized torpedo, so I would remove or fold up the seats and then place ball matting down that locked to the seat tracks in the floor. After my job was completed, I usually helped the mechanics with their various maintenance jobs until quitting time, around 9 or 10 p.m. World Aviation had the aircraft on a progressive maintenance schedule much like commercial airlines did with their equipment.

The one task I hated the most was cleaning out the chemical toilet. The job involved removing the Dzus fasteners on the toilet cover/seat and setting it aside, lifting out the large, white, two-foot diameter bucket, walking it across the flight line to the men's restroom in the hangar, and emptying the contents into one of the toilets. Most nights it wasn't bad, except for those evenings when they had transported a lot of cargo or a torpedo that day. I say it was a bad night because on those flights I knew that a certain cargo loadmaster would have been on board. This man stood out because he was probably 5-foot 9-inches tall and tipped the scale somewhere around a robust 300 pounds. And for some biological reason, while on these flights he ALWAYS dropped a deuce in the aircraft's chemical toilet. Now, this would not be so bad for a normal person with, let's say, regular bowel movements. But this guy was either downright sick or had a serious internal plumbing problem.

Every time he flew, I would reluctantly open the tank lid to find, and I swear that I am not exaggerating, a single dense, spherically shaped, softball-sized deposit half floating in the white chemical water. I could not for the life of me imagine trying to pass an object of this size without excruciating pain. Anyway, my problem would come when dumping the bucket's contents into the restroom toilet. The bucket and water were heavy enough (about 25 to 30 pounds) that I had to stand almost directly over the toilet while slowly pouring the contents out. The conundrum was: How do I roll this large, dense object out of the bucket down into the bowl without the inevitable splash back? No matter what technique I experimented with, it always ker-PLUNKED into the toilet water like a granite rock! And like any rock dropped into a pool of water, it always resulted in a tubular surge of liquid that rebounded vertically and landed somewhere on my face. Having found no positional solution, I resorted to donning a full-face shield to eliminate the problem. (Another pebble of knowledge—more like a boulder: Even the crappiest problems have solutions.)

After about six months into my second job at World Aviation, I learned another lesson when my supervisor told me that they liked my work and wanted to know if I would consider working for them full-time. I inquired about the duties as well as the salary. The pay increase was an incentive, and the job itself was enticing because I would have the opportunity to work as an aircraft mechanic, the field that I had trained in. I shared that offer with my Pratt supervisor, who apparently also thought my work was good. So, without me asking for anything, Pratt made me an offer that matched the one from World Aviation. I decided to remain at Pratt and turned down the offer at World, although I continued to work for World part-time for another year or so. Over the course of my career I used this leveraging lesson a couple of times with positive results.

8

Pranks at Pratt

At Pratt, there was a sense of camaraderie in our office that I had not experienced before and, unfortunately, have never felt again, at least not to that degree. No powerplays, no backbiting; it seemed that everyone appreciated and participated in a cooperative, team-oriented office culture.

Oddly enough, the countless practical jokes played by almost everyone in the office helped fuel the camaraderie. Any and all victims could be counted on to retaliate, keeping the trickery rolling along through even the most stressful of times.

Dilbert Dumb-Ass

A blunder at work, or even at home, could result in being nominated for the Dilbert Dumb-Ass Award. This award was constructed as cheaply as possible from a sheet of blue 6-inch by 10-inch plastic with a picture of Mickey Mouse pasted on both sides. An impromptu jury voted on a candidate's worthiness, and the recipient was required to hang Mickey from the ceiling by a string, directly above his desk for all to see. That is, until the next Dumb-Ass came along.

John Lillberg earned this award after cutting his grass one weekend. He accidentally stuck his foot under his rotary lawn mower while it was running, shearing off the laces and most of the top of his tennis shoe, exposing his shredded sock and parts of his miraculously unscathed foot. He wouldn't have received the award except for the fact that he visited another engineer from our office, Al Nagelrieter, without changing his shoes beforehand. Of course, Al had to share John's faux pas with the office Monday morning; John's unanimous nomination and vote quickly followed.

Cones and catapults

During this time, I learned several valuable office skills, like shooting 2-inch rubber bands with deadly accuracy and enough power to cut through three sheets of newspaper from ten feet away. Over time we all became bullseye shooters!

The office desk configuration was the same throughout the plant. Two engineers sat facing two others in an opposing quad desk arrangement. Each four-desk quad had one standard black dial telephone on a rotating swing arm that was clamped at the intersection of the four desks. A common trick was to cut a 1-inch high cone or pyramid out of black foam rubber and tape it to the earpiece of the receiver, then go to another phone and dial the number for that targeted quad and wait for the person to answer. Now, answering a phone is like tying your shoes, an unconscious act that you do without thinking or looking. Imagine picking up the receiver while your attention is focused elsewhere and shoving a cone into your ear. Victims' reactions ranged from a headshake and a chuckle to looking around the room and calling out the alleged perp with a few choice words.

Another popular trick was to create a catapult from common office supplies. We would cut off the bottom two inches of a Styrofoam cup and discard the top, then take two paper clips and attach them to the rim 180 degrees apart, affixing a rubber band to each paper clip on the cup. Attach another paper clip to the opposite end of each rubber band. Open the victim's center desk drawer and stretch the loose paper clip ends, attaching them to the right and left sides. Preload the cup assembly by rotating it in such a way that it will rapidly unwind when the drawer is pulled opened. Before closing the drawer, and for the *coup de gras*, empty the dots from all available paper hole punches and load the cup to the brim with paper dots. Then close the drawer slowly and carefully, with the loaded cup up under the bottom of the desk top.

If done correctly, when the desk owner opened the drawer, the cup would rotationally unload and cover the unsuspecting victim from head to waist in a spray of paper dots. Quite a shock for someone just looking for a pen!

Chinese Lung Tester

Practical jokes were not limited to the engineering office; mischievous acts were very much alive all over the plant. A mechanic on the engine assembly floor, Bill Richey, had designed and created a beautiful little device that became a well-known plant-wide prank, the Chinese Lung Tester. When he opened his toolbox each morning, the first thing he did was to place his Lung Tester in a conspicuous and honored position near the top lid. It was a bright red lure for any unsuspecting fish that came walking by. Rich made the Lung Tester out of what would now be called a "vintage" Prince Albert tobacco can. It was flat-looking viewed from the front and oval-shaped from the ends, about the size of a person's hand or a little larger than a pack of cigarettes. He painted it candy apple red with realistic gold Chinese characters emboldened on the front and back faces. Protruding out one side of the top were two brass posts that supported an ornate brass windmill on an axle. A tube came out just a little past the middle of the top, and was angled to point directly at the windmill blades. Another tube curved away from the windmill in a slight arc. On the end was a larger cylindrical brass part with a pinhole in the middle. Altogether, it looked like a piece of art.

A sketch of the Chinese Lung Tester

One day I walked by and, noticing it for the first time, I innocently picked it up and asked Rich what this strange-looking thing was.

"A Chinese Lung Tester," Rich replied.

"A Lung Tester? How does it work?"

"You blow into the mouthpiece on the right side to make the windmill turn. The faster you can make it turn, the better shape your lungs are in. You're welcome to try it if you want."

"No thanks, I'll pass," I said, sensing a setup.

Just then, Tom, a mechanic my father's age who had been listening to our conversation, stepped over and said, "Here, I'll show you how it works."

He blew into the mouthpiece and made the wheel turn rapidly. Trusting Tom, I put my suspicions aside, took the Lung Tester from him, and gave a good hard blow into the mouthpiece like he had done.

Unbeknownst to me, there was a tiny, almost invisible hole drilled into the end of the can body just below the mouthpiece that pointed directly at my chin. When Tom had demonstrated the Lung Tester, he must have placed his thumb over that tiny hole and blocked it.

My competitive nature had kicked in, and that wheel revved up pretty well. Rich solemnly confirmed that I had indeed performed quite well.

"Do you smoke cigarettes?" he asked, without a trace of amusement.

"No, I don't."

"I didn't think so. I could tell by the way you spun the wheel."

Well, because I had not known to cover the tiny hole with my thumb when I blew on the mouthpiece, air blown through the tube was partially diverted from the windmill to the inside cavity of the can which, again unbeknownst to me, was filled with powdery graphite. Once pressurized by my effort, the cavity had sprayed a fine mist of black powder all over my chin and most of my neck. As designed, I had absolutely no idea that this part of my anatomy was now completely covered in black graphite.

I have to give them credit: The two of them, with absolutely straight faces, never let on to my appearance. Thinking I had been successful, I put the Lung Tester back on top of his toolbox, thanked him, and walked out of the assembly floor. Passing several mechanics, I strode confidently through the door, down a 100-yard-long busy corridor filled with people, out the building's west door, onto a crowded shuttle bus, and rode to the test area. Disembarking the shuttle bus, I passed the shack where the guard was sitting, nodding for me to proceed, and headed to A-1 Stand. Not once did any of those people I had passed do a double take, make mention of the huge black circle painted all over my chin and neck, or tip me off in any way about my predicament. That is, until I approached the test stand and was about to pass

Tom Beyer, one of our operators from A-1. He stopped for a split second, looked at me with a smirk, and said, "Have you been screwing around with Richey's Lung Tester?" I knew then that something was wrong and rushed to the restroom to see myself in all my graphite glory. I was had, big time!

Later, I found out that I was not the only sucker; almost everyone had fallen for it. Once you were duped, the unwritten rule was to keep mum when you encounter the next victim.

Female impersonator

Another borderline trickster was one wild and crazy engineer, Clay Travers, who could convincingly imitate a woman's voice and with a highly sensual tone. More than a couple of gullible men fell prey to his telephone advances, including me. I was single and, like any other 21-year-old single guy, was always looking for a weekend date. With five thousand people working at that Pratt facility, there were certainly several eligible bachelorettes. One morning I received a phone call from a sweet-sounding young woman who said her name was Pam, claiming to be from the Materials and Processing Department, located on the first-floor way over on the other side of our huge building. She commented on how she had seen me several times in the halls and wanted to know if I would be interested in meeting up. I said "sure" and suggested that we meet during the morning break at a particular Coke machine halfway between us. The sweet voice agreed and we hung up.

No private conversation was ever really private in our little office area, and, as I hung up, I was aware of an odd, deadly still pause in the activity all around me. Then someone finally asked, "So, Bob, who was that on the phone?" Knowing these guys, and suspecting a setup, I was a little reluctant to answer. But, like a dumb ass and too excited to keep quiet, I shared that it was a girl, Pam, from the first floor, and she wanted to meet me. Like every other victim, I had no idea that Pam was really Clay.

Playing along, one office mate said, "Oh, I know her. She's really good looking and has a nice figure." Still a little suspicious, I decided that I better confirm Pam's existence and remembered that Pete Largent, a guy we dealt with in Purchasing, worked right next to Materials and Processing. I immediately called Pete, and without hesitation he said, "Yeah, I know her. She's pretty hot and would be a good catch, if you could land a date with her." The hook was now set—Clay had a big one on the line and was ready to start reeling.

Break time arrived, and I nervously left for the designated Coke machine. I was the first to get there. George Matheny happened to walk into the alcove, then Norm Jones, both peers from our office. I thought, *Damn it, why do these guys have to show up and embarrass me?* Just then, Clay Travers walked in, slapped me on the back and said, "Hey, Bobbie old buddy, how's about buying me a Coke?" By then I was willing to do anything to get rid of these bastards and hurriedly put a dime into the machine while Clay, or shall I say Pam, made his selection. None of them left, and unfortunately, or maybe fortunately, Pam was a no-show. We all went back to our desks with yours truly most disappointed for having been stood up.

Early in the afternoon, the phone rang again; it was Pam on the other end. Completely engrossed in the phone conversation, I didn't notice Clay hunkered down behind some books just one row of desks away. With a convincingly innocent voice, she started off by apologizing that her boss had given her a last-minute urgent job and said that she would still like to meet me, asking if we could set another time. Without waiting for my reply, she then added in a more seductive voice, "because I think you're really good looking and because . . ."

A short pause followed while that S.O.B. Clay stood up from behind the books in the next row and yelled out for everyone's benefit, ". . . because I heard you have a REALLY BIG DICK!"

There was a loud roar of laughter from all within earshot. I was mortified, both for the anatomy comment as well as my gullibility. I wanted to just crawl under my desk and hide but realized that it was all in good fun; it was just my turn in the barrel.

Security formality

One early morning in January of 1974, I was at my desk, which had a good view of the back-entry door that led to the first floor and shop area. The door opened and in walked a guy I had never seen before, striding with an air of confidence and authority as if he owned the place. He went directly to a desk that had been vacated by Mike Dowd, who had left for a job in San Diego a few months earlier, and went right to work.

His name was Arnold Gunderson. He was a heavy-set man of average height in his late twenties with thinning red hair, which was cut short on top of his head and much longer on the sides and back. It reminded me of Bozo the Clown hair. Like the rest of us, he dressed fashionably for that time, the seventies, otherwise known as the decade that fashion forgot. Arnie wore double-knit bell-bottom pants, a shirt with a large collar, a thick polyester tie, and shoes with stacked heels. He adapted quickly to the job and blended in with the group. Little did I know that this man would become a lifelong friend and mentor, who would make a significant impact on my successes throughout my career.

Arnie became one of the top-notch engineers and jokesters of the group. He was one of those rare individuals capable of using both the right and left sides of his brain—he was artistic as well as having strong logic and cognitive abilities. One example of his talent as a practical joker happened shortly after I left the company. The J-58 group had moved to a much larger area in a room where there were 150 to 200 engineers with all the desks arranged in the same quad-desk configuration. A young engineer, whom I will call Harold, was hired into one of the groups on the floor. Harold pretty much stuck to himself, having little interaction with his peers. Today, we would say that he was "wrapped a little too tight." Arnie and a couple of others thought it appropriate to play a friendly joke on him in order to break the ice and loosen up his stiff demeanor.

All the resident engineers in the area were aware of this pending initiation. At the appointed time, Arnie, pulling a Clay Travers, hid behind a pile of books a couple of quads away and dialed Harold's number. When Harold answered, Arnie introduced himself as Security Officer George Bradshaw, who was processing his clearance paperwork.

"Unfortunately," Arnie said, still in the George role, "there is a missing formality that has to be completed before I can send your clearance request to Washington."

Harold offered to go right down to the security office, but George, aka Arnie, replied, "No, not necessary. I know that you're busy up there, and I don't want to interrupt your work. We can take care of this matter over the phone."

"Sure, what is that I need to do?"

"It's very simple and will only take a minute. I need you to stand up at your desk, put your right hand over your heart, and recite the Pledge of Allegiance."

Without hesitation, Harold stood up and followed the instructions to the letter, but he only got as far as "to the flag" when the whole floor erupted into laughter. Knowing he had been had, Harold slammed down the phone and went straight to the administrative supervisor to complain.

As a result, Arnie was hauled into the supervisor's office to be disciplined. Behind closed doors, he was told in no uncertain terms how unbecoming his behavior was, to never do it again, and to behave himself from here on out, or suffer dire consequences. However, as Arnie was walking out, the supervisor said "By the way, that was a good one."

Arnie Gunderson at a Chili Cook-off contest 20 years later in CA

After I left Pratt, Arnie and I remained in touch via mail over the next five years while I was in college. My good fortune in meeting Arnie was the first of many times that I had the feeling of someone, out there somewhere, looking out for my well-being.

9

Grumman and Giving In

In January of 1975, the company instituted a plant-wide 10 percent workforce reduction, and I was part of that group. I learned that none of the five hundred or so affected by the downsize were degreed engineers. Preferring to stay in the warm weather of the South, I looked for engineering aide work in Florida. With no opportunities on the horizon, George's words kept popping into my mind: *You're smart enough to go back to school and get your engineering degree. Your salary would double, and you'd be much more valuable to any company out there.*

Unconvinced, I didn't share his vision at that time. I resorted to working several odd jobs until I was hired in the spring of 1975 as a mechanic with Grumman Aerospace at the Witham Airport in Stuart, just north of West Palm Beach. Grumman was headquartered on Long Island, New York. The Florida facility performed heavy maintenance on Navy Grumman G-1 aircraft that was similar to progressive D-Checks in the airline industry. My A&P license authorized me to do these maintenance checks, and I was happy to put that training to work. The experience would also look good on a resume for a future position with the airlines, my ultimate goal.

This facility also modified OV-1 Mohawks, a Vietnam-era two-engine turboprop observation and attack aircraft. The company had a contract to convert A, B, and C models into a more modern D Model. Most Mohawks coming in for upgrades were returning from Vietnam. The airworthy planes flew in, but the heavily battle-damaged ships were crated in by truck. Bullet and shrapnel holes were clearly visible, and seeing them brought home the reality of war.

On my first day, I was told that plans for me had changed and that I was to work on the Mohawk aircraft modification. It was a terrible disappointment and ended up being an assignment I never enjoyed. My only job was to install new and refurbished hydraulic lines in the D models coming down the production line. With each day, I enjoyed my job less and less. It was a stark contrast to my duties at Pratt.

I was even more discouraged when I received my first paycheck and discovered that because Grumman was a New York-based corporation, the state took out New York state income tax from our wages, despite that fact that we lived and worked in Florida. I wasn't making that much to begin with, so every cent counted. Add another pebble, this one labeled "Fiscal Bullshit."

After a couple weeks of this drudgery, I asked a fellow mechanic who had worked at Grumman for five years how much he was making an hour. He was married, had two or three young children, and made $4.75/hour. I was shocked because I was making $4.50/hour. Is this what I had to look forward to? Invest my time in a company for five years only to expect a measly 1 percent a year average pay increase? I was old enough now to start thinking about marriage and children, and I realized that this job was not going to cut it. It was another profound revelation, like the one on Jackie's porch about continuing my education. George's words—that I'd make twice as much as a degreed engineer—finally sunk in!

A day or two after that conversation, I quit Grumman and started to make plans to move back home, go to college and get my engineering degree. At age 23, it was a little late, but better than never. In the early fall of 1975, I drove north to move back in with my parents, return to work at the Sunoco station, and save money for college with the intent on starting in January of 1976.

The aftereffects of a tragic event factored into my decision. In May of 1975, my 19-year-old younger brother Tad committed suicide. As one can imagine, it was a devastating event for the whole family with my parents taking the brunt of the pain. Things were going well for Tad; he was well-liked by all, had lots of friends, and was enrolled in welding school earning good grades. No one had any explanation for what happened and, sadly, we will never know why he decided to take his life. With my parents struggling to get back to a normal life, I thought that moving home might lift their spirits.

Cheating death #1

On a lighter note, a "shocking" incident happened not long before departing Florida. It was another lesson learned the hard way, and this time one in basic electricity. In those last few months, I had been able to pay the bills by working in an auto parts store in Lake Park. My father had recently given me his 1967 Chevy half-ton pick-up truck, and I fixed it up with some body work and a paint job. Nothing great, a six-banger with three-on-the-tree and a plain-Jane step-side bed. No luxury interior features, but hey, it was free—who was I to complain?

As always, that summer had been hot and humid. I purchased an after-market Sears auto air conditioner to escape the heat, at least while driving. Over time I installed all the individual components except the compressor. One hot late afternoon, I decided to put in that last component. Outside in the driveway, I opened the hood, disconnected the battery, and started disassembling the fan, alternator, and brackets to prep for the installation. A light drizzle had just finished coating everything with a fine mist, but I decided that the heat and wet ground were not going to stop my progress. Being a well-adjusted Floridian, I was shirtless, shoeless, and wearing cut-off shorts. Thunderstorm clouds were forming in the area, but I had estimated plenty of time before the big rain hit. Besides, I really wanted to complete this final piece of the job and start enjoying cool, conditioned air.

I was bent over the front grill, my bare chest lying on top of the radiator support, unbolting the fan blade assembly from the water pump. Just then, I was surprised to feel an electric current flow through my body. It wasn't anything high amperage like touching a spark plug or grabbing an exposed electrical cord, but strong enough to get my attention. With time passing in what felt like microseconds, I remember thinking, *How can this be? I disconnected the battery!* I looked over and confirmed that the battery cable was unhooked and lying to the side. *What the hell is happening?*

The flow of electricity increased and lasted a very long three to four seconds before it suddenly quit. The instant it stopped, a bright white flash of light emanated from behind me and lit up the inside of the engine compartment. Simultaneously, a thunderous boom came from the same vicinity and I not only heard it, but felt a small pressure wave hit my back. The obvious conclusion came to mind: *You dumb shit! You could have been fried by that bolt of lightning.* I made a hasty, but wise, decision to complete the installation another day, slammed the hood and tool box shut, and ran into the house.

It was not until forty-three years later, while overseeing a Lightning Protection System (LPS) modification for a launch pad at the Pacific Missile Range Facility (PMRF), that I fully understood what had happened. Just before lightning strikes cloud-to-ground or ground-to-cloud, the cloud builds up a charge much like a capacitor does on one side of a dielectric. The ground does the same buildup, but with opposite polarity. As the charge (voltage field) builds, it collects all the surrounding electrons and moves them to a location near where the stepped leader begins the process of discharge—where the lightning bolt will strike. Once I learned this process, I then understood that my body had been part of the electrical conduit for the electrons in the truck to transfer through me to the ground by means of my bare chest and wet feet. Had the location of the strike been just a few yards closer to the truck, I would have been a 5-foot 9-inch Porterhouse cooked Pittsburgh-style, i.e., charred on the outside, pink on the inside.

Some would say I cheated death; others would say that someone was looking out for me. But I say I was a frickin' idiot for being out there in the first place, and pretty damn lucky.

10

College Touch-n-Goes

Driving north toward Pittsburgh on I-95 in the fall of 1975, I took a detour to the east coast of Virginia for a short visit with my PIA classmate, Dave Rigau. At the time, he worked as a first line supervisor at the Norfolk Naval Aviation Depot (NADEP) in the metal parts and assembly shop. NADEP performed all kinds of maintenance, everything up to D level checks for F-14 Tomcats and A-6 Intruders to overhauling F-110, TF-30 and J-52 gas turbine engines. It was sort of a one-stop shop for repairing Naval weapon systems.

While I was there, Dave took me on a tour of the repair depot, including his shop. I was quite impressed, not only with the enormity and capability of the depot, but also with Dave's position. Here he was, a mere three years out of technical school and already in supervision. Dave has always been a smart guy with an exuberant, likable personality and a consistently positive attitude. I was not surprised that he was promoted quickly, but it did give me pause to think about my own future. His responsibilities and authority intrigued me, and I started to entertain this idea of management. If Dave could do it, then I could too.

Shortly after I arrived back home, I secured my old job back at the Sunoco gas station. This time I was a full-blown mechanic, paid by the job plus a percentage of merchandise sold. Tom had plenty of business and I earned a decent wage. Living at home provided some financial relief to my working budget, and my parents were generous about providing me room and board. In exchange, I helped out around the house as much as possible with painting, wallpapering, and maintaining their cars. Although I'm sure they hadn't planned to have their adult offspring back under their roof, it worked out and we got along well. The money I earned went to tuition, books, car maintenance and operating costs, plus a little spending money.

One evening, shortly after moving home, I was working at the station when Judy, my first serious girlfriend from high school, walked in. It had been six years since our split, and we went out a few times after her visit but broke it off again. We seemed to be traveling on different roads in different directions. I was going back to college with no foreseeable steady income while she was a professional working in the Pittsburgh corporate world. We parted as friends. Another life circle with Judy had gone around again, with one more to go.

Community College

My four-year plan was to attend the Community College of Allegheny County (CCAC), located on the North Side of Pittsburgh, for two years, then transfer to a four-year institution to complete my bachelor's degree. It took me 2½ years to graduate because I had to take several intermediary prep classes. My last semester was taxing, with twenty-one hours of classes in addition to part-time work at the station.

When I first registered for school, they had me take a Kuder Occupational Interest Survey to help determine the career that best suited my talents based on my interests. At the time, I thought it was a bunch of crap because at age 26, unlike students right out of high school, I knew exactly what I wanted to do. When I got my results, I was pleasantly surprised to find out that the highest six out of ten occupational scales put me in various engineering categories with mechanical engineer scoring the highest. It was official verification that I was on the right track.

In hindsight, CCAC provided me with a solid foundation, not only in the engineering sciences but also humanities. Each and every one of the professors and instructors were sincerely driven to teach and help their students. For anyone coming out of high school, or even older folks considering further education, community or junior college can offer a high-quality, low-cost option.

I worked all the way through college, part-time while classes were in session and full-time during the summer. Having started at the gas station, I transitioned to entrepreneurship over time. During that transition, I worked for my brother Fritz wallpapering and painting houses. He taught me the trade, and we were quite good at it, with most of our clientele coming from word of mouth. I branched off on my own, painting, repairing cars in my father's garage, and taking professional photos for weddings and sports events. My uncle Duane, a professional photographer earlier in his career, helped me tremendously; he taught me different techniques and lent a helping hand when I had a big high school prom shoot.

This period in my life was truly fulfilling in every sense of the word. I was in good health with loads of energy, lived in a comfortable home where I didn't need to worry about money (thanks to my parents), and was able to stick to my plan of saving for tuition, books, and spending money.

I even had a decent social life when time permitted. A small group of former classmates who had stayed in the area already had a routine, and they welcomed me into their group. During the week, we would hang out at Mike's Place, a local, small-town bar/restaurant in Leetsdale run by an Italian immigrant and his wife. The food was authentic and delicious. Beer on tap was just 35 cents a glass—at that price, and on our wages, it was an economical way to satisfy our thirst. Saturdays, we'd end up at someone's house for *SNL*, known then by its full name *Saturday Night Live*, drinking more beer and laughing at Belushi, Aykroyd, Radner, and the rest of that groundbreaking cast.

The first two years of college were exciting. Once again I was taking everything in and loving it. From my technical training and experience, I was familiar with the operations of many mechanisms—their physical and chemical aspects—but had never understood the math and science behind them. All those questions that had passed through my mind many times were gradually answered with each class I took.

Flights with Dennis

I renewed a friendship with Dennis Hencher, a Sunoco station buddy. He was working as a diesel engine mechanic at the Conway Rail Yards and took classes part-time with me at CCAC. In addition, he was taking flying lessons at the Beaver County Airport, where he eventually became a flight instructor and freight pilot with several ratings. He later went on to become an American Airlines captain flying heavies on their Far East route. I had always enjoyed adventurous pursuits, and luckily, so did Dennis. I usually came up with the ideas and he provided the unconventional transportation: small planes, with him at the controls.

Of the many flights we took, two stand out in my mind—one in the summer and the other in winter. On the summer trip, we flew to Indianapolis to visit John Marshall, who had moved to Quaker Heights around the time of my high school graduation. John, now a college graduate, was working for a Catholic hospital system in Indianapolis. Our plan was to fly there early one Saturday morning, play golf, visit for a few hours and fly back to Pennsylvania late that evening. The manifest included three guys—Dennis as pilot, Mark Becker from Quaker Heights, and me—and my girlfriend, a young woman I had met during my second semester.

When we all showed up at the airport for departure, Dennis, Mark, and I all had on the same type—I'm talking same color, same style—of rugby shirt and pants. What were the chances? Dennis rented a fast Piper Lance with a retractable landing gear and we made good time on both legs. When we landed in Indy, Dennis, Mark, and I got a ration of crap along the lines of looking like "members of a fourth-rate loser rugby team." John also had a pilot's license. After golf he rented a plane and both he and Dennis flew in formation while I took some air-to-air photos. We had a great time (despite the fashion critique).

My photo of Dennis piloting the Piper Lance over Indiana

The second memorable flying adventure happened the following winter when Dennis and I made plans to fly north one afternoon to a ski resort, Cockaigne, in western New York state. "Resort" being a relative term around Pittsburgh—anything with some space and a decent slope would suffice. This trip included Dennis, my girlfriend, me, and another couple, Bill and Debbie Walker. Debbie was the sister of Nancy Failoni, my Pratt buddy Dennis's wife. Bill was in Dental School, and Debbie worked for a downtown Pittsburgh corporation.

Cockaigne was about 140 miles NNW of Pittsburgh, an hour flight in the six-passenger plane that Dennis planned to rent. This destination was a small, lighted resort nestled in a shallow valley that happened to have a landing strip adjacent to it, about 100 yards to the northeast. I use the term "landing strip" loosely because it was simply an extension of the back stretch of an oval snowmobile racetrack. Consulting Google Maps will reveal the details. Although the slopes were adequately lit, the landing strip was not. The moon that night would be a new one—too dark to provide any residual light—so we had to plan the trip with an arrival before sunset. If we arrived late, it would be too dark to land and we would have no choice but to turn around and fly back home.

It was a clear night. Dennis's VFR flight plan had us departing Beaver County Airport, flying to West Mifflin Airport (same location as the A&P school I had attended) to pick up Debbie and Bill, and heading north to Cockaigne, where we would ski for a few hours and fly home, retracing the outbound legs.

All had gone well with his carefully planned flight, but unfortunately a slight head wind caused a delay in arrival, leaving us with about a minute or two before the last bit of the setting sun would disappear below the horizon. As we flew in from the southeast, looking out over the surrounding terrain in the diminishing sunlight, I noticed that the landscape colors seemed to disappear, making navigation that much more difficult.

As we approached the valley, Dennis lowered the flaps and landing gear and descended quickly from his cruise altitude, dropping below the surrounding hilltops in order to make a slow pass. By doing so he was able to scope out the terrain and landing strip, planning his touchdown point. But as we buzzed the field at a hundred feet, we saw several snowmobiles with their headlights on, racing around the oval track—and our landing strip! With the light quickly fading, Dennis pushed the throttle forward, sharply pulling up on the controls into a high-banking 180-degree turn, and set up for his final approach. The roar of the aircraft engine was louder than that of the snowmobiles, and the drivers fortunately looked up and saw us, pulled off the runway to the opposite side of the oval track, and lined up side-by-side facing the runway. It looked like they were sitting in front row seats at some sporting event waiting to witness the spectacle of this half-crazed pilot trying to land in the dark. (Or was it to witness a spectacular crash? Who knows?)

With the last bit of light, Dennis had one shot—and one shot only—to make it good. A missed approach meant climbing up, heading south for Pittsburgh and kissing our ski trip goodbye. At the end of his turn I glanced around at our passengers. Bill wasn't looking so good; his face was completely expressionless and a sort of pale white. Not me! I was enjoying a great adventure at its peak. Dennis made a skillful landing with adequate braking that left a short distance before depletion of useable runway. Without mentioning names, to some pilots (yes, Dave Rigau, I'm talking about YOU), a foot or two at the end is all you need.

Dennis executed a 180 at the end of the runway to set up for the takeoff, then shut down the engine and had us get out to manually push the plane off the snowmobile track so the snowmobilers could resume their fun. Just as we were unloading our skis and boots, a hay-filled horse-drawn sleigh approached us. The man at the reins gave us a warm welcome and offered us a ride to the resort which we gladly accepted. On the way, we shared our wineskin flasks of brandy with him. In the back of the sleigh, I was thinking, *What an unbelievably wonderful way to start this evening of fun!* The timing was perfect, Dennis's execution was masterful, and the sleigh was a pleasant surprise—and it all came together with that recurring pinch of luck.

Burnout and bullshit

Academically, the first two years of college went by smoothly and all was going well until I hit my junior year in the fall of 1978. After graduating from community college, I had transferred to West Virginia University's main campus in Morgantown for my last two years of school. But living in an apartment there and coming home on weekends to work was much harder than I thought it would be. My girlfriend and I were having a hard time getting along, and it looked like it wasn't going to last. Emotionally, these things took a toll on my attitude, my studies, and my overall outlook. I struggled trying to cope with it all, and dropped out of WVU in the middle of my first semester. Looking back, I was probably suffering from a mild form of depression.

Hoping to reduce my stress, I transferred to the University of Pittsburgh as a commuter but was disappointed on several fronts. Most notably, I discovered that virtually all the professors came across as arrogant and uninterested in student learning. It was a different environment than community college, where instructors took a personal interest in all the students. At Pitt, most seemed to prefer sitting in their offices, smoking their pipes, and reflecting about how important they were. To be fair, there were one or two younger professors who took an interest in students, but they were by far the exception. Teacher's assistants, whom I could barely understand, were in charge of complicated engineering labs. I swear, one assistant I had from Peru knew no more than twenty English words.

Another disappointment surfaced when I tried to register for a specific class required to graduate on time. If I did not get this particular class, I would be forced to delay graduation one semester. In order to get in, it would be necessary to camp out in the hall outside the registrar's office the night before to be assured of one of the thirty available seats before they filled up, seemingly impossible for a commuter like me. I was reminded of those Vietnam veterans at PIA who had seen and done much more than their younger classmates—like them, I was too old to put up with that chicken shit.

With increasing frustration, I threw in the towel at Pitt after one semester and transferred to Geneva College, a smaller Christian-based school in Beaver Falls, Pennsylvania that had a mechanical engineering department. The classes were much smaller, professors were sincerely interested in student learning, much like CCAC, and I felt like I was getting a good return on my investment. With only eight mechanical engineers in my graduating class, we received more personal attention than students at WVU or Pitt, a benefit to anyone who enjoys learning.

Interestingly enough, I still had residual feelings from my confirmation ceremony that made me turn away from the Christian overtones at the college. My stubborn disbelief made me reject their ancillary references to God and Christ, but I went along with the flow as I had done in Catechism, not wanting to rock the boat, because I wanted that degree. It wasn't until a few years later that I was able to put aside that rejection; in the meantime, I was content with debating the subject among my peers.

Although a much better learning environment, I still had some issues. Some of the classes, differential equations and thermodynamics, for example, were just not clicking in my head. I couldn't relate to ethereal concepts like enthalpy or entropy and struggled to memorize Diff-E equations. Being a nuts-and-bolts guy, I had to see these images in my mind to comprehend and absorb their meaning. Real-life examples would have helped, but most of the explanations centered around isolated equations with little or no connection to how they would be used in practice.

I became increasingly frustrated in our Humanities labs. Admittedly, it was not one of my favorite classes, but I made a diligent effort to do well. In the first lab, grades were solely dependent upon a student's verbal participation in the discussion topic of the day. No tests, homework or quizzes in the curriculum—just discussion. The more a student participated in lab discussion, the better the grade they received. This lab happened to be taught by the middle-aged department head who, as it turned out, apparently had a thing for young female college students. My best female friend at school, Sharon, was in the lab with me. During the semester, I was right in the midst of almost every discussion and I NEVER heard Sharon say a word the whole time, not one! I did notice throughout the course that the instructor's eyes constantly drifted toward her legs and other assets. At the end of the semester I received a C, while Sharon got an A! Not willing to take this sitting down, I discretely and diplomatically complained to my instructor—without mentioning his ocular ogling—and my grade was promptly changed to an A. Score one for diplomacy.

Another lab episode taught me a valuable political lesson. The fourth and final required Humanities class included a lab that offered a wide variety of topics to choose from. One that caught my eye centered around the Pacific War and the bombing of Hiroshima. With my natural interest in all things WWII, I did not hesitate to sign up. It seemed much better than studying Baroque paintings or the architectural style of buildings with flying buttresses.

Well, the first class was a real kicker! Within ten seconds after the lab assistant introduced himself, he explained that he would be focusing on the atrocities that the United States had perpetrated on the thousands of innocent civilians of Hiroshima who were slaughtered by that one atomic bomb. He chose to completely ignore the atrocities committed by the Japanese military in Burma, the Philippines, Pearl Harbor, and China, especially Nanking. The fact that the Hiroshima and Nagasaki bombs potentially saved hundreds of thousands of lives on both sides by ending the conflict was flagrantly disregarded. He went on to say that anyone who felt that the bombing was justified could simply raise their hand and state their name, and each would be excused—not to worry, we would be marked present throughout and receive an A grade for the lab, no questions asked.

I was old enough to know that he didn't want to cope with dissenting students who were also versed in history and might dispute his skewed indoctrination. I felt that his omission of critical facts amounted to revisionism bordering on propaganda. So, I, along with two other engineering students, took him up on the offer. Thinking about it afterward, I feared his views would do unnecessary damage to my younger classmates' minds, but didn't realize until later that this experience was a small sign and a slow burn of what was to come in higher education.

Maybe I was too old for college, but these experiences clouded my opinion of the university system. I was simply not getting the quality that I was paying for. Like the PIA vets, once again I called chicken shit. I was also burned out. Taking heavy loads in tough courses and working part-time was having its toll. I was tired of not having enough money and longed for the fun days working at Pratt.

In my junior year, Tom, the owner of the Sunoco station, offered me a full-time job with a good salary working as his chief mechanic. I came damn close to quitting school and accepting his offer if it weren't for my father's intervention. He was insistent, more so than I had ever seen him, that I knuckle down and finish school.

Job hunting

In the middle of my senior year, I started to apply for jobs. I wanted to get back into the Aerospace Industry, especially at Pratt & Whitney in Florida. In addition, I submitted resumes to General Dynamics, Lockheed, Link, Grumman, and a few others. It was May of 1981, and Jimmy Carter's single term in office had plunged the defense industry into a slump. Few companies were hiring; even the commercial airlines were sluggish in taking on new employees. Students from a select group of schools and at the top of their classes were the only applicants considered—and I was neither.

The June following graduation brought no prospects and I was getting discouraged. My father and Bill Bergman, a neighbor in Quaker Heights, tried hard to get me to consider working for Armco (by then, a division of U.S. Steel) in nearby Ambridge. Armco needed people, but I really wasn't interested in the steel industry. Aviation was my love, so I politely resisted their argument that it might be my best chance for a job. I was happy I stuck with my gut because the Armco plant shut down less than four years later.

Since Pratt was not hiring in Florida and no longer an option, I turned my eyes westward. The application I had sent to Lockheed in Burbank went unanswered. I got a personal letter from my Pratt friend, Arnie Gunderson, asking me how the job search was going. While I was in school, he had transferred from West Palm Beach to Palmdale California as a J-58 engine field representative and was now enjoying life in sunny Southern California. Arnie was put in charge of Pratt's engine repair shop right next to the Lockheed

SR-71 maintenance depot on the north side of the Palmdale Airport. Pittsburgh natives called California the "land of fruits and nuts," but I had a different vision in my mind. It was the land of the Beach Boys, hot cars, beaches, mountains, and beautiful blonde women. If I could land a job out west, it would be great for a young, single guy like me!

I gave him my status and he said he would mail me a second application. I was instructed to send the application and my resume directly to him instead of to the human resources department. I promptly acted as instructed and patiently waited. Arnie gave my resume to Bob Murphy, the head of Lockheed manufacturing in Palmdale. With Arnie's personal recommendation, Mr. Murphy in turn gave my resume to a program manager, Gene Salvay, in Burbank. As I found out later, Mr. Salvay's program was a proposal effort for what was to become the Stealth Bomber. Lockheed Aircraft Company was competing with Northrup to get the design and production contract applying Stealth Technology to a long-range bomber. (If you are interested in more details, do a Google search for Lockheed Stealth Bomber.) As a result, Lockheed was ramping up in anticipation of receiving the contract.

It didn't take long to get a reply. One afternoon about a week later, I was out in the driveway washing my car—again in cut-offs, but no lightning this time—when the phone rang. I answered in the garage, and the voice on the other end introduced himself as Gene Salvay from Lockheed Aircraft in Burbank. He told me that he was with Advanced Development Programs (ADP) and he had reviewed my resume and wanted to ask me a few questions.

"You mean the Skunk Works?" I asked.

Hesitating briefly, he said, "Well, we don't use that term on the phone."

Holy Crap! I thought. *I am actually talking to someone from the Skunk Works.* I tried to hide my excitement.

After I answered a couple of his questions, he said "When could you start?"

This time it was, *HOLY SHIT, did I just hear him correctly?* I couldn't believe my ears. Gathering my composure, I asked him when a formal interview would take place.

"No need for that," he replied. "Consider yourself hired." He said that I would receive an offer letter in the mail along with a Personal Security Questionnaire (PSQ) and information about relocation. Pack my bags and drive out as soon as possible!

I hung up the phone and sat down on the garage steps, totally dumbfounded. I had expended all that effort writing letters, sending resumes, and making phone calls, with no results. And all it took was a connection—one person who knew another person who knew a program manager—and BANG, not only am I hired in aerospace, but straight into the Skunk Works!

Thank God I took my father's sternly worded advice and stuck it out. It took me 5½ years because of those early prep courses and withdrawing from WVU, but I had made it. Finally achieving my graduation goal gave me a wonderful feeling of personal accomplishment, and it had landed me a job I never would have been considered for without a degree.

After packing my Chevelle, I said my goodbyes to family and friends and left home the last week of June 1981, heading straight for California.

Driving west

The drive westward was exciting with a whole new countryside to see. Having never been west of Tulsa, it was my first experience with the huge thunderstorms in the Texas plains, the colorful canyons of New Mexico, the majestic mountains that dwarfed the Appalachians, and the hot, dry desert of Needles, California, reaching 115 degrees. The only sad part was that I had no one with me to share this experience, something I still regret to this day.

During the five days it took to drive to southern California, there was plenty of time for personal, in-depth thinking. I thought about the time George Rogers at Pratt told me that I could double my salary if I got a degree;

he was absolutely correct. My salary offer was $11.25/hour which was 2½ times what I was making at Pratt before I was laid off.

It all helped me realize how negative experiences, like being laid off from a job I loved, could turn into happy endings. Without the layoff, who knows if I would have ever received my college degree? I remember thinking then that previous stumbles in my journey through life had led to the temptation to open the door of self-pity—the *Why is this happening to me?* persecution complex that sometimes plagued me. But every coin has two sides. Bad events often open opportunities for personal growth and learning on the flip side, as long as we take the initiative. Everyone who experiences a setback in life has two options. One is to wallow in your failure, mishap, or personal loss, or you could lift yourself out of the valley of despair and think, *What can I learn from all this? How can I get back into the game?* It's easy to say but hard to execute. Little did I know that one of the biggest knockdowns in my life was lying in wait for me, a mere three years away—one that almost broke me. But for now, life was great!

The plan was for me to stay with Arnie for a couple of weeks in Palmdale. When I pulled into his driveway and calculated the mileage, I discovered I had driven exactly 2,500 miles. There's no meaning behind it, just an odd feature of the trip. I guess I fit the bill of an engineer.

PART 2

Skunk Works

11

Initiations

My first day on the job at Lockheed was a shocker. After the new hire clear-in process, my administrative supervisor told me that I would be working temporary assignments in the "unclassified world" until my interim clearance was granted, and then I could work on the program that I was hired for. It was taking about four months to get an interim Top-Secret clearance and six months for a full clearance to go through.

Late that morning, he escorted me to Building 90, just east of the Burbank Airport (now Bob Hope Airport) and up the elevator to the third floor, where the Design Department for the L-1011 Lockheed Commercial Jetliner was located. The elevator door opened to a huge sprawling office space that took up the entire floor with no dividers; it was filled with a sea of drafting boards and designers. When I first scanned this overwhelming scene, I saw nothing but faces much older than me. My eye caught a heavyset man crossing the room in the requisite white shirt and dark thin tie, shuffling his feet down an aisle at a snail's pace. *This place looks like a senior citizens' retirement center,* I thought. *What the hell am I getting myself into?*

The seating arrangement contained row upon row of drafting boards, each with two wooden drawer cabinets about 36-inches high and 40-inches deep. A drafting tabletop made of tongue-and-groove joined wood, 1¼-inches thick and lying at a slightly elevated angle, spanned each set of cabinets. Attached to the top of each table was an expensive-looking drafting machine, something I had never seen in engineering school.

I was assigned to one of these drafting boards in the area responsible for the plane's cockpit section and was briefed on my responsibilities: 1) incorporate Engineering Orders (EOs) written against drawings by rolling them into the parent master vellum drawing, 2) make a full Letter Change Revision to the drawing, entering all the changes into the upper right-hand change block, and 3) submit each completed drawing for release after obtaining an approval signature.

EOs were quick change mechanisms to a drawing. Without the EO process, designers would need to submit a full-blown drawing Letter Revision, even at the nuts-and-bolts level, and then wait for the official release, a process that would surely hold up production. Plus, EOs were created by designers in the engineering office or liaison engineers on the manufacturing floor, and could be done in a manner of minutes. Company rules allowed only five EOs total against any one drawing; anything over five triggered a full letter revision. Despite this rule, some of the drawings on my desk were accompanied by twenty-five EOs—not an easy task to incorporate at one time. I had days of boring work ahead of me, but I also learned a lot about Lockheed's design drawings and their release system.

Back then, the design of the L-1011 was done by handmade drawings, mostly J-size, typically ink on vellum. J-size drawings, 34-inches tall and ranging from 48- to 144-inches wide, were the largest available. We had only drawn with pencil in college, so I had to quickly learn how to draw in ink, an art in itself. Fortunately, the tall, lanky engineer sitting in front of me, John Kenney, was helpful. We developed a lasting friendship and, soon after meeting him, we became roommates and rented a three-bedroom house in

Lancaster. During this time on the L-1011, I was sent to a class on Computer Aided Design and Manufacturing (CADAM), an IBM mainframe-based computer electronic drawing tool that was a powerful state-of-the-art device in those days.

A little over four weeks later, and still waiting for my clearance to be approved, I was rescued from that icebox job and moved to a building directly across from the Skunk Works engineering department (Building 311) to work on updating the company Drafting Practice Manual (DPM). There were several young new hires like me in one small room and, although the work was absolutely boring, my peers were closer to my age group and I was a little more comfortable. Four weeks after that, I was granted my interim security clearance. Some of us were taken over to the design area and briefed on the program: a proposal to build the B-2 Stealth Bomber. Lockheed was in direct competition with Northrup for that effort. I was there for less than an hour and only got to see two views on a drawing, but it was the damn coolest drawing I had ever seen! Man, was I excited!

Before I could be transferred over to the new assignment, we got word the first week in October that Northup, not Lockheed, was awarded the B-2 contract. I was totally flummoxed! I felt like I was sitting on a limb that was about to be sawed off. Lockheed had moved me cross-country to work on a really cool program, and now it was canceled. I started to relive my Pratt layoff. *What the hell was going to happen now?*

Behind the curtains

By this time, I had stopped driving my car to work and started taking the Antelope Valley bus for my commute. At quitting time, I would wait for the bus outside a large hangar called Building 309/310 that backed up to Hollywood Boulevard. That October was still pretty hot, and with no air conditioning in the building, the hangar doors were left wide open with several enormous tarps covering the opening for visual concealment. Second shift for the hourly employees would have already started, and I could hear air drills running and rivet guns pounding behind the tarps. From my work at the Grumman factory in Stuart, I knew that something really big was going on and concluded that there might be an opportunity for me behind those curtains.

It so happened that on my bus commuting trips, I had met a fellow rider who was a design engineer, Terry Putnam. I had no idea which program he worked on, having learned by then not to bring that up in conversation. I shared my predicament about the canceled program and expressed curiosity about the activities going on behind those tarps. He didn't reveal any details, but told me that he might have some connections and asked what I was interested in doing. I replied that I was hired as a structural design engineer but felt a little insecure being placed right away on the drafting board with no experience. Being a mechanic or an engineering aide was quite different from designing aircraft structures. I asked if there were any jobs where I could become familiar with the inside workings of manufacturing and the details of structures. Terry said he would check into it and let me know.

My honesty about my lack of design experience must have impressed him. Blam! Just like that, I was transferred to the Liaison Group—and completely in the dark about what I would be doing.

Initiation #1

Larry Wise was the Liaison Group's manager responsible for my new program as well as several other classified programs around the plant. A Liaison Group worked as an intermediary organization between the Design Group and Manufacturing. They were mostly seasoned mechanics or two-year-degree folks who played an important part in the aircraft manufacturing process. Design engineers were busy creating any remaining drawings, making modifications as needed or incorporating necessary changes resulting from oversights. They could not effectively spend time on the shop floor while dealing with these higher priorities. Stationed on the floor at various locations of the production line, i.e., the wing, fuselage, final assembly, etc., each liaison engineer dealt with design problems or fabrication errors that had to be addressed ASAP to keep production moving.

I learned from Larry that my assigned program was the F-117 Stealth Fighter, later to be named Nighthawk. Despite the name, it was actually not a fighter but an attack aircraft. The payloads were 500 and 2000 lb. precision laser-guided bombs, both fragmented and penetrator types. Of course, at the time I had no idea what the F-117 was.

Our first stop on his initiation tour was the design area on an upper floor in Building 311, where he made a few cursory introductions to the structural design engineers and their leadership. Because the designers' building abutted the final assembly area, it was a short trip down a staircase to a walkway that circled above all the activity on the manufacturing floor. Kelly Johnson, creator of the Skunk Works in the early 1940s, had insisted that his designers work right next to the manufacturing operations to optimize communication between the two groups. That concept was still in practice when I hired on.

After the introductions, Larry took me down those stairs. When I stepped onto the walkway and looked down, I was STUNNED! I had a full, unobstructed, panoramic view of the entire interior of the building that housed all the drilling and riveting I had heard from my Hollywood Way bus stop. Now I could see everything that was happening—and there was a lot happening on that floor!

To the best of my recollection, this hangar was about 120-yards long and 60-yards wide, three industrial levels high, with a full-length bridge crane. If one were to Google "SR-71 manufacturing" the larger color images would show what was once the factory floor of Building 309/310 where the final assembly work on the F-117 was performed.

I had never seen anything like it in my life—outside of a *Star Wars* movie! It was as if several Star Fighters were below me, being prepped for battle with the Death Star, and any minute Luke Skywalker might appear. I was speechless. I stood there, my mouth hanging open in amazement.

Larry tried to move us on, saying, "Let's go down to our Liaison Group office and I'll introduce you to the other engineers."

Normally I would have been right on his heels, but at that moment I couldn't move. "No, please, just let me stand here for a minute to take this all in." He understood.

Once I was able to tear myself away from the scene below, we continued on to the next stop while Larry explained that other buildings in the Burbank plant made many of the piece parts and subassemblies, but it was here where it all came together. After completion of its final assembly, each aircraft would then be moved under the cover of darkness to the fuel barn, located in another building on the airport complex near the runway. After it passed functional fuel systems and leak checks, the aircraft was moved to a third area where special treatments were applied to its exterior. The last move consisted of removing the wings and tail feathers, loading the fuselage and disassembled components onto a C-5 transport in the middle of the night, and flying it out to a classified test site for reassembly, full systems check, flight test, and Air Force acceptance.

A pencil drawing hanging in my home office of the F-117

Once on the ground floor, and having passed all the assembly work, we arrived at the Liaison Engineering office and I met my fellow coworkers as well as my new lead, Lance. My peers were from all walks of life, with ages ranging from mid-twenties to early sixties. They included a Vietnam veteran as well as a Marine, Stan Holowski, who had fought in the WWII Pacific Island campaigns.

Stan was an easygoing, likable guy and I enjoyed working with him. He somewhat reluctantly spoke about his wartime experiences, but when he did, I found them fascinating. One philosophy he shared about religion has stayed with me all these years: "Religion was created by man to make himself feel good about being bad." It helped me understand that there was a difference between religion and spirituality—a new perspective that I hadn't considered before. The idea of separating the two made it easier, in some ways, to consider a relationship with a spiritual being, but without the parts of organized religion that I had a hard time reconciling in my mind.

Another older gentleman, Leo Yukubian, had been with Lockheed since the 1950s and had worked on the YF-12 and SR-71. He also had some good stories to tell.

Gene Beauchamp was another interesting fella who worked in our group for a short time. He was a fast-talking, fast-walking, middle-aged man with a quick mind. I tagged along with him to learn about cabling and electrical systems. In the process of showing me the ropes, he taught me some things about people as well. Over time, he had come to realize that Lockheed employees fell into two categories, Strokers and Green Backers. Strokers were those whom you could make happy simply by giving them awards and telling them that they had done a great job. They would proudly display their plaques on their walls and desks, their stickers on their notebooks, and their buttons on their lapels. They desired approval and respect from their peers and subordinates. Unconsciously, Strokers tended to place their office desks opposite the door so that a visitor would approach as if seeking an audience with an authority figure.

Green Backers, according to Gene, were the complete opposite; they did not give a damn about any of those things. They just wanted to be monetarily compensated for their hard work and performance.

This little tidbit proved valuable over the years. I learned to see my future bosses, peers, and subordinates through the lens of those two categories, a useful tool that helped me better understand how to interact with others.

Most of the men from the Liaison Group were great to work with and they all went out of their way to pass on, in addition to the technical intricacies of the job, their collective tribal knowledge. And I absorbed every detail.

Initiation #2

For the first few weeks, my job was to tag along with various liaison engineers and learn as much as I could. My first assigned rotation matched me up with Emil Kaspersak, who worked the Wing Jig (wing assembly tool). Emil was one of those always-happy older guys. Short, round, and gentlemanly, he got along with everybody. To me, he became a father figure. Working with him on my first large structure, I took in as much as I could, writing down everything he taught me in my carry notebook. All the mechanics and supervisors liked and respected Emil, which was fortunate for me because it helped them accept me as well—and led to their decision that it was initiation time for the new kid.

The opportunity for this initiation presented itself when the supervisor, the inspector, Emil and I, along with several mechanics, were huddled around a structure examining a serious and potentially costly issue affecting an attachment between the wing plank and the spar. It was late fall, but still warm, and I was wearing a short-sleeve shirt. Right in the middle of an explanation, with everyone appearing to be a little tense, the mechanic standing behind me sneezed and I felt a spray of wet saliva and snot on the back of my arm. In a split second, I went from listening intently to thinking *What kind of asshole wouldn't have the courtesy to cover his mouth?* Outraged and scowling, I turned around to give this low-life bastard the evil eye. As I did, I caught a glimpse of a spray bottle. The person holding it had a big grin on his face, and I knew I'd been had. Everyone busted out laughing. Agreeing that it was a damn good trick, and realizing it was their way of accepting me into the fold, I ended up laughing along with them.

Calling a design god

After a couple of weeks on the wing assembly, I was rotated to the Aft Body, an all-titanium structure unlike anything I had previously worked on. Titanium was processed differently than aluminum, requiring different cutting angles on drill bits and other unique processes. I also learned that if cadmium comes in contact with titanium the result is embrittlement, so we had to avoid using cadmium-plated tools.

A short time later they moved me again to work on the fuselage structure, which was all aluminum. I learned about the various types of aluminum, such as 2024, 6061, and 7075, their tempers, and their other characteristics. By the time I was moved to the final line, at the end of four weeks, I was feeling more confident in my job. On the final line, all the major subassemblies—wings, aft body, fuselage and tail feathers—were mated for the first time. Some functional checks were performed at this location, and then the aircraft would be transported out to the fuel barn.

After the final line, I did a short rotation in the fuel barn and then the Special Coatings area, which I found the most interesting. I got to work with materials that had been developed specifically for this vehicle and had not yet been produced in substantial quantities. Structural composites had only been around for a short time, and I enjoyed learning about them. I was in an ideal position because the older guys, who were much more comfortable with structures, were reluctant to take on mastering new materials. Over time, I became the main liaison engineer for this discipline. Soon it would become my ticket to moving back into the design organization.

During the next eleven months, I worked all areas of F-117 production, including a rotating second shift. We only had two liaison engineers on second shift to cover all production areas, and we didn't have design support, which meant added responsibilities for us. But they were on call if needed.

One night, I had to make that call. A bird had just arrived from the fuel barn and was in the Special Coatings area. Mechanics were re-attaching the wings to the fuselage. This required precise alignment of each wing to its fuselage mating surface via the manipulation of a wing support cradle that moved on wheels and had several hand-operated jacks. Once alignment was perfect, several large diameter bolts would be used to mate the wing fittings to the bathtub fuselage fittings. Manufacturing was always in a hurry and often took shortcuts, probably because performance evaluation criteria for floor supervision included staying on schedule. However, the alignment process took time, and, because it was second shift, oversight was limited, making it easier to take some of those shortcuts.

That particular evening, I received a call from an inspector in the Special Coatings area advising me to come over and watch the wing alignment and installation process. I hung up and rushed over to his building. When I arrived, I saw that they had gotten close with their alignment, but it wasn't perfect. To overcome this misalignment, they had forced two bolts into the wing side bathtub fittings and used those bolts to pull the wing assembly into alignment. The first wing mating didn't go well and had to be separated before trying again.

I took this opportunity to walk over with the inspector and get a closer look at the fuselage bathtub fitting bolt holes, where we saw severe thread gouges and aluminum shavings. This was unacceptable, because sharp, helical gouges were a defect that could crack highly stressed bathtub fittings as a result of the normal wing flexing and cycle fatigue that aircrafts experience. And that could lead to a catastrophic failure—a bad day for the pilot, for sure.

I mentioned the gouging issue to the floor supervisor, but he essentially blew me off, saying that the wings were going to be mated his way. In other words, he did not care one iota about our concerns. The physical condition of the fittings was bad enough, but his arrogant attitude and condescending tone made my blood pressure spike. After a couple of days to think about it, I realized that it was more than arrogance on his part—it was also ignorance of the sound technical reasoning behind the concern. Arrogance and ignorance in tandem are key ingredients for disaster.

So here I was, a young liaison engineer, caught between the two powerful departments of Quality and Manufacturing, each with an opposing opinion and objective. With my lack of experience and new employee insecurity, I opted to call the wing designer, Bill Bissell, at home. Bill had designed the 117 wings, as well as the wings for the SR-71 and the U-2. In my mind, I was calling an engineering design god. When he answered the phone, and knowing that I had interrupted his dinner, I nervously explained the situation. Bill confirmed that I had made a good call and yes, it was a serious problem. I asked him what to do, as we were at an impasse with the supervisor. He told me to have the inspector write a squawk in the log book and for me to disposition it by ordering manufacturing to halt production until he could look at it in the morning.

Halt production! Wow, those were powerful words for a peon like me to hear. I did as he instructed and, as you might expect, the shit hit the fan. My instructions in the disposition forced the floor supervisor to stop work in that area for the evening. He was not happy, to say the least. My name was used, most likely in vain, by Manufacturing in the next day's morning meeting. I went in early on second shift that next day to speak with Bill directly. He reassured me that it was the right call and, consequently, he created a standard repair procedure to be used in the future.

What did I learn from this stressful episode? The lesson was that if and when I find something wrong, and the ball is in my court to prevent it, I need to set my insecurities aside and do the right thing. If it turns out to be a bad call, so be it. I would take my medicine and do it differently next time. Better to make a few mistakes by exercising more caution than to be responsible for a catastrophic event. That would be harder to live with—much harder.

The Lone Ranger isn't real?

Since Special Coatings was a newly developed area, there were naturally many problems to solve, processes to refine and implement, and lots of hands-on training for the mechanics. During the subsequent six months or so, and working with Kent Burns and Duane Grant, the designers responsible for this area, I helped by modifying and writing new Process Bulletins, recommending staffing changes to include an increase in the number of qualified composites mechanics, and completing several other not-to-be-mentioned tasks. After a while, I was invited to meetings with Design, Manufacturing, and Inspection (now known as Quality Assurance). Professionally, I had achieved name recognition and had a decent reputation in the Design Group.

Another enlightening experience came out of working closely with the mechanics on the floor. I was able to see them performing difficult tight-tolerance and high-quality work using basic tools. One particular task in the Special Coatings area took many man-hours to perform and had a low success rate, which meant that with every improper application of this special material, they would need to remove the initial material and start those sections all over again. This task involved clasping a bare, single-edged razor blade as if they were scraping paint off a window, with their fingers right up to the glass, to trim off excess material that we called butter.

As I watched this tedious operation, I had an idea for a tool that could potentially cut that process time by 90 percent and lower the rejection rate. I believe the specifics are still classified and the details cannot be discussed. What I can say is that I designed and created a prototype tool by modifying a small modeling block plane. I first tried it myself in several locations, and then asked a couple of mechanics to test its functionality. It worked well, and the mechanics loved it. I drew up a sketch, including dimensions, and showed it to Kent and Duane in the Design Group. They liked it as well and suggested that I officially submit my "Trimming Tool" to the Tooling Group for a product improvement award. If accepted and implemented, it could be worth between $500 to $1,000, depending on the amount of time it saved—a nice chunk of cash for that time. I submitted my tool and waited for their adjudication and the anticipated incentive award.

After a few weeks, I asked the tooling engineer about the status of my submission and he told me to talk to the manufacturing manager of the Special Coatings area, Mike M. When I did, Mike seemed to beat around the bush with his explanation as to why the approval was held up. After calling him out on his vague explanation, he reluctantly came to the point and said that he was the final approver and would not sign it unless I put his name, as well as his supervisor's name, on the submission form. That would make them co-inventors; I would be forced to share the cash reward and recognition with two people who didn't have a damn thing to do with the idea!

This dishonest maneuver was reminiscent of my experience with the Leetsdale Police Chief who had expected Tom to give him a kickback for towing, and I was angry.

Incensed would be a better word, because I had learned at a young age that dishonesty shouldn't win. Heroes from the TV shows I watched as a kid in the fifties—The Lone Ranger, Roy Rogers, and Hop-a-Long Cassidy—had convinced me that good always triumphs over evil (usually within the span of a half hour). I told Mike M. that his demands were not ethical and that there was no way I would comply. Sadly, the trimming tool improvement, despite the potential cost savings, was never processed and implemented. I ended up giving the prototype to one of the better mechanics for his use. I guess the writers of those TV shows didn't take into account that greed trumps honesty. My idealism took a sharp blow that day.

Don't peek!

My final rotation as a liaison engineer was in the field, at the test site. Once production of each F-117 was complete, it was broken down into sub-assemblies, then transported on a C-5 aircraft from Burbank to the test site in the dead of night. This was and still is a classified location that much is written about but few have seen. After arrival and unloading, the mechanics would assemble the aircraft for the final time, perform a full functional checkout of all systems, ground test the engines, apply the remaining pieces of the Special Coating, and perform flight tests. Once our customer, the Air Force, was satisfied, the final step would be to sign the DD-250, a government form that formally accepts products and authorizes payment to Lockheed.

On my first visit to this location, I had no idea where I was being taken or what was in store for me. Transit to and from the test site for all personnel was on the Red and White, the Lockheed-leased Boeing 737 that I reference in the first chapter. It had previously been in commercial service, operated by Western Airlines. The aircraft traveled twice a day, out in the morning and back in the afternoon, then it would overnight in Palmdale and fly back into the Burbank airport each morning to pick up passengers and repeat the routine.

Processing into that location for the first time was an unusual experience due to the many precautions implemented to maintain security. On my first flight, when we were about halfway from our destination, we were told to pull the window shades down to mask the surrounding terrain, as well as any hardware that might be visible from the plane when we arrived. After landing, cleared employees were permitted to deplane, and first-timers like me were told to stay in our seats. After a brief wait, we were escorted directly to a security/badging shack where we were briefed on how Base rules were enforced; in a nutshell, break a rule, any rule, and your ass would be hauled out of there. No questions asked.

We worked two 12-hour shifts, which meant plenty of overtime in our paychecks. I was assigned to second shift, so I had to get my sleep during the day. It reminded me of my father and what it must have been like for him all those years working night shifts in the steel mill. The food was pretty decent, and on Thursdays they served high-quality steaks and beer and provided entertainment (the kind that would be politically incorrect by today's standards).

One night we could tell that something special was going to happen. During the day shift, the flight test aircraft had been rearranged, and some foreign aircraft assets had been moved to the end hangar. Early in my shift, I was able to climb all over those aircraft, which was quite interesting from an engineer's perspective. I realized that they were designed with a different set of requirements.

Around midnight, everyone was herded into the end hangar and told to stay there until further notice because Vice President George Bush was going to pay us a visit and tour the F-117s. When we heard this, we were excited until Security informed us that under no circumstance were we to open—or even peek through—those hangar doors, or we would be shot. That certainly got our attention!

Sure enough, at the designated time we heard a two-engine turbo prop aircraft taxi up and shut down its engines just outside the hangar where we were sequestered. I assumed it was a King Air by the engine and prop sounds, but no way was I going to chance a peek to confirm. When his tour was over, forty-five minutes later, the aircraft fired up and taxied out. It was the closest I'd ever been to a vice president, and I never actually got to see him! I thought it appropriate that he was the one who implemented the first full-scale use of the F-117 in the 1990s Gulf War.

We had some fun in off-hours at the test site. Our department had a WWII-era Willys Jeep and, if requested in advance, we could use it to explore certain areas, with strict instructions about avoiding stay-out zones. We commandeered the Jeep one day, and it was a blast!

While tooling across the dry lake bed, one of the guys told me a story that had happened a few years earlier. Like us, some explorers had driven across the same dry lake bed and had stopped to examine something on foot. Unbeknownst to them, a B-52 in the process of a flight test saw the guys from a distance. The pilot decided to drop down to about a hundred feet off the deck and do a high-speed approach from behind, with the obvious intention of scaring the shit of them. When an aircraft is flying at high speed, you can't hear it coming until it's directly overhead. As planned, they didn't hear it until it blew right over them at what must have felt like mere inches away, and the subsequent engine roar, as well as the wake turbulence, certainly did the intended trick—the scaring part, that is. I didn't get any details about the inevitable excrement expulsion.

This test site was adjacent to a nuclear underground testing facility. We were briefed on that as well. A test was scheduled one late afternoon, meaning, a nuclear bomb placed deep underground was going to be detonated. Although it was a safe test, there was always a remote possibility that something could go wrong. We were issued badge dosimeters to wear and told that if they turned a certain color we would be evacuated immediately. I must admit that experiencing this for the first time, it was more than a little unnerving. The bomb went off as scheduled and the ground shook like an earthquake for a few seconds. I was looking out of our hangar door when the detonation occurred and saw the telephone poles swaying back and forth. Thankfully, my badge color did not change, and everything went quickly back to normal.

This last—and in my view, the crowning—rotation assignment, the test site, had fulfilled my desire to gain detailed knowledge and specifics about how aircraft were built. Looking back, I think that Lockheed was interested in grooming young engineers like me for advancement and technical growth, and I was one beneficiary of their plan.

Apparently, working hard and taking on extra assignments had caught someone's attention. In September of 1982, a design engineering position opened in the Special Coatings and Composites group and I was asked by Chris Fylling, the group lead, if I wanted it. Without hesitation, I said "YES!"

That fortuitous discussion on the Antelope Valley bus, just a year earlier, went from a conversation about some noises behind a green tarp to an assignment at a highly classified test site, and more pebbles of knowledge that brought me closer to being a better aircraft design engineer.

12

Living the Dream

In September of 1982, I moved from the Antelope Valley to Granada Hills in the San Fernando Valley, which was a much shorter commute of eleven miles. Right before I moved, my commute took an upturn (pun intended). I was still renting a house in Lancaster, and the bus wasn't working out as well with shift work and overtime, so I started driving. My one-way commute was a little over an hour each way. Thinking outside the box, I knew that our B-737, the Red and White, started its daily runs early in the morning from Palmdale and returned in the evening. I asked my new boss, Hank Pfenning, if I could take the plane to and from work instead of driving. He said that because I already had the access clearance and special badge to the test site, which gave me permission to board the plane, he didn't see a problem with my request. My driving distance went from fifty-nine miles down to four miles, plus a quick hop over the mountains! So, for a month or so before I moved, I commuted to and from work in a 737. As Dana Carvey in the role of the Church Lady on *SNL* would put it, "Well, isn't that special?"

On one of those afternoon trips home, I boarded the plane as usual, but takeoff was delayed by the Burbank tower and the pilot was held short of

Runway 15. For some unknown reason, the pilot chose to do something out of the ordinary. Perhaps he was pissed that the tower had held up his departure and he would be late for dinner. Or he had a hot date. Or he had bet his copilot that, despite the delay, he would still make schedule. Whatever it was, something was eating at him.

When the tower finally gave him clearance for takeoff, he taxied to the end of Runway 15 and lined up on the center line as usual. Then he did something that he hadn't done before: he held down on the brake pedals and firewalled the throttles. Only when the engines had spooled up to full thrust and the aircraft was shaking like an earthquake did he cut loose of the brakes, slamming me back into the seat. There were only four or five of us on the plane, and he had a minimum load of fuel, so we were extremely light.

After the brakes were released, we shot down the runway like a rocket. Instead of the usual twenty seconds, it took less than eight or nine seconds for rotation, then he yanked back on the stick, sending us up at one hell-of-an angle of attack climb—it felt like straight up! It reminded me of my flight with John Lillberg back in Florida, but instead of a small Pitts, I was on a commercial airliner. We then blasted north over the San Gabriel Mountains and dropped down like a rock into the Antelope Valley, entering the Palmdale approach pattern. Higher than normal speed forced him to make some much higher than normal g turns through base and final.

As soon as the nose wheel touched the runway and the squat switch was closed, the thrust reversers came on full blast as the pilot simultaneously laid on the brakes as hard as he could without locking them up. I knew it was max performance braking because my whole upper torso bent forward into a horizontal position from deceleration and my head almost struck the seat tray in front of me. I think it was the wildest ride any civilian has ever taken on a commercial B-737, and it was pretty cool!

Pinch me

Fifteen months after I started working for Lockheed, I was now where I had wanted to be. Being immersed in the fast-moving environment of a cutting-edge development program gave me the experience I was looking for. About this same time, I also became engaged. My fiancé was an engineer working at TRW and, like me, was from the Pittsburgh area. The following spring, we were married and we bought our first house in Granada Hills. As an interesting financial side note, our initial mortgage included a 13 percent interest rate, which was considered a good deal because the going rates were on their way up even higher. It was quite a contrast from today's financial environment.

My first week in the Design Group, I kept wanting to pinch myself because I felt like I was living a dream. There I was, with 105 of the best design engineers and leads in the world. The personalities, age groups, and backgrounds were mixed, and my recollection is that nine out of ten were middle-aged to near retirement, and the remaining 10 percent were around my age. Almost all had worked the U-2 and SR-71 programs, veterans of two of the greatest plane design efforts of the previous thirty years.

The two large rooms that housed the F-117 design engineers included a diversity of backgrounds, a rich collection of talents, and a great depth of experiences. One was Al Weddell, who had designed the control surfaces. He was a Merchant Marine during WWII and served on convoy ships in the North Atlantic. His ships were sunk twice by German U-Boats.

Freddie Patton was born in England and, in his younger days, he worked as a mechanic for the Royal Air Force during the Battle of Britain. The last part of the war and during the years immediately following, he was with BOAC (also known as British Airways). BOAC operated routes from England to Egypt, South Africa, and India. The airline had built refueling and stop-over stations along the African route, and Freddie was stationed at several of these remote locations, some in the deep jungle. His experiences gave him plenty of stories to tell, and he enjoyed entertaining us with some wild—bordering on the unbelievable—tales.

Because we all thought that he might have been prone to exaggeration, I took a chance one day and challenged his veracity. Conceding that his stories did seem a little outside the realm of possibility, the next day he brought in two thick albums packed with black and white photos from his assigned locations, including ones taken during the Battle of Britain. Each and every tale was supported by one or more photos. I had no choice but to humbly apologize. It was all in good fun, because we liked each other and got along well.

Klaus Hendricks was born in the Netherlands and was a member of the Dutch Underground during WWII in the resistance movement against Nazi occupation. Doug Freshwater was a Canadian who worked on the Avro CF-105 before it was abruptly canceled by the Canadian government.

Boris Diadyk was a one-man team who had created all lofting for the F-117, using only a hand calculator to generate that beautiful piece of quality work. Loft drawings accurately depict the exterior mold lines and surfaces of aircraft. Each subsequent drawing is based on the original loft drawing, so it must be 100 percent accurate. I was told that Boris was born in Russia and fled west along with the retreating Germans during the last months of WWII. A consultant, who had been a Messerschmitt pilot during WWII, visited our area once or twice, but I never officially met or spoke with him, and I cannot recall his name.

Maurice Chambers and Brian Duckworth were also from the U.K. and worked in our group. I played golf with Brian and it was always a good time. Maurice shared with me that, as a child growing up in southern England, his parents moved him out of their city and into the countryside to avoid the bombing. One afternoon, while walking on a country road, a badly damaged German Messerschmitt Bf-110 fighter-bomber, trailing smoke, flew low overhead and crashed nearby in a field. He and his buddies ran over to see two aviators smoking cigarettes standing over a third airman who was obviously dead. A farmer was standing guard with a pitch fork, waiting for allied soldiers to arrive and apprehend them. It was a surreal experience for a young boy, and it left a lasting impression on him. And on me as well, listening to him retell it.

Others whom I respected and felt privileged to work with included Jim Walters, aft-body lead; Russ Rose, roll over door; George Soto, canopy; Bill Bissell, wing; Sam Kelder, fuselage; Gary Wendt, structures; Hank Pfenning, structures lead; John Dennis, stress; Toni Rose, drawing release; and Bob Allison, Technology Group. Other names from various positions included Bob Shuster, Bob Herold, Dale Lehman, Terry Putnam, Chuck Buhman, Ed Gehring, Tom Swift, and Ed Baldwin. And there were many others with colorful and diverse professional backgrounds whom I came to know.

Jim Walters earns a personal special mention because of the invitation he extended to me during a sad period in my life. That invitation and its subsequent events led me to meet my second wife, which will be discussed in a later chapter.

Moving up our organization chart, our program manager was Alan Brown, who has been interviewed on many TV documentaries about the F-117 along with several other members of upper management. My big boss in the Skunk Works was Ben Rich, replacing Kelly Johnson, who had retired six years earlier. Both are well-known from history and aviation books, engineering journals, and news sources.

Our design area and the adjacent management offices contained some of the greatest aviation engineers and managers in aerospace. And here I sat, this nobody farm boy from Western Pennsylvania who started out as a car mechanic, trained as an A&P mechanic, and now was a junior member of an unbelievable collection of great design engineers. I thought, *Man, I'm only 30, and already it's been a great ride!* Need I mention I had a shitload of luck?

All the men and women that I talk about, along with hundreds of others from manufacturing, inspection, logistics, test, and subcontracting, deserve credit and recognition for making the organization work so well and for creating products that would have a prominent place in aviation history. And while it takes great leaders, it is regrettable that little is written about the many others, including the wrench turners, riveters and pencil pushers. These people are also the ones who made it happen. Twenty or thirty years from now, Kelly, Ben, Alan, and other leaders will still be receiving accolades, but sadly, the regular folks will have faded into obscurity. Hopefully this book will shine a spotlight on at least some of those who worked in the shadows; all have my humble admiration.

Role models: Chris, one of many

My new boss, Chris, was a Norwegian by birth—average height, thin, and sporting a neatly trimmed, slightly graying beard. He was quiet and mild mannered with a quick, dry wit. I could tell right away that he was an intelligent, creative, and talented engineer. He had been the designer for composites components on previous aircraft: the SR-71, D-21 Drone and Have Blue, which was the predecessor to the F-117. On the F-117, Chris again designed all the composite components, in addition to the top surface of the engine exhaust exit platform, called the platypus, and another fragile section in the engine exhaust area. He was also the design lead for Special Coatings, the Radar Absorbing Material (RAM) applied to the exterior surfaces. Chris had two other young engineers working for him at the time, Duane Grant and Kent Burns, who were later joined by Mike Mullaney.

My new design lead, Chris Fylling

Moving from the manufacturing floor to the design office was an adjustment. It meant transitioning from asking for an engineering decision to becoming the one making the decision. I would also be going from an interactive, hardware-touching, walking-around job to mostly sitting at a drafting board producing paper. It was a similar adjustment I made when I went from car mechanic to engineering aide at Pratt. But getting to know my peers and leads was not much of a problem, since I had worked with most of them in my liaison role. Fortunately, a short time later, I was back to more interaction with the manufacturing and support areas.

My responsibilities at first consisted mainly of oversight and working with the technicians and mechanics out in the shop. Chris was responsible for all exterior surfaces on the F-117. I covered and assisted with all his hardware along with our two other engineers. The hardware included over forty leading and trailing edge panels, the platypus, exhaust trailing edge pieces, and all exterior RAM. We had responsibility for maintaining over sixty drawings and over a dozen process bulletins, controlled documents that gave specific instructions on how to apply or install hardware and coatings.

At that time, we had five aircraft in a full-blown Flight Test Program at the test site, and the first production bird, tail #785, was coming down the final line and about to be delivered. Like any development program, bugs would surface and our job was to rectify them. These issues were reported from various production levels, i.e., labs and parts fabrication buildings, assembly areas, and even the test site. Instead of dealing with local onesie squawks and quick fixes, as we had done in the Liaison Group, we were dealing with more complex issues that required us to dig back to root cause and institute fixes at all levels. All this added up to more responsibilities over a broader range of technical areas.

Chris turned out to be a fantastic and creative design engineer, as well as an excellent teacher willing to share his knowledge and experience, both at work and from his personal life. I was reminded of George Rogers back at Pratt. One valuable lesson Chris shared was that a designer for a part or subsystem should never limit his or her knowledge to just that one item. A good designer is fully versed with each adjacent or interfacing part and subsystem to ensure that everything functions seamlessly as a whole.

Changes

About nine months later, in the early summer of 1983, several things began to change on the program. First, it transitioned from development to limited production. This forced many process changes too tedious for this story, but to provide one example, we were instructed that all removable parts, from that point on, had to be modified to become interchangeable. The way we had been operating, most removable parts required some trimming or tweaking in order to fit correctly from plane to plane.

Another change was that folks from unclassified areas were transferred onto our program to help us with the transition, and several of them, arrogantly assuming that we were clueless about aircraft production, tried to tell us how to do our jobs. Because of the increase in non-designer staff and our restricted office space, we were told that we would be moving off the Skunk Works campus to the old L-1011 building, now vacant, the same location I had been taken to on my first day.

Finally, there were two significant personnel changes. At the top of our Org Chart, our program manager, Alan Brown, moved over to lead the Technology Department (RCS) and his replacement was John Sheridan, who transferred from the now-defunct L-1011 production effort. At my level, Chris transferred to the new E Program, and he turned his old responsibilities over to me. He had referred me to replace him; apparently, he felt that I was experienced enough to handle the job.

This increase in responsibility prompted me to further my education, as I would be working more directly with people as well as having more technical responsibility, and I enrolled in several management classes offered by our internal continued education department. These included: *Transition to Supervisor, Employee Communication and Discipline, Business Ethics,* and *How to Deal with People,* along with some technical classes, *CADAM Surface, Aircraft Design Seminar,* and a follow-up class, *Advanced Composites,* at UCLA. But despite the opportunity to learn new skills, I started to become bored and look elsewhere. The fast-paced environment of development had been more challenging, and I realized that I was not cut out for the slower pace of production.

Another change pushed all my buttons and motivated me to move. Since we had transitioned to limited production, several hard-core designers, who had not liked the new culture that was creeping in, jumped ship. Not wanting to lose the tribal knowledge, the new PM declared a freeze on transfers off the F-117 program. That was too much of an edict for me to accept, and I didn't like the idea of someone other than me controlling my career path. I kept putting feelers out for a better place to land.

NO STEP

But until I could find a new program, I was in charge of Chris's hardware, and a critical issue popped up regarding one of his parts. Several pieces of special material, which were on the Trailing Edge (TE) of the F-117 behind the engine exhaust and known as "bricks," were bonded to the structure. They were fracture sensitive, meaning they would crack easily if struck. Because of reasons unknown to me, it had been determined that these bricks would be installed early in the production cycle, and subsequently travel with the aircraft all the way down the line to delivery.

At delivery, when the engines were fired up for the first time, sections of several bricks would blow off and need to be replaced—a costly and avoidable fix happening late in the game, right before aircraft acceptance. So, in an attempt to come up with a solution that would prevent this recurring damage, Quality Assurance (QA) called a meeting and invited the related disciplines (Design, Manufacturing, Tooling, Inspection and a couple of leads) to discuss the issue. As the member of the Design Group responsible for the hardware affected, I was invited.

For a little more background, the aircraft, while moving down the production line, would remain in an elevated position above the floor, easing access to its belly. Elevated work platforms, about halfway up the structure, surrounded each aircraft so that workers could easily access the top and internal surfaces. To protect these bricks from damage during the process of stepping off the platforms onto the aircraft, the Tooling Department had designed a large, V-shaped cover made from several pieces of ¾-inch plywood, which turned out to be quite heavy. It was painted bright red with "No Step" in white letters on the top surface, directly over the fragile pieces.

The protectors not only covered the bricks, but were unnecessarily extended forward onto a sounder structure that did not need their protection.

There were two functional problems with this cover/protector design. It was heavy and cumbersome, requiring two people to install and remove it, a process likely to cause hairline fractures, which may have been one reason that bricks were blowing off at initial engine start. And the cover appeared sturdy, giving the false impression that it could be stepped on without causing any damage.

It was becoming a design-by-committee meeting. I waited for the other participants to weigh in before describing what I thought were the two main issues, as indicated above, suggesting a complete redesign of the cover: make it out of clear Plexiglas and only large enough to cover the fragile bricks. That way, anyone who approached it and saw a glass-like cover would instinctively step over it for fear of breaking it, and the bricks would be better protected.

Well, the reaction to this logical suggestion was as if I had said something like, "Your first-born babies were all butt-face ugly." Seriously. Most used body language, which I "heard" loud and clear, to completely dismiss me. To my amazement, nothing more was discussed, other than a decision to reconvene the following week.

The week passed with no further feedback, but when that next meeting began, I noticed a large, brown-paper-wrapped object leaning against the window in the front corner. The Tooling Department lead started the meeting off by proudly stating that one of his tool designers had come up with a concept for a newly designed cover and wanted to share it with the group. The two of them proceeded to unwrap the package and, lo and behold, it was a smaller, Plexiglass cover—my suggestion from the previous week. He then rattled off all the advantages of this concept which, of course, sounded familiar, because I had used those same justifications. All the participants began nodding their heads in agreement, the new cover concept was accepted, and the problem solved.

For a brief moment I was pissed and thought, *WTF?* It reminded me of my trimming tool invention that was never implemented because I wouldn't let someone share the credit for work that he never did. Then I realized that the important thing here was to prevent damage, regardless of who took ownership of the fix. I kept my mouth shut and chalked it up to "not invented here" syndrome, suffered by people or organizations who oppose any ideas, inventions, or solutions that originate outside their purview. Truthfully, I have seen the same drama played out countless times over my career. It's frustrating when you propose a solid solution, and it's either ignored or shot down.

Counting Dicks

Despite the frustrations of the new reorganization, we continued to keep a sense of humor and rarely missed an opportunity to find something to laugh at. During the transition to limited production, but before moving to Building 90, the other designers and I were struggling to keep up with the increase in paperwork and the conversion to more cumbersome processes. One especially annoying new requirement was to create and attach a Separate Parts List (SPL) and release a Letter Revision Change for every drawing. Until that requirement, parts quantities had been called out on the face of the drawing. To complete this job was a pretty big effort—the fuselage alone had over 1800 drawings. To assist us, the program brought in several admins to help with the implementation. A woman who was part of this group, whom I will call Sherry, was from the L-1011 program and had the unfortunate job of working with the stubborn, often surly design engineers, who really didn't see any benefit from what they were being forced to do. She was a great gal with a pleasant, patient personality, and most of us most got along well with her.

One day, in the larger engineering office, Sherry approached a not-so-cooperative designer whom I happened to be standing near. She needed to talk to him about one of his drawings that had been submitted to her group for incorporation of the SPL. The conversation was not going smoothly, and she was obviously getting increasingly frustrated by this designer's uncooperative stance. His name was Dick, the only designer in the area with that name, and it went something like this:

Sherry: "I found several errors on your XXX Drawing change. Could you please correct them and resubmit?"

Dick: "I didn't make those entries."

Sherry: "Yes, you did. It has your name, Dick, here in the upper-right-hand corner."

Dick: "Dick who?" At this point, he was just being a smartass.

Sherry, raising her voice, now totally fed up: "What do you mean, DICK WHO?"

By this time, all heads within earshot had spun around, and the room had gotten very quiet. Dick ignored her question, raising her level of frustration even higher.

Sherry put her hands on her hips and yelled, "JUST HOW MANY DICKS DO YOU THINK THERE ARE IN THIS ROOM?"

To their credit, they both realized her hilarious faux pas immediately. Everyone busted out laughing, including Sherry. Sure, today, that exchange—and probably the laughing—would be considered politically incorrect, but at that time it was merely a funny ice breaker that helped loosen everyone up. And Sherry, because of her willingness to laugh at her own comment, gained respect from even the most cantankerous engineer.

13

Uppers, Downers, and Filler-Uppers

Living in the Los Angeles basin wasn't just all work. Regarding activities and new experiences, my expectations of Southern California were met and greatly exceeded. The area was filled with history, landmarks, attractions, and any activity you could possibly want. Huge pine trees covered the mountains. The high desert, just forty miles north of us, cycled through the seasons with a series of contrasts. Summer was scorching hot during the day and shivering cold at night. Winter brought occasional snow most years, and in the spring, the poppies and countless other wild flowers that emerged after the rainy season were outstandingly beautiful. As far as the eye could see, an infinite number of colors blanketed the ground.

Up north, Lake Tahoe, with its surrounding mountains, was the most spectacular place I had ever been, on a par with the Swiss Alps. Living where I did in Granada Hills, I could go to the beach and swim in the morning, then drive up into the San Gabriel mountains to snow ski that evening.

The cities in the basin offered a diverse nightlife scene, excellent restaurants, and fun sightseeing opportunities. Hollywood, Beverly Hills, Long

Beach with the Queen Mary and the Spruce Goose, aircraft and art museums, the La Brea Tar pits, and historical sites like the old Spanish Missions were all available for weekend excursions. It was always a pleasant surprise to run into an occasional celebrity. I had the opportunity to speak to Ernest Borgnine of *McHale's Navy* fame, and I had a short conversation with Leslie Nielson soon after his first comedy movie, *Airplane*, was released.

The Rose Parade, with all its colorful floats, was beyond belief. The night before the parade, we would walk along the staging area and watch workers putting finishing touches on floats illuminated by high intensity flood lights. I was simply awestruck by their beauty, and it would be an understatement to say that television does not do them justice.

Not a public tourist attraction, but just as exciting, I was offered and accepted a tour of my friend Arnie's J-58 overhaul shop in Palmdale. He showed me all the operations performed there and the official shop banner, which bore the signatures of famous people who had visited. Among them was Frank Whittle, one of the fathers of the gas turbine engine. Arnie's tour ended at noon, which happened to be when the SR-71 mechanics who worked in the overhaul hangar were at lunch, so we were able to go into the hangar without disturbing them. Three SRs were undergoing various stages of overhaul. The highlight of the tour was when I got to sit in the cockpit of one. What an exhilarating experience!

Polar opposites

I can't emphasize enough the range of talents and personalities on our F-117 program. As mentioned before, about 10 percent of the engineers were under 30 years old. Among them was one engineer, John Kalisz, whose talents made him stand out from the crowd. He was a couple of years younger than me and worked in the Aft Body group. John, who was hired right out of college, was a quiet guy, but always willing to help anyone in need of information or an opinion. We became friends and have remained in contact over the years. After getting to know John and observing him in his professional and private life, I came to realize that he was one of the three most talented and creative design engineers I have known.

To underscore just one of his many talents, shortly after moving to Building 90, a conceptual design engineer in our group was tasked with designing a vertical displacement bomb deployment mechanism for the F-117. He had been struggling for a week or two trying to come up with a linkage configuration that would function properly. This particular bomb was almost as long as the internal payload bay and would not clear the forward and aft structure using the current trapeze mechanism. It had to be lowered vertically instead of swinging down into the airstream before being pickled (dropped). Also, it was important that this new mechanism be interchangeable with the current configuration.

During this time, John would walk by the designer's drafting board on the way to the coffee pot and either look over his shoulder or chat with him about the issues he was having. Later, I saw John hunkered down over his drafting board, feverishly sketching out a 2-D side view of this same vertical deployment mechanism. About two days after that, he completed the sketches and arrived at work with a box under his arm. In it was a scaled, working 3-D model of a deployment mechanism with an attached model bomb that met all the requirements. This earned him a U.S. Patent, one of seven more to come over his career. In his spare time at home, he managed to build three aircraft and one helicopter, and restore two older sports cars.

In contrast to John's positive, can-do attitude, we had a few folks who always seemed to have a dark cloud hanging over their heads. One was Paul, who, despite being a friendly person, was one of those glass-half-empty kinds of guys. For a couple of months, he sat directly across from me in the next row such that our drafting boards were face-to-face. We couldn't have a simple conversation without him casting a shadow of gloom over my work area!

One morning, coming into work, I noticed that it was an exceptionally beautiful day. Cool, no smog for a change, small, white, puffy clouds dotting the crisp, blue sky, and unlimited visibility. When I arrived at my desk, in a great mood, I exchanged greetings with Paul and tried to strike up a friendly conversation, saying, "What a beautiful morning today!"

"Yeah, but it's supposed to rain Friday."

I have to laugh today, but at the time it struck me as odd. I asked myself: *What is it about this man's life that makes him so negative? An unhappy marriage? Did he have a terrible childhood?* Who knows? I never deemed it worth my time to learn the answer.

Another co-worker, Maury Chambers, was the exact opposite of Paul. I never saw him in a bad mood. One morning, a couple of months after weathering Paul's dark clouds, it was my turn to come into work in a vile state of mind. Traffic was a snarled mess. I was late. It was raining and I got soaked walking from the parking lot, having forgotten to bring an umbrella. I said something in passing to Maury about how I detested rainy days—they were just so miserable. His nicely put reply was that he looked at rainy days as a way for God to cleanse the air, cool us off, wash dirt off the pavement, and water our vegetation, all making the world a happier place to live.

Two completely different ways of interpreting a rainy day! It made me reflect on my life, especially the low points. After all, it was a low point that had nudged me back to college, a move that resulted in the best possible outcome. Unfortunately, Maury's words weren't enough to convince me about that silver lining business until something I saw one day, a few years later, made an even deeper impression.

That day, I showed up at work in a particularly foul mood, feeling that my state of mind was justified. I set my thermos down on the drafting board and accidently knocked it on the floor, shattering the internal glass and spilling my morning tea. I really enjoyed my morning tea, so that compounded my misery. My sour disposition lasted all day—no break from my self-imposed dark cloud. That afternoon, I left work early for my weekly allergy shot. When I pulled into the parking lot outside the doctor's office, I noticed an elderly man struggling just to get out of his car. He walked slowly to the other side to open up the passenger door for his elderly wife. After he helped her inch out, he gently and lovingly handed her a walker. I watched this scene play out and felt utterly ashamed. *Bob, what the hell do you have to complain about? A broken thermos of tea? Are you some kind of special idiot?*

I continued to beat myself up: *You have two of the most important things in life, your youth and your health. Man, you have absolutely nothing to complain about!*

Many times since then, life has thrown me curve balls, and I've reacted like most people and started to complain. But the memory of that scene has helped pull me out of those emotional valleys. Even now, when something negative happens in my life, I remind myself, over and over if necessary, *Life is good enough.*

Great mileage!

To end this chapter with a humorous story, I'm passing along an anecdote told to me by Jim Walters, a design lead in our structures group. Back in the mid-sixties, one of the more nerdy engineers in their group had purchased a new Chevy Impala. Obsessed with data, he meticulously recorded each tank fill-up, calculated the mileage, and graphed the results. This was not so terribly unusual, because many of us, including yours truly, have been known to track our fuel consumption at times. But this guy apparently bored the crap out of anyone who came within earshot, elaborating on his car's performance ad nauseum. So, some of his fellow engineers decided enough was enough and came up with a scheme. Over a period of a month or two, they would sneak out during lunch and dump some gasoline in his tank between fill-ups. Each time they added gas, they put a little more in than the previous time. To his plotting amazement, the mileage improved with every fill-up, and he had the graph to prove it! Of course, he had to share this remarkable fuel efficiency miracle with everyone, but now his audience had a reason to enjoy his pedantic monologues.

Well, when he reached mileage in the upper 20-mpg range, virtually impossible for a carbureted V-8 engine of that era, his fellow workers began to reverse the process and siphon out gasoline at an increasing rate. The poor guy was devastated when his mileage nose-dived to below 10 mpg!

After hearing that story, I have to admit that I was jealous of the perpetrators' creativity—and wished I had thought of it myself.

14

Kelly Johnson's World

This chapter takes a few steps back from my story to provide rare insight into the Skunk Works culture of the 1980s. It deals with Kelly Johnson's management style, which was still maintained by Skunk Works leadership when I was there, and it impressed me so much that I think others may benefit from my observations.

The history of the Skunk Works can easily be researched on the internet, so I won't repeat it all here. I recommend reading Kelly Johnson's autobiography, *Kelly: More than My Share of it All*. Ben Rich, who headed the Skunk Works from 1975 until 1991, chronicled his experiences in *Skunk Works: A Personal Memoir of My Years at Lockheed*, another recommendation.

Kelly, who designed over forty aircraft in addition to being the first team leader of the Lockheed Skunk Works, created a set of rules that framed his business model. Originally called "14 Points," it is now known as "Kelly's 14 Rules and Practices," all of which I saw put into action on the F-117 program.

Restricted access

For example, two of the fourteen rules emphasize the importance of restricted access, limiting both the number of engineers on a program and the amount they could say about it. If I were to guess, no more than two thousand people in the U.S. knew about the F-117 and what was going on behind those walls and at other related locations. Just like its predecessors, the U-2 and SR-71, the F-117 was destined to be a historically significant aircraft, providing a powerful tool to the warfighter that adversaries couldn't beat. Our relatively small group was making a significant contribution to our nation's defense, and we felt like members of an exclusive club.

But despite the magnitude of our project, we never focused on that part of it. Never once did I witness any evidence of braggadocio among our group. We quietly went about our business and did our jobs.

Outside our design room, not a word was spoken or a hint ever given about how designers had spent their day. Our wives and families knew nothing about what we did or where we went. If we flew to the test area, family members had no way to get directly in touch with us. We essentially disappeared. If anyone from the outside needed to reach one of us, they had to call a designated number in Burbank, and a message would be relayed to the recipient via a special line.

Staffing and efficiency

Moving up to the top of the leadership chain of command, Kelly Johnson, the founder, was an honest, intelligent and strong leader with a clear vision. From the beginning of the Skunk Works in 1943, he planted the seed of efficiency by handpicking his team, the cream of the crop, for the kickoff of the XP-80 Shooting Star, the first operational jet aircraft. The crew he ended up with came from the Bomber Plant, a name coined when they were producing B-17s during WWII. The XP-80 was completed in less than five months with twenty-three engineers (Johnson and Smith, 1985). After the success of this program and the next, this culture of efficiency was nurtured and perpetuated under his watchful eye. That culture was still alive and well when I joined the Skunk Works.

Our leadership—the group lead, manager, program manager—for the most part were promoted from within the organization. Those whom I knew or had reported to in my early days were former worker bees in their respective disciplines. The hierarchy, from my position to the top dog, Ben Rich, had only four levels: Chris, the lead; Baldy, the fuselage lead; Alan Brown the program manager; and Ben Rich, the head of the Skunk Works. Amazingly lean by today's standards!

Efficiency went beyond the org chart; it filtered down to all locations and facilities. Almost all of our program's engineering disciplines and staff were located in the same large room: designers, loads, weight and balance, stress, and configuration control, along with their leads and managers. Secretaries and program managers were in smaller adjoining rooms. Our F-117 design area was located in Building 311, as mentioned before, directly adjacent to the Manufacturing & Assembly hangar, Building 309/310. If a design problem cropped up on the floor and assistance was needed, the appropriate person could be there in forty-five seconds or less. By way of comparison, the L-1011 Tri-Star commercial airliner was built in Palmdale, forty-eight miles away from its Burbank engineering office.

Our drawing revisions were typically controlled by the designer, and it was their decision to make a letter change. Many times, in the interim between letter revisions, and to save time and cost, the mechanics would build from red-marked drawings that had been modified right on the floor. Once a letter change was completed and signed by the lead and a stress engineer, the designer submitted it for release by taking it to the back of the room to the release clerk, Toni Rose, who then logged it in for configuration control, had several copies made, distributed them, and returned the original vellum to the designer to file. This entire process rarely took more than two days.

Systems Engineering was non-existent in our organization—that function was integrated into the design engineer's role. Each system on the F-117 program, cockpit environments, as one example, came under the purview of the Skunk Works designer responsible for knowing all requirements in his mechanical or electrical dominion and how they were incorporated into the vehicle. There was no design by committee; each engineer worked alone on his hardware or assembly—but never in a vacuum. The design engineer was intimate, not only with his hardware, but with adjacent hardware as well as the next higher assembly. He alone was responsible for the success and performance of his design, and his boss and peers counted on him to get it right.

Management by walking around

Kelly was big on his style of "management by walking around," and one day, long before I arrived, he passed by a drafting board that caught his eye. It was a detail outline of the F-117's rudders. First thing he said was that the rudders were too small and needed to be larger for yaw control. The designers standing around the board included the lead aerodynamicist, who said that they were just right and showed Kelly the wind tunnel data to back up his assertion. Well, after the first couple of flights demonstrated yaw control problems, they determined that the source of the issue was that the rudders were too small and needed to be enlarged. Apparently, Kelly had an innate ability to visualize airflow and vehicle response to control surfaces.

As a side note to the story, enlarging the rudders was going to have a huge impact on cost and schedule, and there seemed to be no way around it. However, Chis Fylling, my boss, came up with a quick fix that alleviated the need for redesign by scabbing on extensions to the edge panels—a tribute to his creativity.

Don't reinvent the wheel

One standard design practice at the vehicle subsystem level was that we never developed any system or subsystem if we could borrow from another aircraft that was already in production. The F-117 and its predecessor, Have Blue, utilized this practice. Have Blue's landing gear came from an F-104. The F-117 engines and Aircraft Mounted Accessory Drive (AMAD) were from the F-18. The fly-by-wire flight control system was borrowed and modified from the F-16. And most of the Environmental Control System (ECS) was based on the C-130. Some components unavoidably required development and the program paid for it in cost and schedule, including the external treatments, the platypus exhaust system, canopy glass, and air sample probes.

By applying these techniques, using existing processes and maintaining the engineering culture and discipline, unbelievable records were set in the design and production of Skunk Works aircraft. The time it took on the U-2—from the first line on the initial drawing to first flight—was only eight months with 50 engineers. That same process for the record-shattering YF-12 took only thirty-five months, and for the SR-71, twenty-four months (Johnson and Smith, 1985). The F-117 went from go-ahead to first flight in about thirty-two months using 105 engineers. Given the complexities of the programs, those timespans were unheard of, and I would be hard-pressed to find other programs outside the Skunk Works that either beat or matched them.

Postscript: observations

Throughout my professional years after leaving that organization, I heard several program managers publicly boast that they ran their program "just like the Skunk Works." But none of them—with the exception of one—even came close.

They were full of crap. For one, they failed to follow Kelly's 14 Rules. Even if they were familiar with them, they discounted how much these rules affect results. But the most likely reason was that none of them had ever been part of the Skunk Works to see how it really worked.

That one exception—where I found a program run like the Skunk Works—was a classified satellite program in Sunnyvale with limited access. It also had a limited budget, necessitating a lean, carefully selected staff with an emphasis on efficiency. And it was run quite successfully by a program manager, Bob Thompson, who BTW had worked at the Skunk Works earlier in his career.

In my forty years in aerospace I also witnessed changes in the relationships between government and its contractors. It's a different environment today than it was during my time at the Skunk Works in the 1980s. The relationship and trust that once existed, in my opinion, has deteriorated over time, and government oversight has grown exponentially.

It may be a question of the chicken or the egg, because contractors are driven by profit, and the government has reacted to being burned by implementing more specifications and controls. Yes, there are shady companies, and there are less than diligent program managers out there taking short-cuts. But trust has to start somewhere. A trusting relationship is no different than a marriage. Both partners need to set aside any tendencies toward greed or control. And, as in any relationship where partners split responsibilities, the government, by establishing requirements and writing the checks, sets the tone in the contractual relationship. If the contractor or vendor chooses to participate irresponsibly, then consequences should follow, but with the objective of steering the relationship back to the tone of mutual trust. From what the older engineers told me about Kelly and everything I've read, he was unfailingly honest, and it was reflected by his long-term relationships with many of his customers.

Later in my career, I had the opportunity to exercise what I had learned in Burbank regarding fairness and building trust with one of our subcontractors. During Thermal-Vacuum testing of a brushless motor, it was discovered that the test fixture was extremely heavy and consequently required a forklift to safely install and remove the Unit Under Test (UUT) from the chamber. The subcontractor unfortunately had not quoted this capital investment in their proposal (an honest oversight) and consequently it was not funded. The price tag was large enough that it would have severely eaten into their profit. We needed them, not only to complete this development test but also to deliver several follow-up production units scheduled long into the future, and I wanted to maintain a good relationship with them. Understanding their predicament, I worked with our subcontract manager to creatively, but legally, provide funding for the forklift. Some folks I know would not have gone the extra mile to assist them. It paid off for both of us, in the short term and on those future endeavors.

As an example of how relationships have changed, our F-117 contract was with the U.S. Air Force, and I've been told that the original program specifications document was only sixty-nine pages long with three key performance parameters. That is extraordinary in today's world for a fighter-type aircraft.

During my time on the program, I never met with a customer in person and had only one verbal conversation, which was a conference call with a colonel at Wright Patterson AFB in Dayton, Ohio. When a customer did come to our facility for a meeting, the gathering typically consisted of three government representatives sitting around a small table discussing specific problems with the various design engineers responsible for the different areas. The discussions were straightforward and succinct: "Here is our problem; here is our proposed solution." "Okay, sounds good; go ahead." Occasionally, lengthy discussions would occur, but they resulted in prompt decisions.

Over time, I came to some general conclusions regarding customer oversight: The higher the program classification, the fewer government folks looking over our shoulder. The type of product also helped determine the amount of oversight. As an extreme example, more customer reps would be involved on a satellite program than for a ground telemetry antenna. A satellite's cost is very high, and it demands near 100 percent reliability/mission success, so nothing short of perfection is acceptable. Near the end of my career, I was on a $200 million-plus program, and over fifty customer representatives attended our Systems Requirement Review (SRR).

Staying with changes over the course of my career—but regarding engineering training—I'm observing some deficiencies that concern me. Academic areas of concentration have shifted from foundational descriptive geometry to software- and computer-centered skills. Specifically, when I started, design engineers had, or rapidly developed, the mental capability to visualize their products in 3-D and to render that vision onto a 2-D paper drawing. I was fortunate enough to have this ability, and it was honed over the years, becoming an asset that I used to my advantage many times.

In my opinion, colleges should go back to teaching descriptive geometry and basic pencil/paper drafting techniques. Current educational programs place too much reliance on computer-generated solid modeling. Don't get me wrong; computer drafting and solid modeling are powerful tools that provide tremendous advancements in cost savings, production and accuracy. But these advantages also have shortcomings; the ability to zoom in or out, for example, thereby losing the relative sense of three-dimensional space, is one unintended consequence of the technology. It often leads to issues involving inadequate wrench clearance, mechanic's arm reach and manipulation ability, machine tool producibility and others.

To illustrate this situation, almost thirty years after getting my degree, I had a conversation with a bright young engineer about his assembly drawing. He asked me to take a look at it and do a sanity check. He had created his assembly on a Solid Modeling CAD machine and printed a paper copy. When he laid the B-size paper copy in front of me, I immediately saw that his Top View (TV) was not lined up with the Primary View (PV), a must for accuracy and quality. After listening to him half-jokingly claim that I was seeing things and needed to get my eyes checked, I reached down into my desk drawer and pulled out two triangles, a 45-degree and a 30-60-90, basic tools from my days on the board. I then placed them on the paper drawing, drew a few orthogonal lines and quickly proved his error. Somewhat embarrassed, he paused, looked at me with a confused expression, pointed to the triangles and asked, "What're those things?"

I was stunned! An engineer, a little over a year out of college, and he didn't know what a drawing triangle was? Yeah, yeah, I can hear the trash-talk from young people reading this: "Hey, Old Man, what about the slide rule? Did you have one of those in your desk too?"

Yes, as a matter of fact, I did have one, and although I never use it, it's still in my desk today. The point I'm making is that these are basic tools that continue to be useful but, unfortunately, those who make higher education decisions seem to no longer value them and probably think they belong in museums.

15

Serious Stuff, Old Films, and Greener Grass?

In June of 1984, my wife of only one year decided that she wanted to end our marriage, and we discussed filing for divorce.

It was the worst emotional experience of my life, and I was in bad shape for several months. Although I enjoyed my new work environment, I struggled to maintain interest in my job and keep up my productivity. My personal emotions were out of control, and while I hid them as well as I could, nothing I tried was helping. It was as if my plane had stalled, then gone into an uncontrollable spin, and the only certainty was that the ground was coming up fast. Every morning I had to push myself to get out of bed and go to work. Each night I would fall asleep for a few hours. Waking around two a.m., I'd stay awake the rest of the night. After some personal counseling, I learned that I was suffering from depression.

Depression was not fun. It would have been easier to deal with a physical injury—a knife wound, a broken limb—than living with depression. If nothing else, with an injury, I would have seen some evidence of healing and felt like I was making progress toward recovery. But depression seemed endless.

My personal self-confidence was destroyed. I feared that, as a divorced man, I would be viewed as a failure at relationships. Who would be interested in a loser like me? Rejection, I learned, was tougher than I had ever imagined it could be.

Up until that time, I had lived only in the physical world and disparaged anything spiritual. That would change very soon.

Days before we officially separated, I was returning from a visit to a friend's house in Sacramento, where I had spent the weekend in an attempt to escape reality. On that Sunday morning, before packing and departing for the six-hour drive home, I was channel surfing on my friend's TV while he was out taking a run. I stopped at a station that was broadcasting *The 700 Club*, a religious show. I had always been totally turned off by the overly simplistic messages in those broadcasts, but I left it on while I started to pack. I heard Pat Robertson preaching that he knew people were suffering out there—that all they had to do was pray to God and ask for help. Already irritated, I thought, *What a bunch of horse shit.* I switched it off, showered, and finished packing. On the long ride home, anticipating the disaster awaiting me, his message kept gnawing at me until I finally yielded to it. *Oh, what the hell? I'm at the end of my rope with absolutely no options. What do I have to lose?*

About forty miles south of Sacramento, I remember thinking, *I'm alone in this truck and no one can hear what I'm saying.* So I started to pray aloud, awkwardly, but too desperate to care anymore. "Please, God! I need help and I have nowhere else to turn!" Less than a minute later, the thought of my deceased brother came to mind, and I fell through an emotional hole, sobbing uncontrollably. It scared me. *What's come over me? Why are my emotions so out of my control?*

Then, suddenly, I felt a deep feeling of cleansing from within. All those emotions—anger, hatred, and tension—were replaced by an overwhelming sense of pure love. Even thirty-five years later, it's still hard to capture that intensity in words.

I'm not preaching or marketing any flavor of religion. I'm simply putting this out there to share my own experiences from the other side of a curtain of enlightenment. I had no doubt that what I felt was the presence of Christ, despite having doubted His existence for so many years. I later remembered the lie I had told during confirmation, when I said that I believed in God. But it didn't matter. All was forgiven. That sense of cleansing helped me, over the next few months and years, choose a different direction for my life and change my underlying attitude.

I didn't immediately become a different person in all things Bob. Instead, I equate my experience to one I had remodeling one of my houses. It was a major renovation; all drywall, plumbing, HVAC, wiring, and some interior walls were stripped away and discarded, leaving just the framing, roof and siding. When I felt that change come over me, it was as if I were given a new set of architectural plans, a clear vision showing me how to rebuild my soul (house) from the inside out, and I began reconstructing one section at a time.

Climbing out of this depressed mental mess was a slow process, but after about three months, helped by my determination to put to use the gift I was given, I began to feel like I might get through it.

Fortunately, my boss and peers realized what I was going through and cut me some slack. If not for friends like Arnie Gunderson and my old roommate John Kenney, I don't how long I would have spent in that state, but I'm sure it would have been much longer.

My recovery pace seemed to accelerate after meeting a young woman from our security department who was also recently divorced. She was a loving, caring, and intelligent person who restored my faith in the opposite sex as well as in myself. The "loser" spotlight that had been shining on me finally went out, and I accepted the challenge of a new relationship.

Thankfully, both my professional and private lives returned to normal by Christmas of 1984. I had managed to climb out of that miserable, dark, and emotional hole.

Pass the popcorn

That summer of 1984, and while my separation was going on, I had found a way to get off the F-117 program—despite the program manager's transfer freeze edict—and moved to the E program. Once again, I was working for Chris Fylling, who asked me to handle Special Coatings. The details are still classified, so there is little I can say about the program, other than it was a much smaller vehicle than the F-117, and our Design Group was proportionately smaller as well.

One difference that I noticed right away was that, of the thirty or so designers, ten were under the age of 28. We seemed to have more fun and a somewhat less intense work environment with this higher ratio of young people.

Tom Weatherall, one of the younger mechanical designers, and I came up with an idea that we named "Lunchtime at the Movies." Tom dug into the NASA and Edwards AFB library, finding a variety of interesting films. I looked for the same at the Lockheed library. We procured a 16 mm projector, set it up in the conference room, and featured a different movie each week. Most of the time we had no idea what we were about to see. Some were great and others were a bust. The films included documentaries, company marketing films, and raw flight footage of various tests at Edwards Air Force Base, including several crashes.

One week, Tom brought in a double reel with the title *Home on the West Coast*. It turned out to be a one-hour black-and-white television show filmed sometime in the mid-1950s starring Arlene Francis and Hugh Downs—probably aired only once. For history buffs like me, it was fantastic. Film crews had been set up in two locations. One was in front of Building 304/305, a hangar facing Runway 15 housing the final assembly line for the Lockheed Constellation L-1049, and the other at a Lockheed engineer's home in the hills above the Burbank airport. The premise of the show was to relate to the viewing audience the benefits of living in sunny southern California and working for Lockheed—a promotional documentary. Several enticements for considering a move to the Los Angeles area were casually slipped into the script.

During the course of the show, the moderators interviewed several employees, ranging from a flight line mechanic to the chief test pilot, Tony LeVier, with the camera capturing him taxiing up in the new F-104 Star Fighter. At the engineer's home, his wife, neighbors, and kids swam in his pool while he barbequed hamburgers and hot dogs. It was obviously staged and pretty hokey, but we all had a couple of good laughs. Other parts were really interesting, including the old aircraft and a glimpse at the much simpler, less frantic way of life thirty years earlier.

The one scene that stuck in my mind the most was an interview with two engineers, a South African married couple who, despite being Lockheed employees, were not permitted on the property. It turned out that they in the icebox, that term referring to the waiting period until their final security and immigration papers were processed, similar to what I had experienced right after I was hired. The interview took place at the fence on the south end of the Lockheed property, adjacent to Runway 26. The brief segment shared them talking about how they enjoyed California and looked forward to starting work. It was one of those insignificant but memorable human-interest stories that I filed away, never expecting it to emerge again. Boy, was I wrong! Stay tuned—more on this in a few chapters.

A memorable tour

Remembering Arnie Gunderson's J-58 tour the previous year, I thought some of the younger engineers on our program would enjoy it; they were all enthusiastic about their work and it could only add to their motivation. So, one afternoon, arrangements made and clearances approved, six of us made the trek to Palmdale—Tom Weatherall, Ralph Medina, Gary Taylor, Mike Reider, Steve Justice, and myself. We learned upon arrival that our visit would coincide with a flight test. Shortly after introductions, Arnie gave us a tour of his engine overhaul shop and the SR-71 maintenance hangar. He then took us into the Physiological Support Division (PSD) Lab where we watched the SR-71 Pilot and his Reconnaissance Systems Officer (RSO) don pressure suits and go through system checkout.

The tour culminated with us being escorted outside to observe the engine start-up and taxi. Then we walked south to the mid-point of the east-west runway and waited for the full afterburner takeoff. I remember the noise and excitement like it was yesterday. The pilot, in his sleek and beautiful air-craft, rotated exactly in front of where we stood. The long blue and ice-white afterburner flame-cones, with their embedded shock-diamonds, shot straight out of the engines and bounced off the runway surface. It was exactly what our physics teacher had taught us about angle of incidence and reflection. In 2011, I ran into Steve Justice and we talked about that day. His memory was as vivid as mine.

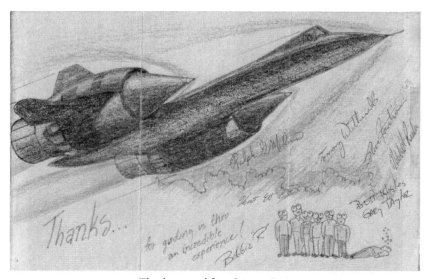

Thank you card from Steve to Arnie

I remembered working for Pratt in Florida and watching J-58 engines run on a ground test-stand—which was a thrill at the time—and here I was in California seeing those same engines power an SR at takeoff.

What was I thinking???

Right as I was finishing the Special Coatings drawings assigned to me on the E Program, it was obvious that the work pace would slow down soon, and I got the itch to see if the grass was any greener outside of Lockheed. My Lancaster roommate and L-1011 drafting board buddy, John Kenney, had left Lockheed and was working at Hughes Aircraft in their satellite division in Hawthorne. He told me they were hiring, and Hughes contacted me for an interview. Two managers wanted to speak with me as soon as possible.

The first was located on an upper floor of their building, which was adjacent to Los Angeles International Airport. His office had a north-facing window that looked out on final approach. During the interview, my eyes were drawn to every plane that flew past that window. I'd note the airline and its configuration—gear and flaps down. Terribly distracting while trying to concentrate on his questions and make a good impression!

The second manager's office was on the south side of the building with no view of the airport. But this time, he was the one distracted. As he began to read through my resume, he stopped and said, "Oh, wow, you work at the Skunk Works?"

I simply said "Yes," and while he finished reading, I sat quietly, hoping he'd soon tell me what my Functions and Responsibilities (F&Rs) would be.

He looked up again, even more excited, "So, YOU work at the Skunk Works. WOW!" quickly followed by, "Do you ever see Kelly Johnson?"

"Just one time in the parking lot, but I do see Ben Rich in the halls once in a while." I tried to get back on track by asking about the position.

He started to fill me in, then abruptly stopped and said, "The Skunk Works—that is so cool!" And he went on to relate what he knew about the SR-71, and what a great plane it was.

His enthusiasm for the Skunk Works, along with my own reaction to the aircraft flying by during the previous interview, made me take a mental pause. *What the hell am I doing here? This guy thinks I'm already working in a fantastic place!*

After finishing the interviews, I got an offer, turned it into a Lockheed counteroffer, and decided to stay at my current job. Yes, it can be true that the grass is NOT always greener on the other side—but it doesn't hurt to take a closer look.

Pole models 101

As it turned out, my decision to stay was a good one. When my work-load had indeed slowed, Chris asked me to help an older gentleman (can-not remember his name but will refer to him as Ed) who was working the pole model for the E program. Because of schedule constraints, he had fallen behind in drawing generation and also needed the help of a CADAM jockey, as he was strictly a drafting board man.

I learned that Ed was assigned to the Technology Group's Pole Model Design organization. Recall that Alan Brown was the project manager for this group, having moved over from the F-117. I also learned that Gary Wendt, from the F-117 Structures Group, became the manager for pole model design after finishing his master's degree. Gary was one of the structural design engineers I had worked with on the F-117, and he was familiar with my capabilities. Ed, slightly over retirement age, was nice enough, but had a low opinion of the shop guys and tended to treat them rudely. He also never admitted to any errors that he might have made, which turned off some of the guys in the shop. Because I worked for Ed, they were standoffish toward me as well.

Because my remaining time at the Burbank plant dealt with pole models, it's worth including a little technical background. The E Program, like all other stealth-type programs, built Radar Cross Section (RCS) pole models to test the RCS of their vehicle, as well as various configurations and materials for optimizing the radar return signature. The lower the return signature, the harder it is for an enemy to see the approaching aircraft. Once design and fabrication were completed, the model/s were handed over to the Technology

Department's test engineer assigned to that program to be tested at various indoor or outdoor ranges. For indoor testing, the model would be placed on top of a Styrofoam column (pole, hence pole model) which was attached to a rotator mechanism that was flush with ground level. This rotator/column mechanism slowly turned the pole model while it was shot with various frequency radar waves from a source some distance away.

Of the outdoor testing options, one was similar to the indoor method. Another was to place the model atop a long, thin, tapered, diamond-shaped structure called a pylon that would rise up from below ground level then mechanically tilt forward toward the emitting radar antenna. Sitting on top of this pylon was a compact, flat, hat-shaped rotator which bolted to the pole model by a standard mechanical interface. The rotator had the capability of tilting at various angles up to 45 degrees and rotating 360 degrees.

Designing and building pole models was always a challenge. They were up-front products in the development phase with aggressive delivery schedules and, usually, lower budgets than required. Aggressive schedules meant that a model had to be constructed of simple, readily available materials that could be fabricated without complicated machining. At the same time the most difficult challenge was that the models had to be dimensionally accurate, both in size and shape.

In addition, the pole model design organization was responsible for development of the pylon rotators, as well as new and sophisticated pylons in the process of being manufactured for Lockheed's Helendale range and a White Sands, New Mexico, range. It was a busy time for Gary's lean pole model group. With only ten permanent staff members, it would almost double in size while I was working for him. When extra staff was needed during times with heavy workloads, he would borrow designers from the pole model's respective programs to assist with design.

Engineer with balls

In keeping with the Skunk Works operational process, Gary's pole model design office was located across the hall from the pole model fab shop, again, only seconds away from the work being performed. The fab shop was staffed by some highly talented mechanics who were more like artisans. These fellas could do almost anything with wood, metal, plastics, adhesives, machining, tooling, etc. You name it, they could build it, and were not afraid to take on any challenge.

My first assignment assisting Ed in his design was to model a turbine engine inlet face, which was much easier to do on CADAM because the software could convert a contoured surface into a flat template. Again, the finished assembly had to look exactly like the real thing and be electrically conductive as well. I finished my inlet face assembly drawing on time and took it to the shop for fabrication. Two days later, I found an error on the drawing that had to be fixed before the shop went any further. I took a fresh revised copy over to the shop, where a modeler had started the build. The modeler assigned to build the inlet face was older and had the reputation of being a grouch. There was no love lost between Ed and this modeler. And I worked for Ed.

When I walked in and handed the new revision to the modeler, I could see he was pissed. I explained that this was an updated drawing and that it should be used to build the inlet face.

The first thing he said was, "Why the hell are you giving me this now? I already started the job and now I need to remake some parts!"

"I'm sorry, I discovered that I made a mistake and got the correction to you as soon as possible."

His face turned red, and he pounded his screwdriver on the workbench. I thought he was going to hit me with it. He then pointed it at my face and said, "You know, you are the first damn engineer that had the balls to admit that he made a mistake. You're okay in my book!"

I was taken aback and didn't know what to say. But that taught me another lesson: Always admit your mistakes. Word must have spread to the rest of the guys in the shop, because from then on, they all seemed more respectful toward me and I got along with them well.

A month later, in October of 1985 when the E Program RCS Model was completed, Gary asked if I would like to transfer to his department. He was taking on more work and could use some help. Wanting to learn something completely new, I accepted. With the move came a promotion, this time to Salary Grade 8, Design Engineer Senior, my third promotion in four years. It turned out to be the best professional decision that, up to that point, I had made.

16

YF-22A and FB-1000 Rips

Now officially part of his group, Gary started easing me into the technology by assigning me to minor modifications for existing small-scale models. Shortly afterward, he asked me to head up a new design for an improved exhaust model to replace one from another program. It had to be a much lower-RCS model than the original. The new model would be used for testing of various turbine exhaust-face assemblies and sidewall configurations, and was in support of the new Advanced Tactical Fighter (ATF) program, later to be called the YF-22. Lockheed, as well as six other major companies, were gearing up for that proposal by conducting studies on internal configuration, aerodynamic performance, electronic architecture, non-afterburning supersonic cruise, and radar cross section.

The Air Force down-selected and issued contracts to Lockheed and Northrup. These companies were to each build two flying prototype-aircraft for a Demonstration and Validation (DEMVAL) competition. The Air Force would then make the final selection to build the production vehicles. Northrup teamed with Grumman and Lockheed teamed with Boeing Seattle and General Dynamics Fort Worth. It was a smart move by the project manager, Sherm Mullin. The two competing engine companies were, as usual, Pratt & Whitney and General Electric.

We were told that there were to be seven categories used to judge the final winner. The top three were aerodynamic performance, electronics system, and radar cross section. The company recognized the importance of the RCS category and provided significant developmental funds to the effort. Gary's group benefited by the increased work, but it wasn't just the ATF program that bolstered his increased staffing—it was also the middle of President Reagan's second term, and defense spending was up.

At the time of my transfer, the current design and construction methods for building RCS models and the previous exhaust model were based on the limited capability of two-dimensional board drawings. The current construction methods did not reflect advancements in what CADAM could provide and, as a result, were not as precise dimensionally as to what was needed for the next generation stealth aircraft, including the RCS models that they represented. In addition, requirements for the models were getting more complex, requiring more intricate configurations, closer tolerances, and detailed components, such as engine faces, along with external surface features and joints. Because I had experience in composites from working the F-117 and attending some UCLA seminars/classes, I thought I might be able to advance our capability and reduce touch-labor costs in fabrication. A couple of other young designers in the group felt the same way, including Paul Thorsen, another outstanding engineer. Unfortunately, the shop manager and my stress engineer wanted to keep building the models as they had in the past and were reluctant to advance the new fabrication techniques.

One enhancement used for the new exhaust model included aluminum Hexcel composite panels, both for the exterior surfaces as well as the load-carrying internal substructures—something that group had not done before. I could see the benefits in weight savings and touch labor. With this new technique, we were able to create computer-generated templates printed on Mylar by a flatbed plotter. The shop, in turn, was able to use those templates to cut intricate shapes with hand tools rather than sending them out for machining, a more expensive process, not to mention that available machine time was virtually non-existent with all the new business coming through the plant.

Changes were also implemented in the edge panel attachments to make them mimic more closely the actual flight-vehicle attachment configuration. I had developed a unique design for a quick-change engine face installation and removal mechanism. This engine-mount mechanism was simple; it used commercial-grade extrusions and inexpensive hardware readily available at McMaster Carr, a popular hardware supply company.

Once completed and tested, the test engineer, Joel Thompson, told me that it was the lowest RCS they had ever seen. Plus, the turbine face change-out was a breeze, saving significant touch-labor time on the test range. It made me happy that these changes resulted in advancing model building techniques. It was also a personal vindication for the past hassles in getting the shop manager and my stress engineer to try something new.

About this time, Tap Kartiala, my neighbor two doors down in Granada Hills, mentioned to me one evening that he was tired of his eighty-minute commute to Northup, in the South Bay, and asked if there were any openings for a stress guy at Lockheed. I agreed to check, and when I spoke with our Pole Model Group stress lead, Rene, the next day, he said absolutely, and added that he had worked with Tap's father several years before. Two weeks later, Tap was hired and joined our group.

A growing professional respect and personal relationship followed that continues to this day. He soon became my lead stress engineer, working with his three staff reports on our full-scale model. Tap always took time to patiently teach me as well as my designers about stress analysis and load paths, to the point where I felt comfortable doing all my rough calculations and material sizing before submitting to stress for approval. This ability became a huge asset for me on future programs. In several instances, I was able to catch load path errors and weak components generated by my designers, and show stress engineers where their part sizing was overly conservative.

Tap also created and taught several *Stress for Designers* classes sponsored by our Lockheed Employee Education Program (LEEP), which offered continued education for our professionals and staff. I strongly encouraged all my designers to take his classes along with me. Overall, Tap became a great asset to my ATF program and to the entire company.

About halfway through the completion of the exhaust fixture, the workload and pace ramped up significantly. The Technology Group on the ATF wanted a new inlet fixture and several modifications to an existing 4/10-scale model. The 4/10-scale model had been completed a couple of years earlier and, although it did not reflect the current ATF aircraft, it was now being used quite effectively in testing various edge-panel configurations. Because of this increased demand, I received additional design help and had to begin delegating, which gave me the opportunity to apply what I had learned in my F-117-timeframe management classes. I enjoyed the new challenge, but I had a lot to learn in many areas, and I struggled with my tendency to micromanage.

The inlet duct for the ATF was much longer than typically found in conventional fighters, having a serpentine-like flow path designed to obstruct the line of sight from the outside to the engine compressor face. The F-117 had a more direct line-of-sight but used a grid panel to hide its engine face.

Starting from the ground up in creating a new inlet fixture, I had the pleasure of working with a gifted ATF configuration designer, John Schuster. He was one helluva likeable character who had grown up in the Midwest and had, by the end of his career, worked at many aircraft companies on countless interesting products. I loved his gritty, down-to-earth, farmland sense of humor. Among his many jobs on the ATF program for the Technology Group was to create a faceted, low-RCS exterior loft (or outside mold line shape) for our inlet fixture that encompassed the entire inlet-duct, engine face, and inlet leading-edges. His group's approved loft drawing was then handed over to us to create the exterior edges, inlet duct, rotator mounting flanges, internal structures, and several other mechanical components.

Once John had finished lofting the inlet model, the hard part began. The problem was not only devising a way to cheaply fabricate the large serpentine duct, but also installing this long, curved component through the tight, volumetric interior space while using a minimum of access doors. With a great deal of hard work, luck, and help from talented designers, the design and fab was completed. Similar to the exhaust model, the inlet duct fixture yielded a successful test and expanded the knowledge and experience base that we would need for the more complicated model to come.

FB-1000

John had more to offer than his lofting ability. He was the certified owner and too-frequent user of a simple device he had concocted with the official name of "FB-1000." Despite its technical name, it was a fart machine, not all that different from one a grade school buddy had made long ago. John had taken a thick wire coat hanger and bent it into the shape of a capital U about 7-inches wide, with two smaller opposing U-shaped bends at the top of each leg of the U. Two beefy rubber bands were attached to a decent-sized washer, 180 degrees apart, and then strung to the small bends.

To operate it, John would wind up the washer with as many turns as possible and carefully place it between his seat and his backside, i.e., butt-cheek. Then, by simply leaning forward just enough to create a slight air gap, the washer would be free to quickly release its potential energy and rip a realistic, crepitating blast. The key to achieving a convincing sound was to use the machine on either a tightly stretched cloth or a Naugahyde chair. A wooden seat didn't work as well—the device had a tendency to leave a good-sized gouge. (These details are not particularly necessary to the story, but are included just in case one might want to build and operate their very own FB-1000.)

Well, John's machine became quite popular and, being dedicated designers, each engineer in his Advanced Design Group devised their own machine, hoping to outperform the previous model. One competitive designer created his from a concrete-reinforcing rod and incorporated surgical tubing to power a large-diameter washer. It wasn't long before every engineer had his own personal machine.

For a special short-term concept study, John and several engineers from his Advanced Design Group were cloistered in a medium-sized closed room with their CADAM scopes. This room happened to be co-located with the IBM mainframe computer. (At that time, computer-aided design scopes were not stand-alone desktops like today's models.) Fortunately, John and the other members of his team were of like minds.

One afternoon, because the IBM repair technician was coming in to perform maintenance on the mainframe, all the designers were required to stop work, shut down their scopes, and secure their classified print materials. Well, boredom quickly set in among that creative bunch. John stealthily pulled out his machine, wound it up tightly while holding it under his desk to conceal the preparation, placed it in the ideal spot on his chair, and leaned back. Moments later he looked over and started a conversation with the designer sitting next to him. In a louder than normal voice he said, "Man, that bean burrito I ate at lunch is starting to really work on me." And he promptly lifted his leg and let out a huge, crackling detonation.

None of his fellow engineers could keep a straight face, and several muffled giggles ensued. About five seconds later, another designer said, "Yeah, I had those burritos, and I'm not feeling so good either," and he proceeded to cut loose with another flutter-blast. Others started in with a musical melody of rotating washers that lasted several seconds, until everyone couldn't help but laugh out loud. The IBM technician didn't appreciate the humor of this impromptu rectal recital and ignored their antics. They couldn't get him to crack a smile. When he completed his work, he walked out and was heard to mumble something like, "THOSE %*#@ing KIDS!"

Occasionally, he would return to that area and the group, once again showing no mercy and after claiming colonic crisis, would engage in an encore performance.

Open-loop

John recently told me about a break activity, "Friday Open-Loop Session," that he had started with his Advanced Design Group and continued with other companies after leaving Lockheed. The objective was enhancing creativity, and it consisted of stopping all work at some point every Friday, closing the door, and just cutting loose, adolescent-boy style. Meaning, pulling out the fart machines and noise makers, blowing paper wads through straws, flying paper airplanes, shooting rubber bands and other various clowning-around techniques. Anything a prepubescent male would enjoy. Then, after each session, they would settle down and get back to work. Surprisingly, many of the problems that had eluded them all week were instantly resolved.

When he told me about this afternoon routine, I was reminded of all the jokes, pranks, and rituals we had at Pratt. The only difference was that he had a regularly scheduled session, while at Pratt, it was spontaneous and spread throughout the work week.

Many studies have been performed on methods for increasing creativity and productivity, including incorporating humor, levity, and downtime. I seriously doubt that researchers specified fart machines, or a replication of John Belushi's zit scene from *Animal House*, not that it wouldn't work. But, as I point out again later on, those antics have unfortunately been removed from the workplace and replaced by behavior expectations straight out of the Victorian-era.

Personal reflection

Ending this chapter on a more personal note, one afternoon around this time, I was looking for a particular drawing in our CADAM library, and as I perused the file, I began to appreciate the sheer number of drawings that we had produced. I also hadn't realized how many drawings I completed on my own during my time on the ATF program, and I felt some pride in the magnitude of my accomplishment. Granted, it was a team effort, and others deserve some of that credit, but looking at the body of work that I could call mine, I felt pretty good.

All my life, I had worked hard for the purpose of trying to prove something to someone—parents, bosses, girlfriends—but also, unconsciously, to myself. I felt like I was an average designer, mechanic, whatever, and when compared to the most accomplished members of those groups, I often felt less than average. That didn't stop me from admiring the strengths and assets of better performers, and their excellence drove me to try to be as good as they were. Still, my insecurities had continued to make me doubt myself and distorted my perception of my achievements.

However, those library drawings helped me realize that perhaps my self-doubt was unsubstantiated; for the first time I understood that I did, in fact, possess value and worthwhile talents.

At the same time, I started to see how important it is to maintain a balance between insecurity and true limitations. That balance allows one to step back and consider their accomplishments more objectively.

Too much insecurity increases the fear of failure, and to a debilitating level if left unchecked. On the other end of the spectrum, failing to acknowledge at least some insecurity, combined with a false sense of overconfidence, merely masks that insecurity with a narcissism that blinds one to their limitations. History is full of examples: General McArthur (WWII), General Arnold (Korean War), the French Generals in WWI, and the Civil War's General McClelland.

This self-realization that started with perusing some drawings counted as another pebble of knowledge, and I pulled it out whenever those doubts started to surface again.

17

Management and Marriage

We were in the phase of the ATF program that focused on perfecting our performance to meet the Air Force evaluation criteria prior to the contract award, with aerodynamic performance, avionics suite, and RCS performance as the top three. Similar to the fly-off competition, the customer required Lockheed and Northrup to build full-scale, highly detailed RCS models. Each company was to complete a suite of RCS tests at their own range, with ours at Lockheed's Helendale Test Range. Then both models would go to the White Sands range separately, and the government would run the same tests for RCS performance and final evaluation to determine the winner of that category.

During this process, I was oblivious to the amount of oversight that upper management would have in the RCS performance category; managers, directors, and vice presidents were all players. My focus was limited to solving the problems, pumping out the drawings, and managing the team. I was not situationally aware of my organizational surroundings and, as I'll share later, that eventually came back to bite me.

The hard part for me, as Gary's lead on the program, was the amount of detail that this model required—to my knowledge, it was the most complicated model ever produced out of our shop, as it was the first one that had to include all of the external features, such as movable flight control surfaces, all exterior doors and access panels, joints, antennae, canopy, radome, edge panels, and inlet duct. We were also required to include both Pratt and GE engine inlet and exhaust faces, along with their thrust-vectoring systems.

The model had to be tested in both normal and inverted positions, so an upper- and lower-mounting receptacle for the pylon rotator was mandatory. To match the flight vehicle, all control surfaces had to be movable. Combined, these requirements were difficult enough, but the added challenge was to make it as light and economical as possible.

The original quote for design hours to complete the full-scale model was another landmine. As always, it was submitted early in the program and well before all the details and requirements were fully understood. This was a classic case of requirements creep, when more and more requirements get added to the project, driving up cost and negatively impacting schedule. Unfortunately, in the mind of ATF management, the quote was set in stone and would not be revised. As we progressed, my budget slipped into an overrun condition and, as a result, I almost lost my job.

Fortunately, the final outside mold line had to be tweaked—an attempt to increase aerodynamic performance—and, as a result, the loft had not been frozen and that bought me some time. Several changes would be made by the Aero Group until they were happy with the performance results from wind tunnel testing. While these final tweaks were made, I worked with my stress lead, Tap Kartiala, on concepts for the internal structure and load paths. I was also lucky to have a creative shop supervisor as the build lead, and he supported us in brainstorming various methods to build this beast. Among the three of us, we developed a solid concept that saved time and money down the road.

Load environments and model details

Author's Note: If you're not an engineer, or have no interest in load environments, you can safely move along without taking time with the following description.

The external dimensions of the pole model were about 64-feet long, 43-feet wide, and 13-feet tall from the belly to the top of the vertical stabilizer. Early weight estimates came in at about 13,500 pounds. We ended up just under 16,000 pounds, including ballast to balance the model. This model had to be as light as possible because there was an operational limitation to the pylon/rotator system at Helendale and White Sands that could not be exceeded.

The operational limitation was based on the model's gross weight, plus wind loads, calculated at a maximum of 40 knots (25 knots steady plus 15 knots gust). The larger the model, the higher the combined loads would be due to increased surface area. This total of weight and wind loads determined what is called the operational Limit Load that all calculations were based on for both pole model and the pylon/rotator assembly. For the pole model attach plate that bolts to the rotator interface, we (stress and design) were required to show a structural analysis that would be safe to three times the limit load, called a Factor of Safety or Ultimate Load.

This hefty Ultimate Load would guard against any unforeseen design oversights or manufacturing defects while on the pylon/rotator. Bottom line, because our model had to be three times as strong as the maximum load that the pole model would ever be subjected to, the resulting structure was pretty damn beefy.

Staffing up

After the outer mold lines of the aircraft were finalized and approval to proceed was given, we still had obstacles to overcome. Staffing was going to be the biggest. The Stress Group was in pretty good shape but we were grossly short of designers. We only had about ten in our pole model group and, with other projects to support, the team was short fourteen designers.

As mentioned before, the usual practice for the Pole Model Group was to borrow designers from the program to supplement the effort. But ATF design management was reluctant to give up personnel. They had been given the go-ahead at the same time, which meant that the structural design team for the aircraft was shorthanded as well. Despite several requests submitted to ATF management, no additional designers were provided at the outset, but as we fell farther behind schedule, ATF management started to relinquish some. Gary hired two outsiders for his permanent staff, Ted and Elizabeth, plus we ended up getting two contractors and ten ATF designers from the program. At the height of the effort, I had eighteen direct report designers and seven support staff for a total of twenty-five engineers on my team.

The additional staff provided was both good news and bad news. The good news was that we received warm bodies to sit behind CADAM scopes and produce drawings. Fortunately, about half of them were A and B performers. The bad news was that the other half were inexperienced in structures, let alone designing pole models. And some were lower-performing employees. The reason for not getting better loans was simple: ATF managers were directed to offer up some of their people, and the natural tendency was to give up lower performers whom they could easily spare. Why would they give up their best?

One contractor who failed in his assignment was a member of the fuselage group. I had put him on canopy design, and he spent two weeks plus overtime sitting on my charge number producing no more than a donut hole. That was the first time I had to fire someone; it was not a pleasant experience.

Back under the good news category, we received a kind, likeable draftsman, Julie King, who specialized in cable and wiring. Julie was eager to help and willing to learn new things. I spent several hours giving her some On-the-Job-Training (OJT) and she came through with quality products. J. J. Burton, an electrical/electronics designer, was another asset, but only available on an overtime basis; he appeared at various times of the day with no regular schedule.

Then there was Jerry, a former General Electric technical rep, who knew almost nothing about producing structural drawings. But Jerry taught me a valuable management lesson. Early on, I realized that having Jerry make drawings would only frustrate him, resulting in a discouraged, non-productive member of the team. However, I also realized that he had some natural administrative talents, and I assigned him to do drawing release status, scheduling, budgets, and metrics reporting. Score! Two of my problems were solved. I was able to delegate some of my administrative duties, and he was happy as hell knowing that he was making a contribution.

At the design kick off, the program assigned an interface Point of Contact (POC) for our model group, Roger Hayes, to handle and direct all lofting and configuration details for the fighter. After the loft was frozen and the vehicle detail design began, management took Roger back and replaced him with Bob Hnat from Lockheed Georgia. Bob was in Burbank on Temporary Duty (TDY) helping with the ATF staffing crunch. He was a gentle man, over six feet tall, quiet and soft spoken. When he did speak, it was usually after pausing a second or two, then he would issue a succinct statement that went straight to the point. We got to know each other quite well and, unforeseen at that time, he would play a significant role that eventually carried me in a very different professional direction.

Management challenges

In my role managing the pole model design effort, I had responsibilities that included: satisfying technical requirements; coordinating across several supporting disciplines including the oversight of contracted parts (exterior skins) manufactured by our partners General Dynamics in Fort Worth, Texas, and Boeing in Seattle, Washington; and overseeing the design and fabrication of engine faces at Pratt, GE and others. Integration of all parts and subassemblies had to be perfect, or damn close. This had to be accomplished without drilled-interface tooling—not an easy task at that time.

For example, the pole model had to accept engine-inlet faces and exhaust-vectored thrust nozzles from both Pratt and GE. Each company was motivated to produce a quality product because they were also graded on RCS performance. On the receiving end, we needed to produce a model that would readily accept those complicated pieces of hardware with almost no mismatch in contour, requiring the least amount of touch labor to make the change-outs while at test.

Test time and field campaigns were always costly; the fees charged for the use of the facilities were based on time used, and those fees were expensive. The more time spent on the range, the more expensive the total cost would be. All operations at test burned time, including efforts to mount and dismount the model, configuration changes, and test time for engineers to conduct their runs. Add in travel costs—flights, hotels, rental cars, and meals. Well-defined common interfaces helped reduce costs on the test site, and we accomplished this by generating Interface Control Drawings (ICD), backed up with CATIA (3D CAD software developed by Dassault Systems) files that were given to both companies. Along with the delivery of the ICD, we had a kickoff meeting with each supplier to lay out our intent, plus several follow-up status meetings to check progress and deal with questions or issues.

Second marriage

My life wasn't only about budgets and schedules—almost, but I did make time to get married in the summer of 1987, after several months of dating a woman from church. I had no children from my first marriage, and I was happy to inherit three girls and one boy, ages 4 to 10. Later, a fourth little girl arrived to our welcoming home and hearts. It took a few personal adjustments to convert from bachelor to uber-family man, but it was surprisingly easier than I thought. And at age 34, I was ready to settle down.

My wife sold her house and we all moved into my small 3-bedroom, 2-bath, 1400-square-foot home. It was a little crowded, so we decided to add another 900 square feet with a two-story addition. We hired a contractor, Pentti Lappalainen, a trusted friend of Tap Kartiala, and paid him by the hour. I added the role of general contractor to my resume, and that turned out to be a win-win situation for both Pentti and me. It gave him a steady job without worrying about quotes and bids, and my wife and I saved money by taking the discounts on the materials and filling in as additional labor. We also picked up reliable references for other tradesmen, and learned a great deal about construction.

My holidays, vacation days, and a couple of sick days were spent working alongside Pentti, doing whatever he told me to do. He gave me tasks to complete in evenings and on weekends in support of what he was about to start or to finish off something that he had been working on. Some nights I was outside until 10 p.m. schlepping truckloads of lumber around back and stacking it in a specific order.

The whole addition took about seven months to complete. The only parts of the project where I didn't participate were installing the sewer lines, roofing, and stucco. All in all, it was a great learning experience.

With the full-time job, family obligations and the home addition, I had absolutely no free time. But I enjoyed everything I was doing, and few issues out of my control kept me up at night.

Just a paint bubble

Midway through our renovation, I was returning from a personal trip visiting my sister in Texas, flying on one of those airlines that made several stops along the way—a bus with wings. My itinerary had me on the same plane for the duration and, on the first leg, I took a seat next to a port side window near the middle of the wing. After takeoff, I noticed that the #3 spoiler had a 4-inch-diameter bubble on the top surface that got larger as we climbed out to cruise altitude. When we descended and landed at the first stop, the bubble had gotten smaller and was barely visible.

Being a somewhat aircraft-savvy engineer, I felt that this defect should be reported and got the attention of the flight attendant, advising her that she should inform the pilot. A couple of minutes later, before passengers started to board, the captain came back and asked me to describe what I had seen.

After I explained, he said, "Don't worry about that. It's just some hydraulic fluid."

"No, not that spot," I replied. "I'm talking about the bubble on top of that spoiler." I pointed to it through my window.

"Oh, that? It's just a paint bubble. No need to worry."

Sensing some condescension, and understanding that many pilots are not technically informed about that type of anomaly, I just let it go. The bubble was growing in size on ascent and deflating when we came down to land, so I knew it was a simple de-bond, a delamination existing between the top skin and whatever substrate it was bonded to, e.g., honeycomb, and most likely not a flight safety issue. However, it should have been written up in the pilot's squawk book for inspection and, if necessary, repaired.

In the middle of the second leg, I got up to go to the bathroom near the cockpit. The flight attendant was sitting down reading her book. She looked up to ask if the pilot had addressed my concern.

"No, he blew me off and said not to worry, like I didn't know what I was talking about."

"What do you do for a living?" she asked. Apparently, she sensed that I might indeed know what I was talking about.

"I work for Lockheed as an aircraft structures design engineer."

Her eyes grew as big as quarters, and she slammed her book shut, jumped up, and ran into the cockpit.

When we landed, a mechanic boarded the plane immediately to discuss the issue with the pilot. I found it interesting that the information exchanged in the initial conversation led only to a polite dismissal of my concern, but after learning that I was an aircraft designer, my words became credible. The words hadn't changed, just the identity of the person behind them. Lesson to Bob for the future: Don't blow off potentially important information because of rash assumptions. Better yet, don't make assumptions.

18

Samurai Minions and Crossing the Goal Line

After a couple of months, we were finally staffed up and operating like a team marching to completion. Because the schedule was tight, overtime had been authorized, and although it helped with the progress, we were running about 35 percent over budget. This caught the attention of upper management—anything over 10 percent raises a red flag. It was partly my fault because I didn't know that our progress reports were presented at program status meetings by a finance guy who was clueless about technical issues. When he was asked specific questions about the overrun, he either took a guess or said he didn't know, leading to a growing frustration among the managers attending the meeting. Their frustration eventually boiled over, and I got the word in January of 1989 that I was summoned to attend the budget and schedule status meeting to be held later that week. Being naïve, I didn't know what to expect or that I might be walking into a minefield. I was Alfred E. Newman: "What me worry?" *Just go in, tell the truth, and walk out.*

I began to get concerned when Therise, a friend and the head of the ATF Program Security Department, tipped me off that upper management was out to crucify me in that meeting. The next day, Dick Cantrel, one of my managers on the program, took me aside and told me that I better have a damn good justification for my budget overrun condition. I started to sweat, especially knowing that two members of the status meeting did not like me. One was Trevor F., a guy I had reported for blocking the fire exit with empty computer boxes. And the other was Wiley, who was currently dating one of my previous girlfriends from the E Program. Great! I certainly wasn't feeling very lucky that week. I had planned for an explanation; now I realized that I might be walking into an execution—mine.

Of course, there were several justifiable reasons for this overrun condition. The underbid on our initial estimate and requirements creep were inevitable, coupled with understaffing and the lack of experience among several of my designers. Management had not considered their pole model a priority when they provided seating arrangements for our team. I mentioned that Skunk Works always had their designers co-located, but since many of the ATF managers were from the outside (not the Skunk Works culture), that was not important to them, and our team suffered as a result. Of my eighteen designers working on CADAM scopes, only six sat in the same room with me and the stress guys. The rest were scattered throughout the building and across two floors. Communications, both designer-to-designer and designer-to-me, was more difficult, inefficient, and time-consuming.

Stressing about this upcoming meeting, I came up with a plan, but did not know how successful it would be in saving my butt. The meeting was on a Thursday morning, and the previous Tuesday afternoon around 5:30, I walked into Mickey Blackwell's office and introduced myself. Mickey, if my memory is correct, had the title of deputy program manager at the time. I nervously told him that I was in budget trouble and started to explain why. About fifteen seconds into my off-the-cuff spiel he interrupted me, pulled his weekly schedule card out of his jacket pocket, and suggested that I take him around the next afternoon and introduce him to the pole model team.

Thanking him, and feeling somewhat relieved, I took him up on his offer and set a time for the following day.

The next day at the appointed time, we started the tour. I made sure that each team member was introduced to Mickey, along with their department, their responsibilities with the program, and their prior experience, which in most cases was unrelated to our requirements. I had the opportunity to show him firsthand how we were scattered all over the building. After the tour was over, he thanked me and left. No comment from him, no discussion—just thank you.

Thursday morning rolled around quickly. I was seated at the front of the status conference room near the projector screen, with all the managers around a large rectangular table in the center of the room. The podium was to the left and in front of the projection screen where all my status charts were to be displayed. I suffered through watching them grill the person before me, who was in a similar but less serious situation. I knew mine was going to be much worse because my overrun was greater. They started off slowly, asking routine questions, but then increased the intensity, firing more demanding questions at him that required quick, succinct responses. It was sort of like Perry Mason near the end of the hour, when Mason would have the suspected killer up on the stand and hammer him until he screamed out his confession and collapsed from exhaustion. After seeing my predecessor's interrogation, I thought, *Shit! I am a dead man walking.*

During the previous victim's ordeal, I noticed that if the head finance guy, Mr. B., used an accusatory tone when he started the questioning, the others around the table (aka, his minions) would follow with surgically precise questions intended to slice up the presenter. If Mr. B. was nice to the presenter, they all followed suit.

Okay, my turn and I walked up to the guillotine, uh, podium. The first chart on the screen was a graph of my budget with the cost-to-date line rising far above the budget line. Not a great way to start. Following my brief words of explanation, Mr. B. started in with his first question, and by the tone of his voice, it was not good. I answered but was interrupted by one of his proxies, and I thought, *Here it comes.* It was like a Japanese movie—I watched as the Samurai warriors started to pull out their swords in preparation, while I stood there bracing for the first strike.

Just as I began to answer the second question, the door opened. Mickey Blackwell quietly walked in and took a seat in the chair right next to the door, as if not to intrude on the spectacle. Everyone in the room noticed his entry, and the warriors got eerily quiet. After a silence hung for a second or two, Mickey started talking in a low, calm voice. He said that he "had the opportunity to go around yesterday and meet all of Bob's team. And I got the impression that we, as a program, have done a poor job in supplying the tools that Bob needs to build our pole model. His current budget condition is not all his fault."

Having heard zero feedback after we completed the tour the previous day, I was a little stunned that this upper manager would find the time to come to a lower-level meeting and defend me. Immediately, the frenzy in the room disappeared. I visualized the Samurai reluctantly sheathing their swords in disappointment, heads bowed, murmuring to themselves. A muffled affirmation rose above the murmurs. "Yes, you're right, Mickey, we haven't been supportive." No one was making eye contact with me; the only other sounds I heard were paper rustling and throat clearing.

What a bunch of shit heads, I thought. They were all ready to convict me without a fair trial, but then, in the nick of time, one man entered the courtroom, said a few words in my defense, and the demeanor and proceedings flip on a dime. Yes, I was over budget, and yes, I was the lead and the one responsible. But this thwarted attack felt more like a political game, purpose being to make themselves feel important, rather than a serious budget-over-run discussion.

Mr. B. said to me, "Ok, thank you for coming." I was dismissed without any further questioning or conversation about my justifications. I never had to report my budget status again.

Man, what a relief!

I owed my reputation, and possibly my job, to Mickey. One helluva valuable lesson in leadership was on display, between his demeanor and his willingness to admit to the program's failings. It was another great example for me to emulate, and I stored it away with the others.

Back to work

Excitement over! From then on, it was the routine grind of long hours and the fun type of stress—solving tough design challenges. For me, it was OJT on how to manage a team as well as overseeing manufacturing and suppliers.

We went the extra mile for one design challenge, providing movable control surfaces and engine interfaces. As the program and model were classified, they tested at night to avoid optical spy satellites flying overhead during the day. I knew that the test engineer needed a support team of model builders at the test site to make configuration changes quickly, either at night during testing or during the day when testing was suspended. The quicker configuration changes could be made, the more test time completed during a shift, thus reducing total cost.

For example, the horizontal stabilizers needed to be adjusted to various angles for RCS study. We had designed a jack screw mechanism that could be accessed by removing a simple cover, inserting a speed wrench with a socket, giving it a couple of quick turns, and moving the stabilizers to the desired angle. All control surfaces were built with simple mechanisms similar to that design.

After transferring to Sunnyvale, a little later in my career, I had the opportunity to speak with Bob Allison, the head test engineer for the ATF model. He told me that the mechanisms and other time-saving designs had paid off greatly. Northup's team would sometimes spend a whole shift making configuration changes, but we were able to do them in less than an hour. I felt good about our contribution and appreciated him sharing that with me.

The pole model completion date finally came, a proud moment for me and all the designers, stress engineers, and ground support designers. A tremendous amount of credit went to the shop model builders, who had applied their artistic talents to our effort and produced a top-quality product that functioned as intended.

Since we had worked so hard and I was proud of our accomplishments, I nominated our team for an Employee Recognition Award in the category of Productivity, Morale, and Teamwork, and it was approved by the awards committee. We all got a small gift certificate and had our group photo taken, and it was displayed in the building entrance throughout the following month. I also submitted an award for Walt Jensen, my shop foreman. Walt was in his late fifties and reminded me somewhat of my father. He and I got along well, and I depended on him to suggest better designs in fabricating our model. He was there throughout the whole process and was a great asset to me and our team.

Picture taken during the Crew of the Month Award ceremony

Walt's nomination was not accepted as submitted, but was downgraded to an "Instant" award, essentially a baseball cap—recognition far beneath his contributions. The official reason given was that his performance "did not meet the standards for a normal Product Excellence Award." Not willing to accept this explanation, I did some digging behind the scenes and found out that the approval process had gone through his supervisor, Lee, someone who been a real thorn in my side for years, and Lee had put the kybosh on my original submission. He replied in writing to the committee that "This award would undermine my authority by giving an award to someone who was merely doing his job." To me that was downright evil.

I often wondered what had happened in Lee's life that made him treat others with such meanness, especially the subordinates who depended on him. I was disappointed, but recognized Walt privately to show my appreciation.

Our next tasks involved disassembling the model, shipping everything to the Helendale test site, then reassembling it, doing a final weight and balance, and mounting it on the pylon pole in Pitt #3 (the largest of three). One of the first tests of the model was to be inverted, meaning that it was mounted upside down on the rotator/pylon. In order to invert the model prior to rotator mounting, we utilized a huge roll-over fixture and two 20-ton cranes to lift the model about forty feet in the air. Then, using rope taglines attached to the model and fixture, the ground crew manually rolled it 180 degrees and then lowered it without incident—a hazardous operation if the center of gravity had not been perfect.

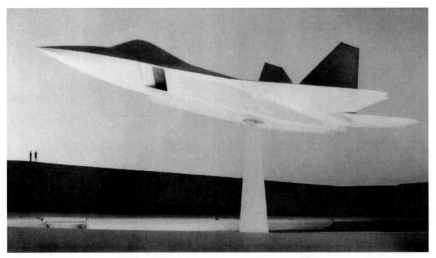

The finished YF-22A Pole Model above Pit #3

I found out later that the category of RCS testing and performance was ruled "exceptional" by the customer, and the team of Lockheed, General Dynamics, and Boeing won the contract for the production of the aircraft.

My wife and I threw a party at our house to say thanks to the design staff, and all had a great time. Even our Special Technology Director, Alan Brown, showed up. After the party, the sustaining engineering responsibility for the pole model and the ATF program was transferred to one of Gary's qualified designers, Ted Dupas. Ted was familiar with the model because he helped on parts of the project. Gary assigned me to oversee his Independent Research and Development Projects (IRAD). It was another new challenge for me, but much less stressful.

Postscript: observations

Toward the end of the pole model build, something happened that stuck in my craw for some time. One day, I went to the shop floor to inspect the rotator structure, at lunch time so that I wouldn't interrupt the crew working. At this stage of the build, the model was looking impressive, and various managers were escorting officials through the shop to feature the product. While I was looking over the rotator mounting structure, the lead for the ATF Technology Group, who had been the head RCS test engineer of the ATF program, walked in with his Air Force customer counterpart. He was giving the customer a personal tour, showing off the quality of our work and its details. I could clearly hear him touting the features that would produce an accurate representative cross section of the real vehicle. As they rounded the fuselage, they walked within ten feet of me, avoiding eye contact and ignoring my presence as if I were invisible or a complete stranger. I wasn't a stranger—I had been responsible for all his models over the previous four years. After they left, I stood there with my mouth open, somewhat confused and disappointed. At minimum, I felt there should have been an introduction.

After a couple of days pondering this brief but annoying encounter, I realized what his actions said about human nature. Some people don't have a strong sense of self-worth, and that makes it hard for them to share credit for accomplishments. I compared his behavior to Mickey Blackwell's—also a manager, but one willing to go out on a limb for a subordinate. Which one deserved more loyalty and respect? Thinking back to my days of cleaning toilets on aircraft, and regardless of where I am on the chain of command, I renewed my promise to show respect for those who might be considered "below" me. After that experience, I expanded my definition of respect to include introducing anyone on my team who deserves even a small amount of credit for their contributions.

Another manager on the program, Bill Tabor, did something that I thought was strange at first, but I quickly realized that he was damn shrewd politically. Knowing that they were cutting chips (slang for machining) out in our shop, he went out and picked up a couple of handfuls of the aluminum shavings from the floor beside the machine. He had someone make several nice-looking desk pen and pencil sets, using pieces of the chips embedded in clear acrylic. A brass plaque was applied to each with the words, "First metal chips cut on the YF-22 Program." Then he went around and gave one to each manager above him on the organization chart. Some would call him a kiss-ass; I called him smart. Few engineers are gifted with that instinct for marketing themselves, and it's not a bad skill to have.

On a later program, I remembered Bill's idea. At the end of testing, we had several well-made parts left over—fairly expensive ones—that were headed for the scrap bin. Pulling them, I had plaques made. I then gave them as awards in a small ceremony to all the key players on my team, which they seemed to truly appreciate.

19

Sayonara Burbank

The last half of 1989 included a culmination of several factors that made me feel a change was coming. One was that production for the ATF Program was scheduled to transfer to Lockheed Georgia, which meant a big cut in personnel in Burbank for those who did not want to move. Production programs were definitely not for me, so Georgia was not an option. We were also told that all the buildings in Burbank were going to be sold, and that operations, mainly the Skunk Works, was moving to Palmdale. Those two changes combined meant that a major cut in workforce was imminent. The third factor was more personal. I was beginning to feel that much of the aircraft industry was no longer a mystery to me. I had learned in 8½ years what it took, technically to produce a development aircraft, at least a small fighter type. Looking down the road, I wasn't seeing anything new to learn in my current environment. It seemed that my collection of pebbles from this road was almost full.

I was at a professional crossroad. Over those years, I had advanced from entry-level Salary Grade 1, Associate Engineer Mechanical, to Salary Grade 11, Research Development Engineer, which was the highest technical grade at that time. Two choices confronted me: stay technical or move into management. Management would offer many new challenges and I was seriously considering a move.

But another carrot dangled in front of me. Bob Hnat from Georgia, my interface POC for the pole model configuration, had moved on and accepted a job as a design manager at Lockheed Sunnyvale within their Astronautics Division. For several months, he had been recruiting me to come work for him as a design lead on a new classified program.

At the same time, a home-related issue was brewing. Our neighborhood had started to show signs of degradation. It had been a great middle-class working neighborhood, but some tagging (graffiti) started appearing on home property walls, which meant that gangs were creeping in. Our oldest daughter, who had started middle school that year, came home one night and said that there had been a stabbing on the playground. My wife and I decided that perhaps it was time for a move. After serious consideration, I accepted the Sunnyvale job and started in March of 1990. There was no promotion involved, but the offer included a healthy raise as well as a lucrative signing bonus.

In the few days before my going-away party, I took some time to reflect on my professional position, evaluating the recent past and considering my future. I thought about those five promotions in less than nine years, and wondered what had fueled that number in such a short time. I concluded that several components had contributed, starting with my age and maturity level. My engineering career started at age 29, after nine years of part- and full-time work experience related to engineering and working with my hands. My peers had far less experience, and most had started their careers at 22 or 23. By comparison, engineers in Germany are required to take hands-on vocational classes when they start college or university. The only engineering school I'm familiar with that has a similar policy is Cal Poly in San Luis Obispo, but I'm sure there are others. It's something I wish all engineering schools in the U.S. would adopt.

I had worked hard on all my assignments, an ethic that I attributed to my German heritage and parental influence. Also, I had great bosses like Chris Fylling and Gary Wendt who focused on the growth of their team members. Chris had taught me many practical engineering lessons and techniques. Gary had encouraged me to take management classes and gave me challenging assignments that stretched the boundaries of my capabilities. For this reason alone, I hated to disappoint him by transferring. But family priorities trumped my career, and Northern California offered a better family environment in addition to the new challenges I was looking forward to.

I was at the right place at the right time with this job opening. My luck was still holding, or else whoever was looking out for me was still on the case.

PART 3

And Beyond

20

This Old House and Course Correction

In March of 1990 when I started in Sunnyvale, my wife and children remained in Granada Hills to keep the kids in school and assist in selling our house. I came home for three or four days every other week. It was difficult living away from them. Our youngest was approaching 2 years old, and I was missing out on many things in her life, along with all the fun activities with the older children.

As spring moved into summer, it got worse because our house was not selling and we weren't seeing much interest. We unfortunately caught the start of a declining housing market, and we kept lowering our asking price but never enough to get it sold. Eight months later, in November, we contracted with another agent and dropped the asking price below the declining comps in order to become more price-attractive. It finally sold, teaching me a valuable and costly lesson that I wished we had learned much earlier. Regardless of the value something has for us, its sale price will be solely determined by what the market dictates—in other words, basic supply and demand—and not our own estimation of what it's worth.

We bought a fixer-upper home near the Pleasanton town center, large enough to comfortably fit our family of seven. It was a perfectly sized house in a perfect location. Pleasanton was a wonderful small town forty-five miles east of San Francisco, with a population of about 50,000, and surrounded by farmland and hills. All three schools and the main street of town were within walking distance of our home. I was reunited with my family and everyone liked our new home. Life was great again after being separated for nine months. I thought I could live in that location for the rest of my life.

Work life was not as perfect as home; my new job in Sunnyvale was somewhat of a professional course correction. The Pratt and Burbank years were periods of learning and absorbing everything possible about technical and entry-level management, while Sunnyvale was an opportunity to apply that knowledge and experience. No longer would I be directed while watching and learning—instead I would be observing situations and making decisions while directing others. Guess one could say that's the description of "responsibility."

I started to understand the difference between what I term the "two-dimensional" versus the "three-dimensional" engineering worlds. Engineers work on technical problems considered two-dimensional—simplistic equations like $y = mx + b$ for calculating the slope of a line or determining heat loss through a wall. They're basically on one plane determined by two axes, X and Y. Of course, the problems are much more complex, but you get my drift.

When one gets into management, they are still responsible for the outcome of those two-dimensional problems solved by their team, plus additional two-dimensional problems like cost and schedule. Still simple enough, just more calculations and more time. But the hardest challenge facing a manager is working with people. That becomes the third dimension, or the Z component, which is superimposed upon two-dimensional problems.

There are no mathematical rules that a manager can learn and apply to this type of three-dimensional problem that will achieve a predictable outcome. I liked and became good at the two-dimensional problems and remained intrigued by them. But that third dimension of management, figuring out how to motivate, retain, and challenge people, was a personal challenge and exponentially more interesting.

Unlike the Burbank plant, with the Skunk Works and the Bomber Plant both building aircraft, the Sunnyvale campus was more diverse. It included four divisions: Missiles Systems Division (MSD), Space Systems Division (SSD), Astronautics Division (AD), and Marine Systems. Eventually I was able to work in all four, and I learned that each had its own core line of business, different operating processes, and distinct cultures. Much had to do with their products as well as the various defense agencies each contracted with.

Coming from Burbank, I transferred into AD, which, like the Marine Systems Division, was primarily development. MSD and SSD had their development efforts, but they were mostly production in various forms. Astronautics had an increasing number of contracts, primarily for space-based lasers and Space Station modules, hitting the door faster than they could keep up with. The government at the time was in a technology race called the Strategic Defense Initiative (SDI), dubbed Star Wars Program, and the goal was to outdo the Russians.

TAV program

The program that hired me was called TAV and headed by our project manager, John R. It was a development program that involved reentry vehicles, something I learned only after my clearance was transferred and I was read in on the program. We were a subcontractor to a Philadelphia corporation, and the managers there were outright bastards to work with. I often thought that they wanted us to fail, because they couldn't have made it any harder for us to succeed. Working for Bob Hnat was pleasant, and the team he assembled was made up of talented, good people, which made the job more enjoyable. Many of them came from Burbank and Georgia. Working on the TAV program for two years, I was the design lead on two projects, one a material development effort and the second a development and limited production effort. The program was not what I had technically envisioned, but I needed to suck it up and do the best job possible.

I can't say much about the technical side of this program due to its classification, but I can share a couple of stories that are worth mentioning. The first is a lesson I learned after an experience with our analysis team. The other is about one of the many eye-openers that marked a turning point in my professional growth plan.

The analysis team issue started with one of our designers, who had been asked to create a two-dimensional curved surface that would provide the lowest possible radar cross section return. Keeping it general, the problem dealt with varying the radius of curvature and then sweeping that two-dimensional curve over x degrees of rotation, thus creating a three-dimensional surface looking somewhat like a section of a split bagel. My designer would create a configuration, and it would be performance-analyzed, then cycled back to the designer for tweaking. After a couple of weeks, they reached a performance plateau, getting bogged down short of completing an acceptable shape. I got involved when we started to run behind schedule, trying to determine the reason for the plateau.

It turned out that our designer, by the analyst's direction, was changing the geometry or tweaking the shape by increments of less than 0.0001-inches, or what we called sub-mil dimensions. As this was a composite part, we didn't have the capability at the time to fabricate the part, and the tolerance was so tight that we couldn't verify the finished dimensions. It was the typical case of the analyst having little concept of reality—living in a pure math and physics world with no understanding of current manufacturing capability. The analyst and his superior objected, but I had to put a stop to this do-loop and go with the 80 percent performance solution.

I consulted with my boss, Bob Hnat, and he agreed with my call, sharing his philosophy on the subject: "You can spend 80 percent of your time and effort trying to get to the last 20 percent in an attempt to reach perfection.

You need to know when you've achieved a 'good enough' design, and then put your pencil down." Later on, working future programs, I generally found this 80/20 concept to be non-existent in the PhD engineering world. At that level, they seem to emphasize perfection and ignore cost and schedule.

This second story, as I mentioned, changed my career path and squelched my desire for moving up the management ladder. After reaching the highest technical engineering level in Burbank, the only option for professional growth was management, and when I transferred, I had intended to take that route.

About one year into my new position in Sunnyvale, I noticed that our interdepartmental communication was inefficient, but could easily be improved. This was before email, so all interactions and directions were verbal or hard copy. While I was in Burbank, the company had provided everyone, from management down to first-line supervision, with a Time File Planner, and paid us to attend a two-day class to learn the planning system, as well as techniques for organizational and communications improvements. Our program in Sunnyvale did not have this tool, and I felt that it could greatly help our team. I persuaded my boss, Bob Hnat, to take the class as a guinea pig, and I made his attendance arrangements. When he returned, he said it was just what we needed and asked me to coordinate budget approval with the operations manager, who I'll call Henry, for the rest of the team to attend the class.

So, I met with Henry, gave him the background story and presented my proposal. All I needed from him was a nod and authorization to spend part of his training budget to train all the leads on our program—I would do the rest. After my spiel, he looked me right in the eye and gave me a sob story about how his "training budget funds were almost depleted for this fiscal year." And added, "Perhaps next year." Resigned to his response, I thought, *oh well, guess my great idea will have to wait until next year.*

A week later, the program manager, John R., invited me and several others to a "skip-level meeting," meaning that the big boss would meet with team members two levels down the organization chart. In the meeting, Brad W., the head of the Analysis Group, asked for some training money, and John R. said "No problem. I have so damn much money, I can't give it away!" My mouth dropped open. I spoke up and told him about my proposal and my meeting with Henry the previous week. Confused, he promised to check into it and get back to me.

The next day Henry stopped me in the hall to inform me that what he said had been very much misinterpreted, and he would authorize the training. I was happy that it was going through, but I thought, *What a lying weasel!* (I actually used another noun, but we can keep it at weasel.)

This event, and a couple of others, helped me realize that if being promoted to the next level of management meant that I would have to work with these types of people, I wanted no part of it. From that point on, I stopped looking for promotional opportunities. I went on to lead large teams and had manager-type responsibilities, but I stayed at a Salary Grade 10 level (the highest grade for individual contributors) the rest of my career. As it turned out, that decision never affected me financially and resulted in much less stress.

Ending my stint on the TAV program on a happy note, during the first Gulf War, we saw F-117 Stealth Fighters used in large-scale combat. I called contacts back at the Skunk Works to try to find out details of the outcome—how the planes had fared—knowing that they had played a heavy role. I was delighted to hear that all sorties flown on that first night and subsequent missions came back to base without any damage. Not even a scratch! I was proud to have been a small part of that success, and thankful that all the pilots got home safely.

I found it ironic that George Bush, the vice president who had made that middle-of-the-night visit to the test range, was the president who gave the go-ahead for the first strike. And the first manned asset to go into harm's way was that F-117 that he had come to see.

21

Program Hopping

I n March 1992, and after two years of working my first program in Sunnyvale, I requested and received a transfer to Missile Systems Division (MSD) in the biggest office building on campus, Building 157. It was the heart of engineering for the Fleet Ballistic Missile (FBM). This is the missile launched out of SSBN-type submarines. The FBM program has a long and successful history with the U.S. Navy, starting way back in the early 1960s with the A-1 missile. Continued improvements brought newer models like the B-2, C-3, C-4, and eventually the D-5. Each new model had longer range and increased accuracy.

The engineering department in MSD was centralized and quite large. At least 140 people were in the department, consisting of approximately 85 designers, 32 material and process engineers, 10 staff members, and 9 supervisors and managers. "Centralized" meant that all engineers were administratively assigned to one department, which farmed out the appropriate talent to various MSD programs on campus as needed, as well as supporting FBM. At the time of my transfer, there were several small- and mid-sized programs in the works within MSD.

While in MSD, I worked some interesting short-term projects and efforts the first few years, described below, then was assigned to larger, longer-term programs, which I discuss in the next chapter.

SCAMP

For the first six months after transferring to MSD central engineering, I worked various small projects and ran one proposal. Central engineering management was still getting to know me, and I, them. Then, in September of 1992, we got word that a small antenna program called SCAMP, run out of Palo Alto (a research division just north of us), was in trouble and needed help fast. The acronym stood for "Single Channel, Anti-jam, Man Portable" and it referred to a light antenna that could be set up in seconds and would be used by soldiers in the field to communicate with their command.

Turns out that they wasted away too much time studying concepts in the DEM/VAL portion of their contract and didn't produce any of the drawings in support of their Conceptual Design Review (CDR) that were required for contract continuation. They had a conceptual configuration layout but no detailed or assembly drawings. And they had one month to produce all the drawings necessary to go into limited production.

My supervisor asked me if we could get them out of trouble by creating the drawings they needed for the big, upcoming customer review. After looking at the scope of the job, I said, yes, it was possible, but I would need some top-notch designers. He gave me four CAD jockeys, one from Lockheed Ontario and three from the Skunk Works who had transferred to Sunnyvale. We all started the next day. I was the lead, and also sat behind a CAD scope, cranking drawings. The Ontario guy was my configuration man, and the other three Skunk Works guys were punching out drawings. The timeframe given was no more than five weeks and a max budget of 800 man-hours.

SCAMP Antenna

At the end of 4½ weeks—720 man-hours (m/hrs)—we had produced fifty-six detail and assembly drawings! An average of 13 m/hrs per drawing—somewhat of a record, I would say. The SCAMP program manager had been in some serious trouble, but we pulled his bacon out of the fire. In the end, he was so happy, I thought he was going to kiss me. Management was impressed and gave us a group performance award. I don't remember any serious bonus money, but I could tell that our status had risen.

ACES Program and Snubber

Right after the SCAMP effort, I was asked to be the design lead for ACES Program. ACES was a joint U.S.-Israel venture to produce a defensive missile system. Lockheed Huntsville (note: little did I know that this division would become significant in my career) had a contract to build a radar-transparent nose cone for their missile. Some managers thought it could be effectively built out of Space Shuttle tile material, which had been developed and produced on our campus. We made good progress in eight months, and built two prototype units, but the contract was canceled by the Israelis for convenience in July of 1993. The actual reason for the termination was never divulged.

After the program termination, I moved back to Central Engineering; within a week they asked me to take over a Failure Review Board (FRB) for the Snubber, a component used on the D-5 Missile. The FRB was stalled and not moving to closure.

The Snubber is an inflated rubber bladder that surrounds the D-5 first-stage motor nozzle. Its purpose is to absorb any shock induced by motor ignition. The missile was designed to be launched from submerged submarines, a requirement that increased complications including the intensity of the induced shock. The bladder reduced the force transmissibility caused by ignition shock, preventing failures in the actuator mounting.

Production of this part was experiencing a 20 percent failure or scrap rate, and the Service Life Extension (SLE) was showing a 50 percent failure rate. SLE was a series of additional tests that existing parts would experience after their removal from initial service. Successful completion of the test meant that the service life could be extended on this relatively expensive part rather than scrapping it after its initial predicted life span.

I had inherited a team of five engineers from MSD, and together we would review data from three years of production records, test results, Navy submarine service records, and failure reports. It was a huge pile of data. We then had to determine the root cause of the high failure rates and make recommendation/s to correct the problem.

We got the job done in three months, including an extensive final report. Management and the Navy were happy, and our team received another special recognition award.

Looking back, I wondered why I was able to take the team to closure while my predecessor could not. To me, this job was pretty simple. When I arrived on the scene, I simply looked at what had been completed and how the goal line was defined, then laid out a plan to get there. As a team, we didn't inject any opinions of our own; once all the data was reviewed and correlated, we let the results speak for themselves.

I also looked at the individual team members and matched their capabilities with tasks at hand, as I had learned to do on the ATF program. We had meetings twice each week to review progress and hand out additional tasks. We then ground through it to the end. Running this FRB wasn't magic, just simple logic to me.

It seemed that I had developed an unspoken reputation for being a project trouble-shooter/rescue guy. From that point on, I was asked to help solve technical problems and bail out projects that were in trouble.

The remaining months were spent on small efforts, such as supporting an evaluation team for procurement down-select between two solid modeling software products, Ideas and Pro-E, as well as some self-training on solid modeling tools.

JDAM

At the start of 1994 they assigned me as the design lead to the pre-contract phase (post-proposal waiting for contract award) on the JDAM program, an acronym for Joint Direct Attack Munitions. We had a short time to ramp up and prepare for the expected contract award, which would be four months later in April. We were competing with McDonnell Douglas and Martin Marietta-Orlando for the win. It consisted of a huge production contract to convert all the Air Force and Navy 500 lb. and 1000 lb. gravity bombs in inventory. The conversion made the "dumb" gravity bombs into "smart" bombs by adding a nose guidance kit and a tail kit with movable fins. This modification would provide the capability to "fly" (a loose term) the ordnance a longer range with pinpoint accuracy.

JDAM was going to be an exciting program for a couple of reasons. It was my opportunity to get back to aircraft, and it was set up to be a very efficient, high-volume production program—something new and challenging. The Executive Summary Letter from the Air Force contract manager at Eglin stipulated exactly what they were looking for in our proposal and the evaluation criteria. Item number seven in this summary letter dealt with the importance of "Lean Production," which was based on the classic book by J. P. Womack, D. T. Jones and D. Roos, *The Machine that Changed the World* (New York: Simon & Schuster, 1990) a must read for every mechanical engineer—no excuses!

The Air Force wanted to introduce into this contract the discipline and processes of lean production that were so heavily embedded in the Japanese auto industry. In preparation, I read the book and became even more inspired, eager to implement those efficient manufacturing methods into our program.

Interestingly enough, and adding to my anticipation of a fun project, my neighbor in Pleasanton and fellow coach for our son's Little League team, Bob Guisti, was a Quality Assurance manager at the Numi plant in nearby Fremont. At the time, it was a joint venture between General Motors and Toyota that produced, among other models, the Toyota Corolla, Geo Prizm, and the Toyota Tacoma. Bob was kind enough to give me a personal tour of his plant, where I got to see firsthand how efficient lean production worked. It was unbelievably fascinating, and the quality was far beyond anything I had ever seen before.

Having read the book and gone on the tour, I asked the program manager and his deputy about our timeframe for implementing lean production processes. A deer-in-the-headlights look came over their faces, and I became a little suspicious. I tried again, saying, "You know what I mean—what it says in *The Machine that Changed the World*?" That got a reply, but not the one I wanted.

"Oh that? We didn't read it. Didn't have time."

What? Were they kidding?

Now it was my turn to have ta blank look. Here we were, potentially about to be awarded an EMD contract, with leaders so arrogant that they couldn't be bothered to learn something so important to our customer. This brief conversation reinforced what I had learned in my Burbank Liaison days—that arrogance and ignorance, in tandem, is a formula for disaster.

We lost that contract to Martin Marietta in Orlando and I was not surprised. I'm pretty confident that the shortcomings and attitudes of our managers weren't factors in that contract award. But if we had won, I believe those inadequacies would have been quickly exposed.

Back to Central Engineering

After receiving the bad news about the JDAM loss, it was back to FBM central engineering, where I continued to work on various short-term jobs for the next fifteen months. I worked on the next level of Ideas solid modeling training, along with other engineers, in the SIM lab. There I met and became close friends with Jim Glasser and Greg Farnham, and our friendships lasted long after we went our separate ways.

Both Greg, Jim and I established a fishing group that we named "MMFT," an acronym for Manly Man Fishing Trip. Once or twice a year we planned fishing expeditions to the High Sierra Mountains. Well, at least that was the advertised agenda. We also partook in card games, drinking, yard games like horseshoes and corn hole, drinking, target practice, swimming, drinking, and hiking. Did I mention we did a little drinking as well? Our group grew to as many as ten long-term members, and, after twenty-five years, and despite being scattered across the country, we still meet every year.

Shortly after my transfer, a political event halfway around the world had a tremendous effect at Lockheed: the collapse of the Soviet Union. One of the unintended consequences was the ripple effect throughout the defense industry over the ensuing years, known as the "Peace Dividend," the political slogan popularized by President George H. W. Bush. Many defense contracts were canceled, including my old program, TAV, and Lockheed was forced to disband its Astronautics Division. Aerospace companies merged, with Lockheed and Martin Marietta coming together a few short years later. Fortunately, our engineering staff was not impacted that much. It was neither boom nor bust, and there was enough work to go around, so no need for layoffs.

Corporate-wide, Lockheed was getting away from manufacturing our components in-house because of the larger overhead costs, and planned to outsource much of what we had once built. On top of that, the NAFTA agreement was signed a year or two later and Lockheed, now Lockheed Martin (LM), sold off a huge percentage of their machine tools. Most of them went to Mexico and China for pennies on the dollar—in my view, a bad decision for our country that we're paying for now.

Future Engineer

Point of historical interest for Lockheed: In March of 1995, when Lockheed merged with Martin Marietta, it was the beginning of several changes in upper management. A Martin Marietta person was brought in to lead the Sunnyvale division, accompanied by a very different culture.

The merger marked a turning point, converting Lockheed, a corporation that had operated like a small, family-run business, to a mega-corporation, and the culture was unavoidably changing. Part of the change was the intrusion of more government regulation that started under the Clinton Administration. We now had mandatory human resources training that spelled out many common sense dos and don'ts. Remembering one training session that still makes me smile, it was called "Sexual Harassment," and we were made to watch a video identifying various types of forbidden behavior. The smile was brought on by irony—the introduction, which addressed the absolutely critical nature of this training, was presented by none other than President Bill Clinton. Need I say more?

While the change seemed like a hassle, one was positive. During National Engineer's Week, the company encouraged and paid engineers to go to schools in their local areas and talk about the engineering profession. As I had children in all three Pleasanton schools, I volunteered and made arrangements to give a forty-five-minute slide presentation to the elementary, middle, and high schools. Leaving late morning, I was able to do the good deed in one afternoon, feeling proud about promoting my profession. I brought various small pieces of hardware that I had worked on, including two space shuttle tiles. The kids loved it.

At the time, I didn't think that much about it, nor did I feel that any minds were altered that day about going into engineering as a profession. But, on a spring Saturday afternoon about three years later, the doorbell rang. When I opened it, the young lady standing there asked "Is Allison home?" Then she looked at me with a startled face and exclaimed, "Oh my God! YOU'RE Allison's father!" She explained that she had been in one of my presentations at her high school and that, because of it, she had chosen engineering as her career path. I felt pretty good about the encounter, and was happy to learn that those couple of hours made a significant impact on a person's life.

A memorable rerun

After completing the SCAMP effort, and right before my next assignment, a bizarre coincidence occurred. An older gentleman, whose name I don't recall, was casually passing through my office cube one slow afternoon, looking for my supervisor. We started a brief conversation and I mentioned that I had transferred from Burbank. He seemed to take an interest in me after that, asking about my background. After about ten minutes of conversation, I began telling him about our E program "Lunchtime at the Movies," and the antiquated black-and-white TV show *Home on the West Coast* that we had seen. When I got to the part about the South African couple, he sat up with a strange, surprised look on his face that made me stop talking and look questioningly at him, curious to know what had elicited that reaction.

He paused, then leaned forward and said, "You're not going to believe this, but that couple being filmed outside the fence bordering Lockheed's property? That was my wife and me!"

He was as surprised as I was totally dumbfounded. What were the odds that ten years after seeing a random person in a TV show—a show filmed thirty-eight years ago, no less—I would be talking to that person in my cube, 300 miles from where both filming and viewing took place? What are the odds that this gentleman would run into a young man who would, in casual conversation, even *mention* a TV show from ten years ago? We were both blown away!

He went on to share behind-the-scenes details and the excitement of later seeing himself on the "telly" when it aired. Our serendipitous encounter, crazy as it was, completed one of those life circles that began with our "Lunch Time at the Movies."

22

More Hopping

In August 1995, I was working various small jobs in MSD central engineering when Mort Parker, a manager formerly with the now-defunct Astronautics Division, put in a special request for me to take over one of his design and fab projects that was over budget and way behind schedule. I didn't know him at AD, and I never figured out why he asked for my help.

His project, PATS, stood for Portable Antenna Telemetry System. The need for this antenna arose from the Strategic Arms Limitation Talks (SALT), where the U.S. had signed an agreement to provide downloaded telemetry data to the Russians from our D-5 missile test flights. They were launched out of a submarine about ninety miles off the coast of Cape Kennedy (Canaveral) and flew southeast over the Caribbean, crossing the equator. The test reentry bodies then fell back into the atmosphere, and the test was terminated by the missiles hitting the water off the coast of Ascension Island, a British-owned island in the South Atlantic, west of Africa. In order to comply with the treaty, the Navy had to pay for P-3 Aircraft to loiter in various locations along the flight path to receive and collect the telemetry data from the booster and reentry bodies. It was an expensive process, and they were looking for something more cost effective.

The Lockheed Martin solution was to build two 24-foot by 24-foot phased-array antennas, mount each on a 40-foot flatbed-trailer, deploy them by C-141, and place them and their control station ISO (International Organization for Standardization) containers along the flight path. One, planned for Rosie Roads in Puerto Rico, was for mid-course recording, and the other on Ascension Island for the terminal phase. A key requirement was that each antenna had to pick up signals from the booster and reentry bodies, lock onto them, and track while receiving and recording the telemetry data. Another requirement was that the antenna must fold up to be loaded onto a C-141 Cargo Aircraft for deployment.

When I came on board, I inherited a few problems. Not only had the project fallen behind schedule and over cost, the project manager couldn't accurately predict the completion date, and the customer was losing faith. On top of that, the project technical lead, who I'll call Richard, was definitely not happy about losing his leadership position.

Another problem I discovered shortly after assuming control was the flawed structural concept for the antenna support frame assembly. Richard kept insisting that his concept for this 256-square-foot structure that rigidly supported the 4096 Yagi antennas was a sound design, and that we needed to carry his concept forward into manufacturing. A while later, he got disgusted after he lost an argument when the stress analyst brought in to assist agreed with me, and he quit. He was a decent fellow, but his downfall came from not being able to admit that his design had major shortcomings, even when the math proved his original concept insufficient.

Completed PATS Antenna during field testing at Moffit Field

It wasn't all bad. The antenna project team came from the Marine Systems Division; they were a smaller, leaner group located off the main campus and didn't have the bureaucracy and union rules to deal with. The team included Doug DeVore, subcontracts; Louise Jordan; materials and procurement; Dave Kennedy, scheduling; Steve Larson, mechanical design; and Cy Joseph, electrical and electronics. The plan was to use the Marine Systems Division assembly shop and technicians to build the two antenna assemblies. It was similar in culture to the Skunk Works, but on a much smaller scale. This was no surprise, because Marine Systems had built the Sea Shadow, which had originated from the Skunk Works and is noted in Ben Rich's book. We also had two good people from Space Systems Division (SSD): mechanical designer Terry Messersmith and controls engineer Jim De Simple.

One way I prepared for my new assignment to ask my longtime friend Arnie Gunderson for some coaching and guidance. Per his suggestions, I first determined what the customer wanted and when they wanted it, then got to know each of the team members and their capabilities. I reviewed design progress, requirements, the budget situation and, finally, the schedule.

With the help of some key staff members and many long hours, we determined that neither the original budget nor the schedule could be met. Fortunately, logic prevailed and we convinced management and the customer that a project re-plan was the only way to execute the remaining tasks. The re-plan showed the new budget at $8 million and it would take 10.5 months to complete.

After the re-plan was presented and accepted, our cohesive team went to work, with several of us from the office out in the shop many times, turning wrenches when we got behind schedule. We delivered the two PATS Antennas only six weeks late, but on budget.

Unfortunately, I failed to follow an earlier lesson from the Skunk Works, which would have saved us from complicating the job's progress. Kelly Johnson is known for the KISS principle—Keep It Simple Stupid. In other words, don't be elaborate in your designs; keep them neat and concise, so they don't come back and bite you.

To better understand the problem we encountered, it's necessary for me to describe the quantities and complexities of the antenna system. Each antenna had four large, intricate electro-mechanical assemblies called Beam Formers. Each Beam Former assembly was 42-inches by 40-inches by 12-inches thick and contained a stack of 16 machined-aluminum frames bolted together. Within each Beam Former there were 512 coaxial connectors called SMAs. So, doing the math for both antennas, the total was 8 Beam Formers, 128 machined frames, 5096 SMA connectors plus 128 large internal printed circuit boards—a lot of components for such a small section of the system.

Because the overall antenna was so large and the incoming radio telemetry beam was curved, the electromagnetic waves that hit each antenna would be out-of-phase from one end to another—meaning the 4096 yagi-antennas across this array would pick up the incoming pulse at different times, instead of simultaneously, and distort the processed signal. The Beam Formers would take all the incoming out-of-phase signals and, by virtue of its shape, would "straighten" out the signal into a crisp pulse and send it out to the ISO shelter via coax cables for processing.

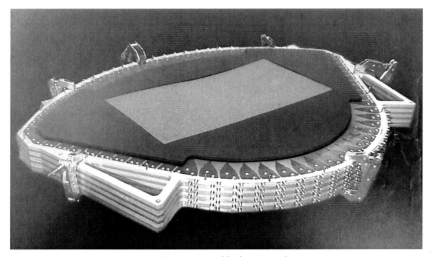

Beam Former Assembly during stack-up

Well, these 128 Beam Former frames had also been designed by Richard before he left the program, and he had insisted they should go out for quotes despite my objection that they were too complex. I gave in—my mistake—and had Doug send them out for quote, and the results were disastrous. We received two no-bids and one bid for $180,000 that would ensure an overrun and an eight-week delay in our schedule. I decided to call in a brilliant mechanical designer from central engineering, Carl Glahn, whom I had worked with on the TAV program. He had a reputation for being what I called a "Design Doctor," a title he earned by coming up with workable designs when others could not. I considered him on a par with John Kalisz from my Burbank days.

Carl spent two weeks redesigning Richard's frames and came up with a simpler configuration that enabled cheaper manufacturing processes. They ended up at $118,000, saving $62,000, and with a shorter delivery schedule that put us back on track.

Because we essentially met our revised plan and restored our relationship with the Navy customer, Mort Parker showed his gratitude by giving several of us significant bonuses. It was one of the few times I received something more than a hearty handshake and a paper award. Mort was a real stand-up guy and I had great respect for him. Much to my dismay, he retired a short time later and I never got to work with him again.

A brief reflection

Even with all the schedule pressure, the stress level had not been that bad because I knew that our well-qualified, trustworthy shop personnel would put in the extra effort to pull through. I had respect for their efforts and tried to make sure they knew it. I also think they appreciated the fact that my designers and I would come down to the shop and get our hands dirty during those schedule crunches instead of cracking the whip and returning to our cushy offices, leaving them to sweat it out.

Reflecting on why it felt comfortable to roll up my sleeves whenever necessary, I believe it was because of my upbringing. Living on the farm, I watched my father deal with the responsibilities of a family, work two jobs, and still get everything done. Helping my father with farm chores and working for the station, sometimes the only one out with the tow truck pulling a car out of the mud, I had to learn to think on my feet and do whatever it took.

And a "briefs" prank

Before leaving the PATS project, I fell victim to yet another prank, this one performed by my lead mechanical designer, Steve Larson. One afternoon near the beginning of our effort, when stress levels were at their highest, Dave Kennedy, Doug DeVore, and I were standing in a large, carpeted office passageway, deep in discussion about a serious vendor problem that had the potential to create another major schedule delay. I was totally engrossed in what they were saying, shutting out everything else going on around me.

Right in the middle of our conversation, Steve abruptly came around the corner and stopped right next to my left side, with his hand in the vicinity of his fly. He blurted out, "Oh, man, do I have to take a leak!"

Now, I had caught what he said, but was too engrossed in our conversation to give it any thought. All of a sudden, I felt something pelting the top of my shoe and heard what sounded like someone peeing on my foot!

Forgetting about a similar incident—the sneeze all over my arm that had turned out to be water from a spray bottle—I was infuriated that he had chosen my foot for his urinal! And, like that previous time, I angrily turned to confront him and got as far as "What the fu . . ." before looking down to assess the damage. That's when I saw his hand. It was holding a pile of aluminum sheet-metal plugs, one-eighth inch in diameter, that looked like miniature dimes. He was letting them dribble out of his palm, creating a continuous stream onto my shoe. I swear, it felt and sounded like the real thing! My profanity quickly turned into an insult regarding his spurious heritage, followed by a really good laugh. Then of course, we all had to have a go with this newfound toy.

I understood that, if the boss falls victim to a prank, especially one this crazy, it means that the team feels comfortable enough with their manager to pull the prank. I can't imagine working for an asshole and pulling a stunt like that. It's just not done.

Airborne Laser Program

After the Portable Antenna Project, it was back to Central Engineering again, assigned to various small projects for the next six months, until January of 1997 when they needed someone to head up a design team in Palo Alto for a newly awarded contract, the Airborne Laser (ABL), later known as YAL-1. ABL was a demonstration program; the customer, the Air Force, wanted to put a megawatt-class chemical-oxygen iodine laser in a B-747 and shoot down missiles during their boost phase. Lockheed Martin and TRW were subs to Boeing, the prime contractor. We would build the Beam Transfer Assembly (BTA), a large, complex composite bench with a bunch of mirrors on it, the Beam Control/Fire Control Assembly, Beam Path tubes, all the software for our components, and a huge movable turret mounted in the nose of the aircraft and aptly named the Turret Assembly. TRW was to provide the laser, which would be mounted in the aft section of the aircraft, and Boeing would provide the aircraft and be the integrator.

Because Palo Alto was several miles north of Sunnyvale, my commute had now increased to over an hour each way on a good day. I met a young design engineer who was assigned to our team, Dan Correia, and we started commuting together, as he lived in Livermore, the next town east of Pleasanton. We quickly became good friends and remain so to this day. I invited Dan to our Manly Man Fishing Trip that year, and he has been a member in good standing ever since.

Like all the other programs I had been on since transferring to Sunnyvale, this one was a mixed bag. I had the opportunity to work with some extremely intelligent colleagues at the Palo Alto facility, which was mostly staffed with PhDs. It was a pretty campus, and for once, my office had windows with a great view, quite a contrast to the environment of my former classified programs.

Working with several PhDs on the ABL program, I made some general observations about the areas where they tend to excel versus areas of strength for hardware designers. PhDs are good at figuring out how something will work theoretically, based on research and data, but then they need to hand off the project to those of us who are better at designing, planning, costing, and scheduling. This was highlighted in my first weeks after starting the detail design effort.

The Palo Alto group won the proposal to provide the Laser's large and complicated subsystems, as stated above. When I arrived, we were supposed to take the proposal concept and start generating drawings based on their work-to-date. When I got past reading and understanding their technical volumes, I asked to see the CAD files, drawings and/or sketches that supported the proposal. The answer came back that there were no such things. Mother Hubbard's drawing cupboard was bare. They had nothing other than a pretty picture in the proposal, a few technical descriptions in paragraph form, and several concepts stored in their heads. I later discovered that the Beam Former Bench was too large to get through the aircraft entry door and had to be resized, something no one had realized, but that would have been obvious with some conceptual drawings.

Dan and another engineer helped us punch out several drawing trees in an effort to get an idea of how big this elephant really was. When we finished, the drawing tree drafts showed a total of 1,143 drawings. Not a small effort, and this was where the rub between management and me began.

Program management and I had a basic difference of opinion and approach about the execution of the design portion of the program. For example, when we finished the drawing trees, we placed them up on the wall so that everyone on the program, not just the designers, could see and understand what we were building. It was one of my forms of communicating and had always worked before. Shortly after hanging them, I saw Bob L., my immediate manager, perusing our newly hung products, and I stood there watching him. When he got done walking the wall, he hung his head and shook it as a sign of disgust, as if this was all bullshit. From that point on, he treated me as though I was a C player and with zero trust in my capabilities.

A few weeks later, the Boeing program manager came to Sunnyvale and personally interviewed each lead in the building to fully understand what they were doing. When my turn came, I shared the drawing trees with him, attempting to demonstrate that I had a good understanding of all the hardware that we were required to produce, along with the metrics and a detailed schedule to back it up. In other words, I implemented all my learned skills from the past, or at least, that's what I thought. When I finished, he gently informed me that it was good work, but that I had overachieved. My first thought was, *This guy doesn't have a clue.*

To be fair, ABL management may have had some political justification for pushing back on a more traditional program-design execution, but if they did, it wasn't shared with me. Consequently, I was a little confused, and, not having the benefit of explanation, my confusion turned into frustration. How could a person who had just been rewarded for rescuing a manager's project be viewed as having so little credibility? I just didn't get it. My time on ABL lasted a total of fourteen months, and I did my best, despite our differences of opinion.

On the positive side, I did get to meet several intelligent, productive engineers, including Dan Correia and Chris Cirves. Another person who stood above the crowd was Al Gegaregian. I briefly knew Al from a year or two back in Central Engineering when he was working on various IRAD projects. When he transferred to ABL, he was two offices down from me and I got to know him both professionally and personally. With an amazingly broad range of knowledge of all things, from race cars to sound systems, he was a brilliant engineer with three U.S. Patents and the brainchild behind the ABL turret design and fabrication. Photos of the aircraft show his product prominently displayed on the nose. He was also a patient, low-key person, especially when graciously helping other engineers. I was a beneficiary of his patience and tutelage, and appreciated that he was willing to help me brainstorm any problems I had with design or analysis.

Al, John Kalisz and Carl Glahn were among the most creative engineers I ever met. Their contributions to aerospace were significant enough to regard these three as national assets.

In the past, my supervisors had advised me that gaining some experience on satellites would enhance my potential for growth and add value to the company. So, I started to make some phone calls.

Connecting to my roots

While working on ABL, I saw that the ABL turret contained a 1.3-meter primary mirror built by Contraves-Brashear in Pittsburgh, Pennsylvania. Contraves had bought the mirror blank from a company in Hanau, Germany, called Herraus.

Circling back to college days, I had become interested in my ancestry during that time, and had done some genealogy research on and off since then. I had unusual luck finding past and present family members on my father's side, and I was able to follow the paper trail back to Germany. After some correspondence, my brother and I took a trip in 1999 and had the great fortune of meeting our cousin and his family, who happened to live in Hanau. It turned out that he and his son owned a construction company, and that they had put up the building for Herraus—the building where our mirror blank had been made. What a coincidence!

"In my day, young lady . . ."

One last note before leaving this program. One of our young engineers, Karen, caught me completely by surprise while on a business trip with Dan Correia to the Boeing plant in Seattle, Washington. We had finished our meeting in the engineering building early on the last day and took the afternoon off to tour Boeing's museum. It was a fantastic aviation museum with many vintage aircraft, including an SR-71 Blackbird along with a J-58 Engine exactly like the ones I worked on at Pratt in the early seventies. When we got to the engine, I showed Dan and Karen all around it, pointing to the various components and explaining their functions.

When we got done and were walking away, I felt pretty proud of myself for remembering almost everything about the engine and showing these young engineers something from my past. That is, until Karen stopped, looked at me, and asked, "So, Bob, how does it feel to be old enough to have something you worked on in a museum?" Wow, that question not only made us laugh, but it made me think, *Am I really that old?*

23

Satellites and Three Amigos

Good fortune shined upon me once again, and in February of 1998, I found an opening on a brand-new program that would mean transferring out of MSD into the SSD organization. The new program was called Space Based InfraRed Satellite, SBIRS, which offered an opportunity to learn a new technology. Satellite experience was something that would round out my resume and enhance my value to the company, a move that was encouraged by my administrative supervisors.

The purpose of the program was to design, build, and launch several satellites into geosynchronous orbit for the purpose of detecting foreign missile launches anywhere in the world. This would enable our defense system to receive early warning of any threats against us. The design lead on the program was Bob G., who had worked for me on SCAMP. I was so burned out from being a project manager on PATS and design lead on ABL that all I wanted to do was chill for a bit as a below-the-radar designer while picking up a new skillset. And, as I soon found out, there was a helluva lot to learn.

A satellite operating in space for the extent of its useful life has many challenges. After launch and on station, it must generate its own power from on-board solar arrays, coupled with batteries, and use hot or cold gasses in propulsion systems for station keeping and/or orbital maneuvering. Navigation using star sensors was yet another challenge.

Hardware and components must be built to survive extreme temperature spans from -150°C to +100°C. Electronic components are wrapped with mylar thermal blankets to protect from these extremes.

Satellites require radiator systems to dump excessive heat generated during operation. The solution was heat pipes that absorbed heat from an electronic box, and then transferred its thermal energy to a radiator pointed out toward the blackness of space.

Special processing and materials were used for electronic soldering to prevent the growth of tin whiskers. And something as simple as motor brushes have a limited life span in space because of the lack of humidity.

Probably the biggest issue facing designers was that everything had to be built super light and the structures extremely stiff. The launch and the subsequent ride into orbit are harsh, to put it mildly. Satellites had to be designed to survive extreme vibration, shock and acoustic environments.

It was amazing to learn how phenomenally detailed the manufacturing, assembly, and integration was, including the associated paperwork. Each process and operation were written in precise detail, then followed, observed, stamped and signed-off by several people, and finally photographed before completion. Everything was performed in a clean room. While in the integration area, all personnel were required to wear bunny suits, especially where optics were involved.

I started my first assignment by creating what is called Process Flow Diagrams, or PFDs. A PFD is a series of highlighted steps showing the different processes that a vehicle, subassembly, or complex part must go through from start to finish. Bob Hnat on the TAV program had taught me the importance of this document as a tool for making complex operations understandable, as well as an effective communication tool. I took his process one step further in the generation of my documents for SBIRS.

The traditional PFD format shows each step as a simple rectangular box with text describing each specific process. Arrow(s) point to the next block(s) in a series or parallel flow. This could run several pages with those same monotonous blocks depicting important chunks of program information.

I worked to enhance this process on the SBIRS program and take it to the next level. No more boring blocks putting the reader to sleep! The new product included isometric computer-generated or hand-drawn sketches to replace the blocks—a progression of images similar to a comic book. My intent was to make the format clear enough that the customer or the least knowledgeable member of the team would have a much better understanding of the process.

I continued to create and make improvements to PFDs on future programs, to the delight of both management and customers.

After completing the PFDs, Bob Gardner had me oversee the production of the Jitter Test Vehicle. We had a vendor in Orange County, California, build the structural portion of the satellite, which we call the spacecraft, for a test to determine how much the vehicle vibrated and/or dampened with all its components attached. Since SBIRS was an optical bird, they had to verify the coupled-loads analysis, insuring a stable platform for quality images. The principle is similar to taking a photograph with a hand-held camera. If you're riding on a Harley Davidson motorcycle at the time you take a picture, the vibration coming from the bike and up through your body will make the camera vibrate, and your print image will be fuzzy. To obtain quality images, the optical devices on board were required to have stable platforms.

Jitter Test Vehicle and crew at delivery in Sunnyvale

Ramping up the pranks

The Jitter Test production and delivery went extremely well, and I got to work with engineers who, again, remain good friends to this day: Doug Kobbel, the lead mechanical designer, Carlos Rodriguez, our manufacturing rep, and Robert Ivanco, one of the program's test engineers. After SBIRS, Doug and I went separate ways until twelve years later, when our paths crossed again. Carlos, Robert, and I—also known as Lettuce Picker, the Crazy Czech, and the Nazi, nicknames that would get us fired today—worked on another classified satellite eight years later. We called ourselves the Three Amigos and had the best of times everywhere we went together—work, business trips, golfing, or camping with our daughters.

Three Amigos: Robert, Carlos, and me

Mid-program, Robert was away from the office for an extended period of time for a business trip, followed by vacation. The tradition in Sunnyvale for anyone leaving a program was to have a send-off luncheon or dinner. So, the day before he was to return, I drew up an announcement for his fictitious going-away luncheon, as though he were leaving the program, and posted several of them all over the building. When he came in, and before he could get to his desk, he was bombarded by people congratulating him on his new job and asking when he was leaving. By the time he got to his desk, he was thinking that he had been transferred—or even fired—while he was gone.

Another time when Robert had been gone for a while, Carlos and I came up with the idea of turning his cube into a crime scene. We found some police tape and strung it across the entrance to his cube. I then lay down on the floor next to his desk, making like I was a dead body, and Carlos took a big piece of white chalk and outlined my body, so it would look as if Robert had been murdered next to his chair.

Soon after those pranks, Robert and Carlos paid me back while I was on vacation in Germany. Upon returning to my office, I discovered that they had inserted pictures of Adolf Hitler, Himmler, and Goering into my family photo frames. Even more embarrassing was that one of them was somewhat hidden, and I didn't discover it until a couple of months later.

We played more practical jokes while working together on the program. Both Carlos and Robert could tell several embarrassing stories about me, but darn, those stories ended up on the cutting room floor.

Container Experiment

The last leg of my SBIRS career had me working as the mechanical design lead on a classified effort that I'll refer to as the Container Experiment (CE). CE was a small experiment associated with the program that encompassed a crucial subsystem and electronic control boxes slated for proof-of-concept testing. My responsibilities included the structure for this experiment as well as completing the design, fabricating and testing two units, and delivering them to final integration. After the integration, the CE assembly would be shipped out to another aerospace company, attached to the mother satellite, and launched.

Four months later, management removed two of my direct reports due to "slow schedule performance," and asked me to take over their project lead responsibilities and complete the project. It was a similar situation as the PATS project, but much smaller and easier to get back on schedule. The CE project was successful, with our team delivering the completed structures only one week later than originally forecasted for integration on the mother bird. Despite Karen's museum crack on the ABL program, it's nice to think that, as of this writing, some of my hardware is still circling the earth.

This success bolstered my reputation locally, both on the program and in the satellite division. Unfortunately, a short time later, my supervisor gave me only an average performance rating for that period and wrote in his evaluation, as his justification, that I was a "bottleneck" to the design group. Considering my recent CE project success, that clearly did not compute, but despite my protest, I wasn't able to have the rating changed. He was not the type to reconsider, nor did the system permit score adjustments. Fearing that my career future would be in jeopardy if I continued working for him, I started to look for a new program. Besides, two years on SBIRS was long enough, and they were moving into production. I had gained the satellite experience I desired and was now marketable on other similar programs.

A look in the mirror

I admit that there is a harsh, and sometimes abrupt, side to me. Diplomacy is not always my strongest suit, especially when I'm confronted with ideas or ways of tackling a problem that I know won't work. And I'm sometimes hard on colleagues who arrogantly insist that their proposed—but unworkable—ideas are the only solution.

We often used the phrase "many ways to skin a cat" while discussing various options, and I'm not afraid to acknowledge when someone else's proposal is a better solution than mine. I'm good with accepting the alternative suggestion, complimenting and giving credit to the originator, and moving on.

However, I did seem to have a recurring issue with management finding ways to knock my rating down despite my successful performance. A few years after the CE performance evaluation, a casual conversation with a friend who happened to be a manager revealed a plausible explanation. He shared that within my salary grade, I was one of the three highest-paid engineers on the Sunnyvale campus, exceeding the salary of many, if not all, of my supervisors. Personality quirks aside, and not making any excuses, I'm speculating that jealousy and even resentment may have contributed—and continued to be a factor—in decisions regarding my ratings. If so, that was a situation that I couldn't control and just had to live with. It became even worse when I later transferred to Huntsville, bringing my inflated California salary to a much lower cost-of-living area.

24

Concept 9 Nirvana
and a Diagnosis

O nce again, luck smiled on me and I quickly found a new position. In May of 2001, I transferred to a newly awarded classified
program in a closed area, which meant that the program was
off-limits to everyone except those who were read in. Another term we
used to refer to closed programs was "the black world," with "white world"
meaning unclassified. All anyone from the outside ever saw were employees entering or leaving a restricted access building. It was similar to the
hangar in Burbank that I observed from the bus stop. Landing this new
job was easier because I had an active Top-Secret clearance and the right
technical experience in areas that were important to the program.

After being read in, I reported for my first day, and I couldn't believe
my luck! This was the program I had been looking for since leaving Burbank.
And the program manager, Bob Thompson, was from the Skunk Works! I
jokingly told a friend that my job was nirvana, and of course he ribbed me
every chance he got.

This was a development program that I'll call Concept 9. Lockheed
Martin was awarded this contract to build subscale test hardware—a

preliminary effort that would validate the manufacturing feasibility, reliability, and performance of the design. Funding for the program concentrated in three major hardware areas, which I can only refer to as C, S, and V.

Believe me, I had never seen anything like it! It was like my first vision of the F-117 from the hangar catwalk, but this time I was involved from day one. We, as the program team, faced incredibly difficult technical mountains before we would achieve our respective performance goals. We were pushing the envelopes of current technology, physics, and manufacturing ability. Dimensional tolerances were, in most cases, sub-mil or to the fourth decimal place. Each of the C, S, and V areas were tasked to build fairly large full-functioning scaled demonstration models and operationally test them. If successful, Lockheed Martin would most likely get a larger follow-on production contract.

Cheating death #2

Once I had settled in and was starting to be productive assisting the project lead for the C effort, I went in for my annual physical. One of my favorite parts of this exam was the digital prostate check—NOT! Since my father had died thirteen months earlier from prostate cancer, it was an ordeal I couldn't skip. He was almost 85 at the time, and I was only 49, so my risk was low. When my GP finished this uncomfortable but brief procedure, I could tell by the look on her face that it was not good news. She strongly suggested that I have a biopsy performed to verify her suspicions.

Dozens of bad scenarios shot through my mind in those few seconds after she spoke, feelings that I hope never to relive. I had been having a little more trouble urinating, but wrote it off as getting older; however, that symptom, combined with her facial expression, said all I needed to know. The death of my father and his painful last days were still fresh in my mind.

Two weeks later, my wife and I were in the urologist's examination room, waiting for the doctor to arrive and start the biopsy procedure. I was lying on my left side facing the window, wearing a skimpy gown that exposed the required anatomy. My back was to the side of the room that contained the lab equipment. After my wife scanned the machines behind me, she leaned over and whispered in my ear, her voice a mixture of horror and humor, "Bob, if that's the biopsy probe they're going to use, it looks like a giant penis!" I quickly rolled over, looked at the huge ultrasound probe, and thought, *Ahh crap! That's going to hurt.*

The doctor then came in with two lab assistants and, sure enough, he pulled the giant penis over and started to explain his plan for using that lethal-looking device. The last thing he said before starting was, "Now, try to relax." Yeah, sure, pal!

I swear he did a bait-and-switch job on me and substituted an even bigger probe from under the table. Man, was that uncomfortable! While dealing with the pain, I remembered my World Aviation days and thought, *I now know what it was like for that loadmaster to make those deposits in my chemical toilet.*

When the biopsy test results came back positive a week later, I was surprisingly relieved. The interim weeks since my doctor had made the initial diagnosis were full of sleepless nights, loads of stress, and all kinds of fearful scenarios. I say relieved, because I had a confirmed problem and could attack it as if it were a failed component on an aircraft or satellite. All I had do now was research and select my options: do nothing and roll the dice, radiation, implants, freezing, or prostatectomy. All the available options, except removal, were listed showing a 60 to 75 percent chance of living more than five years. Removal was the best option at 99 percent. At age 49, only one was acceptable and that was removal, but it carried the risk of incontinence and impotency.

I continued to do research, and it paid off when I discovered something featured in a couple of news articles. It was called the da Vinci surgical system and was a new form of robotic surgery recently approved in the U.S. for performing prostatectomies. The machine had several robotic arms that probed the abdominal cavity and was controlled by a surgeon sitting at a console that contained a monitor and hand and foot controls. It was invented by the French and used extensively over there. I decided on this removal, using the da Vinci machine, because it would enable the surgeon to guide his important instruments using slow-control motion of the robotic arms and 3X magnification. To me, as an engineer, it seemed better than having a human being with human vision working with his hands deep inside my lower abdomen. The more precise the scalpel, the less chance of nerve-bundle damage or severing something vital, and the less risk of incontinence and impotency.

At the time there were only three locations in the U.S. performing prostatectomies using the da Vinci: Chicago; Greenville, South Carolina; and San Ramon—twelve miles up the road from our home.

My operation was scheduled two months later, and thankfully, it was a success. I took off four weeks to recover, and two weeks after returning to work, I was back to playing racquetball. I was once again very lucky—that the cancer was caught early and that the location and timing for the da Vinci machine's availability were perfect.

To all my male readers, please schedule regular prostate check-ups, starting at middle-age. As I learned, they can be a life saver.

Postscript: I must have been a model patient, because the doctor's staff invited me to be interviewed on a local television airing that featured the new da Vinci machine—my fifteen seconds of fame. His office also asked me to speak with several new patients recently diagnosed with prostate cancer and share my experience. I was happy to do it, as he had pretty much extended my life, and I wanted to give something back in return.

Resolutions

My ordeal with cancer and its eradication was not without lasting effects. It was a painful wake-up call, and just as painful were the recent deaths of my Uncle Duane and my old boss from Pratt, George Rogers. I had planned to spend more quality time with my uncle, but was always too busy. And I had wanted to reconnect with George, but it wasn't a priority, and it never happened. I'd lost the opportunity to express my gratitude for how much they both helped me in my earlier years. So, from that point on, I decided that I needed to make time for traveling cross-country and visit with friends and loved ones.

Up until then, we didn't have that much disposable income due to the obligations of raising a family. No regrets here—it was a choice and I remain happy with that decision. But by this time, all but one of our children were out on their own, and I was earning more. So, I decided that, if all the family monetary demands were met, and I was saving 12 percent of my gross income, I was going to use what was left to buy what we wanted and travel where we wanted to go. This became a problem for my wife. She was frugal and objected to this radical change, but I didn't care. I'd felt what it was like to fear an early death, and I didn't want to wait anymore to live.

Pilot relief tube

Upon my return from recovery in early November of 2001, my boss Kris Forrest asked me to take over the S portion of the contract. The Concept 9 program was staffed with a bunch of pretty rowdy engineers similar in nature to my Pratt peers. They even took my return as an opportunity to welcome me back with a gift designed for my perceived situation. My first morning back, as I turned the corner to my cube, I saw a funnel hanging by several wires attached to the underside of my center desk drawer, about seat chair height. Attached to it was a rubber hose draped down into a one-gallon coffee can. I guess they thought it would be easier for me than walking to the men's room. Very funny.

Not one to let this go without retribution, I found out the culprit's name—won't mention it here to spare him the embarrassment, but no surprise—with a plan in mind. I brought in one of my catheter bags from the hospital. Dave Ellis (darn, it slipped) always drank massive quantities of water from large plastic bottles. I filled my C-bag with water, adding just the right number of drops of yellow dye, and hung it on Dave's white board. I then draped the catheter drain hose into a cheap water filter, and another hose from the filter outlet into one of his drinking bottles. Then I wrote a note on the white board with the words, "Dave's drinking water recycling system."

25

Resuming Nirvana

Putting the welcome back pranks aside, we created a detailed Integrated Master Schedule (IMS) to get my new S effort under control and heading in the right direction. Bob Hnat had taught us to pay close attention to details, starting at the lowest-level tasks across all areas and working up, keeping the same level of detail throughout. Other than Bob, I hadn't experienced engineers or managers creating detailed schedules. Instead, they usually started with a top-down schedule, which meant listing higher-level rollup summary tasks without getting into the weeds. Bob called that a seat-of-the pants approach and cautioned me that it almost always ended up with underestimated costs and durations.

Applying this same bottoms-up principle also works with Basis of Estimates (BOEs), which are used to develop costs for proposals. After several screw-ups, I learned that neglecting to include that level of detail can lead to way too many oversights, which can cripple product credibility.

When I presented my completed schedule in a baseline review a week later, the customer told me and everyone in the room that my schedule should be the Poster Child for every schedule on the program. Boy did I get a razzing for that! From that point on, everybody called me Poster Boy. Bob

Thompson even used that nickname in the write-up for the Employee of the Quarter award.

Over the next six years on the Concept 9 program, I averaged ten hours of overtime per week, peaking at twenty to twenty-five. I was in the groove and loved the job—the extra time and stress wasn't that bad. Besides, we were paid for overtime, and my wife and I were working to replenish savings depleted by college tuition, orthodontics, and the other obligations of raising five children. I had also started to travel quite a bit to Washington D.C. and several states across the country, which I found both enjoyable and enlightening.

Eighteen months into the S project, a power struggle occurred at the Lockheed Martin director and vice president levels. I had no control over the outcome and had to wait it out, knowing it might wreak havoc on program staffing.

Some Sunnyvale white world managers who were not cleared were trying to get into our closed program and control certain technical portions of the effort. They won, our program management lost, and we were directed to clear them onto the program and give them control over the S portion.

Once their leadership and team moved in, I was displaced on S. At the same time, the lead on the V effort was falling behind schedule due to technical issues, and I was asked to take his place. He didn't handle that well and continuously complained to management—and anyone else who would listen—that my technical decisions were going to take the effort down. Think politics, especially presidential campaigns.

The basic issue on the V effort stemmed from the fact that the previous leadership had hung their hats on a vendor who made pots and pans. Literally. And their culinary-product background gave them absolutely no experience with or knowledge of the rigors and processes required to produce spacecraft hardware. I had the painful task of canceling our relationship with them over the former lead's objections and working with our subcontracts group to quickly find a new supplier.

The leadership above Kris had little technical knowledge of the V effort's lower-level details. As a result, they didn't know whom to trust—the lead I had replaced or me. Over the next couple of months, while I worked hard to get the project back on its feet, I dealt with both solving technical problems and keeping vindictive wolves at bay. Fortunately, once we started to make visible signs of technical progress, they went off to howl somewhere else. I was still struggling to catch up with schedule and budget, but I couldn't change history and needed to keep my eye on the goal posts.

Payback big-time

I had been boasting to Robert Ivanco that, because I was behind the doors of a closed program and he was not cleared, he couldn't get to me to play any payback pranks—especially with our computer system and all electronic communications severed from the outside world. Well, that was a mistake. I had underestimated his capabilities and ruthlessness.

By this time, it was 2003 and we were engaged in the second Gulf War. Mohammed Saeed al-Sahhaf, aka Baghdad Bob, was making nightly appearances on CNN and other news organizations, claiming that the clips showing American tanks approaching Baghdad were all a Hollywood propaganda illusion and that they, the Iraqis, were actually winning the war against the imperialist infidels. Those appearances must have been the spark that ignited Bob's payback idea.

As cost account mangers (CAMs), we were required to present monthly status reports, using Powerpoint slides, at a formal meeting in the program conference room, to all inside program management as well as our customer reps in Washington. Our remote audience sat in a similar conference room, simultaneously viewing the same charts on their screen. It was a big deal, and most participants were interested in hearing what CAMs like me, who were behind schedule, had to say about their situation—how we were going to pull a rabbit out of a hat and finish on time. It was a meeting like the presentation to ATF management in Burbank, but I knew that this team would be orders-of-magnitude more respectful than the Samurai warriors. They understood the details better and appreciated that we were pushing a technology envelope.

Each CAM in turn went to the front of the room and spoke from a podium under a huge presentation screen. An assistant would advance through the slides prepared by the finance group showing each presenter's financial and scheduling status. Pretty much standard operation for aerospace programs.

When my turn came to discuss the V effort, I started my presentation with the first chart, which showed a graph depicting the schedule and how far behind we were. The next chart was supposed to be a similar one showing our cost situation. However, when they brought up the next chart, all I could hear was both rooms busting out in uncontrollable laughter. Confused, I turned around and looked up to see that some S.O.B. had slipped a fake chart into the package—a photo of Baghdad Bob giving one of his press conferences, with my face superimposed on his body. Underneath, they had placed a caption that said, "My situation is all a fake story put out by Hollywood, and I'm absolutely, completely within cost and on schedule." *Holy Shit! No wonder they were laughing.*

I turned back and tried to carry on, but the sounds coming out of my mouth were something more akin to the babbling voice of Ralph Kramden, a character from the 1950s classic TV show *The Honeymooners*, "Hum-ah-na, hum-ah-na . . .." So befuddled, I couldn't say a single word that made any sense. While they were all still laughing, Bob Thompson waved me off the stage and brought my "presentation" to a premature end. I give credit to Bob Ivanco for pulling that one off, a classic that set the bar pretty damn high.

Night crew sculptors

Near the end of the manufacturing phase, and right before we were about to integrate our completed V hardware, we were in the middle of a long and continuous ECG machining effort.

One byproduct of traditional machining are the fine particles, called burrs, of smeared metal that remain at the part's edge. Electro-Chemical-Grinding, referred to as ECG, is an unusual type of machining process that enables the removal of metallic material, leaving very smooth edges, i.e., no burrs. The type of material and requirements for the V product were such that traditional machining was completely out of the question, and ECG was our only option.

The ECG process involves placing one side of a direct current (DC) charge on the part to be machined and the opposite charge on a spinning copper wheel impregnated with minute diamond particles. The rapidly spinning wheel makes incrementally small-depth passes over the part, while continuously spraying electrolytic solution which, along with the differential charge, oxidizes the exposed surface. The diamonds in the wheel remove the oxidized material as it passes over. This process is used in making the points on hypodermic needles, which must have a flat, angled surface without any burrs.

Still behind schedule, we decided to run our T-Class ECG machine twenty-four hours a day, six days a week, utilizing two twelve-hour shifts. (T-Class was a decent-sized CNC machine tool that was modified to incorporate an ECG grinding head.) We were lucky to have two of the best machinists on campus, Tom O'Malley and Tim Hanna. Safety requirements stated that there had to be two people in the room at all times. I took the day shift with Tom, and my manufacturing lead, Jim Handley, took the night shift with Tim. I had briefly worked with Jim on the CE project. On this program, he had already proved to be an outstanding leader with great technical ability, and I trusted him managing our production.

Right in the middle of this machine run, Bob Thompson arranged a VIP tour and invited some LM vice presidents to accompany the tour. Joanne Maguire, the executive vice president of Missiles and Space, together with Bob would be shepherding a group of U.S. congressmen and their staff members to various development areas, showing off our hardware in an effort to sell the follow-on program. We all knew the significance of this tour and felt the pressure to put on a good show. Screw this one up, and forget about being looked upon favorably. I didn't want to be on that shit list.

Their tour planned to pass through our ECG Machine shop the next day, and I was asked to give the presentation about our efforts for the V portion and to display some of our hardware. Nothing was happening during that nightshift—other than the machine running its automatic program—so I asked Jim and Tim to set up the shop with some hardware on display tables and to create labels. I drew up a sketch and picked some of our more impressive hardware pieces to display.

Early the next morning, I walked in to relieve them and inspect the display set up. Well, they had done a great job on the display, but had added a couple of, shall we say, extra pieces. Apparently someone had a hidden talent for sculpting, and whoever it was did a good job. Scattered all over the area were exceptionally realistic clay-sculptured penises. Large penises, small penises, and even a huge penis stuck to the top of my hardhat helmet.

The shocked look on my face made all their efforts worth the time. My immediate thought was, *What the hell am I going to do if those VIPs walk in right now?* Fortunately, we had two hours before the scheduled tour.

After clean-up, I asked, "OK, so who modeled and who was the artist?" No answer. Anyone who says that engineers are boring never worked with this crew! Or maybe it was their way of telling me that I was a dickhead.

At the end of the Concept 9 effort, we completed our hardware very close to on time, and it tested as predicted, with passing results. As Kent Nolan, my contracts guy, kept telling me, "After hardware delivery, all sins are forgiven." Management proudly mounted three life-sized photos showing off our team and the products they had successfully created. For me, it was a great feeling of personal achievement, and another challenging accomplishment was behind me.

The Concept 9 V effort Design and Contracts Team

Slow death of Nirvana

With the Concept 9 program successfully over, they retained me to run a follow-on, full-scale ECG development effort. By this time, several changes had been implemented as a result of natural program growth. Many people in the front office had moved on, including Bob Thompson. Others had been added. We had new Systems Engineering and Finance staff, which translated into more meetings, more paperwork, more bureaucracy, and seemingly unnecessary oversight. All reminders of those F-117 days after we moved to limited production, and an environment that I have tried to avoid. My nirvana had transformed into a typical production program.

The changes mentioned above trickled down into all aspects of the Concept 9 program, extinguishing the fire of excitement found in fast-paced development efforts and introducing a political correctness that increased tension on the program. While we were ramping up for production, they brought on board more systems engineers from the white world. After a few weeks, two new SEs started to complain to the program manager that we were using sexist terms in naming the parts of our vehicle. One objection targeted our skirt, a cylindrical-shaped structural part that covered some internal components. Anyone, inside or outside aerospace, would easily make the connection between its form and the term "skirt," one used throughout other industries.

Another objection was the program's use of the words "male" and "female" when referring to molds. These in-process tools take what we call "splashes" from a master shape to accurately mimic a specific part that resembles a cavity or cylinder. Again, those terms are used in many other contexts and professions.

Regardless, after receiving official complaints, the PM made us change any nomenclature that had been specifically mentioned, and we were told not to use the former names even in casual conversations. Once again in my life, I encountered chicken shit. The speech police had invaded our closed program and it bothered me. Was our little world really a better place because we outlawed a few words? Sadly, it made me think of George Orwell's *Nineteen Eighty-Four*, and I started looking around for the memory hole.

Sometime later, we threw a going-away party for one of the major players on the program. Historically these were known to get pretty crusty with foul language and off-color gifts. And we often acted out lively skits. This party was held at a restaurant off-campus and on our own time. We were not on company property; we were not on the clock. After lunch was over and before the ceremony began, one manager, who knew the reputation these parties had, and mindful of the previous issues raised by our two systems engineers, went around and spoke to each table in the room. He cautioned everyone that some content in the upcoming ceremony might be offensive, and since the luncheon part was over, anyone who wanted to return to the office was free to do so. No one did. Well, the ceremony that followed was par for the tradition.

Surprisingly, or perhaps not, a week later, an LM Internal Affairs official investigation began, and many party attendees were questioned. It went on for several weeks. Photos had been taken in fun during the festivities, and the assigned investigators asked several employees for copies as evidence for disciplinary action. Amazingly, none were found. And thankfully, no one was disciplined.

Again I wondered, why does the world have to make a universal change to avoid offending the few who find harmless names and raucous skits objectionable? It was a way for the programs to have fun, to promote camaraderie, to feel as though everyone was part of a cohesive team, and most importantly, to blow off some steam and get rid of the creativity-killing stress of a fast-paced deadline-driven assignment. That was John Schuster's idea behind his "Friday Open Loop Sessions," and productivity increased by having them. Is it really worth it?

Burning brushes

Easing off the accelerator, I took a break from lead positions and wiggled my way into an oversight role as principal for the development of Electro-Chemical Grinding machine processes and the procurement of two 5-axis L-Class ECG machines. I was still associated with the V effort, but the L-Class was a larger-scale machine—our development T-Class on steroids, each machine almost three times as large.

During this effort, I the opportunity to work with a knowledgeable older gentleman, Dick Gattey. While traveling together, he taught me more about machine-tool operations, large-scale buys, and, my personal favorite, techniques for making business travel more pleasurable.

With this assignment, as with several previous procurements, I had the good fortune to work with Kent Nolan, the subcontracts and procurement manager for the program. We both benefitted from our professional relationship; Kent was interested in learning more about mechanical engineering and I needed a better understanding of contracts and suppliers. In addition, we shared some common personal interests, such as firearms and fishing. We invited him to one of our MMFT trips and he continues to be a member in good standing to this day.

Our supplier for the L-Class ECG was Cincinnati Machine, located just southwest of Cincinnati, Ohio, in Hebron, Kentucky. The 3-axis T-Class ECG machine had worked well for our sub-scaled part, but we needed two significantly larger 5-axis machines to meet production demands.

L-Class ECG #1 near completion at Cincinnati with Tom and Tim, our machinists

Working this effort, I learned quite a bit about contracts from the business end. On the technical side, I expanded my knowledge base in the areas of 5-axis Computer Numerical Control machines, CNC programming, Factory Acceptance Tests (FAT), high-tolerance machining, rigging, and how to perform a shitload of on-the-fly trouble-shooting and problem-solving.

ECG Installation Crew in Sunnyvale

One huge issue pertained to the DC brushes inside the grinding head assembly; they were wearing down within a few hours instead of the expected several months. This problem surfaced during the factory checkout runs required before accepting delivery of the first of two machines, and it was a schedule show-stopper. Everyone was puzzled by the accelerated wear and offered several possible reasons, with about as many suggested solutions, but they seemed to be shooting from the hip, and their ideas, while well-intentioned, didn't sound right to me. To further complicate the situation, Cincinnati Machine was behind schedule, and this new delay was eating into their profit. Management on both sides were breathing down our necks, pushing for a quick fix.

As the senior Lockheed Martin team member on-site, it was my job to zero in on the root cause and be 100 percent sure of the corrective action. I made a few phone calls to some experts back in Sunnyvale and to the company Moog, one of the suppliers for this type of brush. From those phone calls and some additional research on my own, I learned that they needed a certain level of humidity to function properly.

So, I had the folks at Cincinnati Machine instrument the brush-housing cavity, and we confirmed that the brush-cavity temperature was running high. Then, looking at some charts from my college Thermodynamics book, I was able to verify that the corresponding relative humidity was considerably lower than minimums. We convinced the Cincinnati Machine folks to make a modification by adding a device that would dump a controlled stream of water vapor into the brush assembly cavity in order to raise and control the humidity.

As could be expected, we encountered naysayers, including the experts at Cincinnati Machine and their subcontractor for the grinding head assembly. This was a precarious position for me to be in: Representing Lockheed Martin, if I was mistaken and the fix failed to solve our problem, then CM would charge us for their lost time and money. Fortunately, I was correct, the change was made, and we had no further issues.

I learned something about human nature from that experience and from similar ones over the years. There is no shortage of helpers who are happy to offer solutions, but they tend to pooh-pooh corrective actions suggested by those at the front of the pack. Then, once the fix is made and discovered to be effective, they look the other way instead of saying "Nice job" or "Congratulations." Good sportsmanship is something that we should all practice, at every level.

I admit it was a little surprising and disappointing, as an aerospace engineer with little experience in ECG machines and brushes, to have solved a problem that the machine designer should have been able to address. *Go cypher that one, Jethro.* (Jethro was the numbskull character on the TV show *The Beverly Hillbillies*, popular in the 1960s.)

I wish I could say more about my assignment during this time period, but the program is still classified. Those efforts were all cutting edge, and I'm proud to have been a part of them.

26

Won the Battle,
Lost the War

In January of 2007, after the two L-Class ECGs were delivered and accepted, I was starting to look around for my next challenge when I got an out-of-the-blue call from another classified satellite effort that I'll refer to as the P Program. Their propulsion shop at the Lockheed Martin Denver facility was having some trouble with an automated welding machine for propellant tanks, and they asked me to head up an investigation team to fix the issue. This tank was part of a program that had gone out of production several years earlier, but the government wanted to purchase more vehicles. For Lockheed Martin, it meant restarting a production line—not always an easy task.

Our small team made two trips to Denver and corrected the problem inside of three weeks. Our success got my foot in the door, and I soon landed a job in the P program's design department.

Because it was a resurrection effort, the program required fewer new mechanical designs or drawings, except for those instances where newer materials or processes would offer better solutions or improved performance. One challenge was that most of the gray-haired engineers on the original program had either retired or moved on when the initial production run ended. LM was then forced to hire several engineers right out of school who had little experience. Three young engineers in my new department were responsible for the subcontracts dealing with restarting the production line for both brushless and brush motors, as well as a couple of large bearings assemblies. They were having trouble getting the effort off the ground, and management asked me to give them a jump-start.

I enjoyed the P program for several reasons. It was a challenging assignment, and solving some of our more perplexing problems helped me gain additional satellite knowledge. I got to work again with Carlos Rodriguez, Jim Handley and Robert Ivanco, and Bob Thompson was our program manager. Plus, it required lots of travel to San Diego, Los Angeles, and, coincidentally, Cary, North Carolina, which happened to be where my cousin Skip, Uncle Duane's son, lived. Out of all the cities in the U.S., how fortuitous that one of the three vendor cities was home to the son of a special person from my youth. Skip and I got together several times during my trips to Cary over that next fifteen months, a valuable and memorable perk from that program.

I worked hard on my responsibilities to help make the program successful. The harder I worked and the more successes our small team had; the more responsibility Peter C., my manager, gave me. Many of the tasks overlapped, and I was juggling several efforts at the same time.

As the brushless motor development wrapped up and production began, Peter C. had me take over the high-level planning for a large and complex subsystem, which was floundering because no one seemed to have the vision to drive it forward. I quickly set up a small team to create a detailed 1400-line Integrated Master Schedule and borrowed one of Dick's engineers to draw up a pictorial Process Flow Diagram. The schedule helped management and manufacturing with planning, and the PFD broke down the extremely complicated assembly and components into easily understandable synchronous pieces. The customers loved it, as they had also been confused by the whole thing since the beginning. When I traveled to Washington, I saw that they had the PFD prominently displayed on an office wall.

When that was finished, Peter C. asked me to help with a large procurement effort that was behind schedule. It involved the machining of forty-three different Beryllium parts that together cost about $1.5 million. Beryllium is a stiff, lightweight metal with excellent thermal properties used in space vehicles, rocket motors, and aircraft applications. The downside to beryllium, aside from the cost, is that breathing the dust generated during processing can cause serious pulmonary and cancer-related health risks, a fact that I was conscious of whenever I visited the machine shops.

Again, to get a complete understanding about procurement, I generated a detailed schedule starting with the required delivery date and working backward. We discovered that it was too large for one machine shop, so we split the job between two different machine shops, one in Burbank and the other in Cullman, Alabama, my first contact with the state, but not my last. We broke production into four staggered phases in order to match the manufacturing need dates. To complicate matters further, I discovered that all raw beryllium billets were available from only one U.S. vendor, Brush-Wellman in Cleveland, Ohio, requiring some schedule juggling. Coordinating all these issues was not an easy task, but we pulled it off.

As an aside, that year, my business trips peaked at thirty-one, totaling about 130 days away from home. While it was fun to travel, meet people and solve problems, it aggravated a declining marital situation.

The last task Peter C. added to my list was assisting in a proposal-costing effort for a follow-on satellite. It was about this time that the relationship between us took a wrong turn. We had a disagreement about my use of a car service to the airport and back, which was permitted by company policy, but he rejected it anyway. I ended up going over his head, and his boss decided in my favor.

Well, I won the battle, but he was determined to win the war. Shortly after the travel expense adjudication, my requests for legitimate comp time were rejected, and he even accused me of being absent from work when I was in another building witnessing a test. The *coup de gras* was his rating on my annual performance evaluation. Despite my team's many successes that made him look good as our manager, Peter C. gave me the equivalent of a C grade and added comments that a supervisor would normally attach to a non-performing, "needs improvement" employee.

This was the second average grade that I had received throughout my entire twenty-eight-year career. I was livid, but there was nothing I could do. LM didn't offer an appeal process for performance evaluations. I had to eat it.

As the final nail in my coffin, Peter C. notified my supervisor a couple weeks later that I was available for reassignment—a politically correct way of saying, "Don't let the door hit you in the ass on the way out." That was a career-first. I had never been put up for reassignment before. The war ended quickly, and I had no choice but to surrender.

The next month I was back in SSD Central Engineering waiting for a new assignment and hoping to find one as interesting as the P program had been. I had a great time, learned many things, saw different parts of the country, and met at least seventy new people who worked for fifteen different suppliers in as many cities. And most important of all, I reconnected with my cousin Skip. All things considered, it was a good run.

I had collected as many pebbles as I needed on this road.

27

To Huntsville and Back

After almost eight fantastic years, I found myself outside the cloistered walls of the classified world. It felt strange—like living comfortably in a small town where you knew everyone, and suddenly the mayor says, "You're outta here!" Over the next few days, I relived this experience. *What could I have done differently to avoid what happened? Could it have been my fault?* I'm sure these are normal questions one might ask.

In SSD Central Engineering, I was assigned to boring busy work while waiting for my next job. Two weeks later, in March of 2009, I got a call from my supervisor saying that a test failure had occurred in Alabama. It was a piece of hardware called a V-band, or manacle ring, at Lockheed Martin Huntsville, home to the Targets and Countermeasures division. I knew what a V-Band was but that was about it. I felt like Sargent Schultz on *Hogan's Heroes*: "I know NU-thinnggg!"

I received a15-minute brief from the stress engineer in our group. LM-Huntsville was performing structural tests of a DO-12 program V-Band, and it had failed twice. The call had then gone out to Sunnyvale for help in determining the root cause of the failure and to come up with a fix. Both the stress engineer and my supervisor said it was something simple—a part-time effort—that I could easily manage from Sunnyvale. Most likely I would need only a few face-to-face meetings in Huntsville.

That was all I was told, other than to reserve a flight for the next day. *Well, okay, but kind of short notice.* I wondered what this new adventure would lead to, having no idea that Huntsville would become my next home.

The program was called Delivery Order 12, or DO-12 for short. It was a small program in which they had built and delivered a Reentry Vehicle (RV) that was used as a target for our offensive weapons to shoot down in a mock attack. The customer was the Missile Defense Agency, MDA, also located in Huntsville.

The deliverable products included the RV packaged with the V-band and an adapter ring. These three pieces combined to make an assembly that was integrated with a rocket motor, sometimes referred to as the booster. The original V-band that had failed testing was essentially a four-piece V-shaped aluminum band that was held together with two sets of hinges and four machined screws. The V-band assembly also included two ordnance-charged chisel devices, called bolt cutters, that would sever the four screws at the desired time during the boost phase of the trajectory, thereby releasing the RV from the booster.

The morning after our conversation, I was on a Delta flight to Huntsville with instructions to meet with an upper-level engineering manager from the LM-Denver office for a breakfast briefing the following morning. We would then drive to the LM-Huntsville program office for further instructions.

After a brief meeting in the Huntsville office, the Denver manager, the Huntsville director, and I drove to the MDA program office, located on the Redstone Arsenal. We walked into a large, corporate-type conference room on the top floor of the MDA office building. The three of us sat in three of the four remaining unoccupied chairs. The manager and director sat at the end, next to where the highest-ranking customer would normally sit. I took the last available chair against the wall immediately behind them. In hindsight, I believe MDA planned the seating arrangement in advance. That fourth empty seat was positioned at the head of the table, and it was obvious that we were waiting for the arrival of the head honcho. The room was filled with twenty or so people, and I had no idea who they were, what they represented, or what they did. All I knew and cared about at that point was that there was a problem and I was identified to fix it. *No big deal.*

Wrong!

A few minutes later, a woman walked into the room and everybody stood up. *Wow*, I'm thinking. In all my years in aerospace, I had never seen this type of protocol. She walked to the head of the table, sat down, and everyone else promptly took their seats. Quick to learn, I mimicked these movements as if I did them every day. Her name was Patty Gargulinski, and she was the big boss for Targets at MDA.

The meeting began with Ms. Gargulinski mercilessly ripping the LM director and manager new ones. My first reaction was, *Man, I don't want to get on the bad side of her!* From what I could gather, this dressing-down was justified. Apparently stress analysis for the design had shown it as good, with a comfortable safety margin, but it had failed miserably in Qualification Testing. This failure had resulted in critical delay implications for MDA's scheduled launch—it was holding up everything. She was not happy, and by the body language of the others sitting around the table, I could tell they were equally displeased. It was like my budget status meeting with ATF Finance back in Burbank: These Samurai warriors kept their swords sheathed, but if blood was about to be shed, they were settled in for the show.

After she quit speaking, the LM-Denver manager started in with an attempt to smooth over this FUBAR. He acknowledged their failure and assured her that it would be quickly remedied. "We put in a call to Sunnyvale requesting an expert to come out and assist with this issue," he said.

Then he dropped the first bomb: "They've provided us with a highly qualified and experienced engineer, Bob Retsch, who has a great reputation for getting things done." As he spoke, he turned around and pointed to me, adding the second bomb. "And Bob here is going to relocate to Huntsville full-time until the job is done."

To anyone looking at me, I was cool. I'm positive that I showed no expression that gave away my true thoughts: *WTF happened to, you can manage it from Sunnyvale?* The meeting ended a few minutes later with a surgically clear message to Lockheed Martin, "Get it right this time!"

As I was not born yesterday, I clearly understood that I needed to keep my mouth shut about the promises made back in Sunnyvale. I also had to get used to the idea of a long-term Temporary Duty (TDY) assignment. It was, as I had hoped, another new experience, and I could see some positive aspects to a TDY. By now, I had accumulated miles and points with Delta airlines, Marriott hotels, and Avis rental car agency, and was reaping the benefits— first-class vacation travel to Europe, free hotel stays, and discounts on rental cars. This assignment would only add to my status.

I also thought that my personal life would benefit from the assignment. My wife and I had developed some issues over the last few years, and some time away from each other might give us an opportunity to regroup. With twenty-two years invested in our marriage, I wanted to make it work.

On the way back to the LM-Huntsville office after the meeting, I thought, *Here I am, again put into the position of fixing a fouled-up situation. Nothing new here—been there, done that.* But I also knew that I had to watch my step; there was no room for error and the customer would be watching my every move. My thoughts were interrupted by the two managers in the car telling me not to worry, that I had an unlimited budget and to just let them know what I needed at any point in time. And added, "Just get the job done!"

When we arrived back at LM, the site manager gave me my own office in the executive area. He introduced me to his secretary and he told her to get whatever I needed. They lived up to their word and delivered on both budget and staff. Another first for me.

What a contrast! I thought on the flight back to Sunnyvale. One day I'm a C-performer available for reassignment, and the next, I'm an expert, with my own office on mahogany row, an unlimited budget, and a green light to cherry-pick the best staff from both campuses. Boy, was I confused!

As an aside, I couldn't help remembering the definition of "expert" that my father-in-law once shared with me: "A person who comes from faraway."

I returned to California, packed my bags for an initial ten-day stay in Alabama, and flew immediately back to Huntsville. My routine for the next seven months was pretty much the same: Monday through the following week's Thursday in Huntsville, home for four days, then back on a plane to Huntsville. Occasionally, I stayed longer in Sunnyvale for coordination, special face-to-face meetings, or vacation. During my weekends in the South, I took advantage of the location by visiting my sister and elderly mother in South Carolina and Skip in North Carolina, and renewing several friendships east of the Mississippi. It was rewarding to spend time with them after living on the West Coast, an inconvenient and expensive place to travel to, which had caused several relationships to wane over time.

Doing what works

Kris Forrest, my old supervisor from the Concept 9 program, was assigned to assist, and I was happy for his expertise and to work with him again. He was experienced, cool under fire, and quick at thinking on his feet. He also filled in when I took vacation.

I requested and acquired the assistance of Robert Ivanco to help with the test failure investigation, planning, and execution—major areas of concern, but I knew I could rely on him to complete them without much oversight. Steve Norman was added to our team for stress. Having no previous experience with Steve, I found him to be a fantastic stress engineer and one of the best I'd worked with since Tap Kartiala from the ATF pole model. Sheryl Howard was helpful in assisting with ordnance.

We had a good staff in Huntsville as well: George Bruegger and Mike Emerson in design; Dusty Howard and Norm Jones, scheduling and systems engineering; and John Colbaugh, stress and material. All shared general insight about the program and the local culture. We did have problems with my procurement/subcontracts person in Huntsville, who was uncooperative and arrogant. But as I'd learned before, no one gets a perfect team every time.

Robert, Dusty and I started out by creating an executable 400-line Integrated Master Schedule to plan our staffing needs and long-lead material procurements. Then I set up a small tiger team in Huntsville to determine the root cause of the test failure. Once the customer and our team came to an agreement as to the root cause, we set about redesigning a new V-Band and executing our detailed schedule.

As I've mentioned before, when the hardest part is complete, i.e., the detailed IMS, then the actual job becomes much easier to execute. Without the IMS as a roadmap, leadership would be constantly creating, adjusting, and (mostly) reacting throughout the process. Unforeseen issues will always pop up regardless of the plan, landmines that need to be dealt with. But once they're taken care of, it's easy to return back to the IMS.

We also started a parallel effort with thermal and stress analysis, looking for a suitable, off-the-shelf bolt cutter. The main hub of our activity had been centered in Huntsville, utilizing local and familiar vendors to reduce schedule time, but the bolt cutter was an exception. Our only option was to choose between two suppliers, both in California. We then set up a Battle Rhythm (a term frequently used in the MDA world for status meeting), both in-house and with the customer to make sure communication was at its peak.

The long pole in the tent turned out to be the bolt cutter and, even with the best option, we still had to perform delta qualification and lot acceptance testing. That was a long, drawn-out process that had me in a sweat, but luckily, Robert Ivanco had it under control and pulled off a miracle. I was fortunate to have such a dependable person who I could absolutely trust to get the job done. Plus, Robert and I got along well and had some fun times, along the lines of his Bagdad Bob stunt.

Within nine weeks, we had a delta-Critical Design Review (delta-CDR), which is a formal presentation to a large group that includes high-level customer representatives. CDR approval would give us authorization to proceed with fabrication. At the end of the review, we received a pass for start of production.

The Chief Engineer from MDA made me feel really good about our team effort with his closing remarks. Among other positive comments, he said, "This was the best CDR presentation I have ever seen from Lockheed Martin." I noticed that Jeff Anderson, my direct report from the Huntsville front office, was writing down every word, and later used them to submit our team for an achievement award. After CDR, we completed fabrication, qualification, and lot acceptance testing. I even got to do some hands-on work with the installation on the flight vehicle, another first for me.

Two of the major tests we performed before delivery took place in Chandler, Arizona, at a subcontractor's test facility. (This subcontractor also happened to be one of our competitors.) The effort involved structural testing of the V-band and an actual separation test where we successfully fired the bolt cutters. This was not an easy task because it required an efficient and well-coordinated series of tasks that involved members from both Lockheed Martin and the subcontractor working closely together, and we did it well. The last day before departure, I took everyone out for dinner to a nice restaurant, Firebirds. What I didn't know then was that a couple of years later and under completely different circumstances, I would be working with many of those same team members again.

Borescope this

After we completed and delivered our hardware for the target in November 2009, my supervisor set me up with another lead position back in Sunnyvale on a NASA project, a small contract that our home organization had proposed and won. It included designing, testing, and building radiator panels for the Orion Space Capsule. The purpose of these panels was to dump excess heat generated inside the capsule out into space while in orbit or on a long journey. I promptly began organizing a team and again created a detailed schedule. It was my first time working on a NASA program, which was very different from DoD, and truthfully, I didn't enjoy it. The overall pace was tedious and upper management decisions were a cumbersome ordeal. Simply put, too slow and bureaucratic!

On the upside, I traveled to some new places: our Lockheed Martin Michoud facility in New Orleans; a prime supplier in Tucson, Arizona; and NASA Headquarters in Houston, Texas.

After an all-day meeting with the Tucson vendor, a group of us went out to dinner, including my boss from Michoud, the vendor's owner and team members, and folks from NASA in Houston. I sat directly across from the vendor's Quality Assurance lead, and after a couple of drinks, we began to tell war stories. He told us one that almost made me pee my pants laughing.

He had been working in Stennis, Mississippi, where they were over-hauling the big Space Shuttle Orbiter engines made by Rockwell. During an overhaul, one of the processes called for Borescope inspections of some tur-bopump or casing, I can't recall which. Borescope operations involve remov-ing an inspection port and sticking a long tube, with a camera and light at the end of it, inside a cavity. The camera was hooked up to a television screen and recording device. It provided the ability to visually inspect various items with-out the need for disassembly, which saved huge amounts of time and money.

It was a two-man operation. A Stennis Quality Assurance guy sat behind the display screen at a console while a tech, who would stand behind him, operated the Borescope. Our dinner companion told us that this particular

QA guy was a surly old-timer with a devious mind and, being the senior inspector, it was his responsibility to train new employees.

He went on to relate that the older gentleman would have new employees sit at the television console with their backs to the hardware and the Borescope probe inspector. Consequently, they could only see the picture on the screen in front of them. At the start of the inspection, the old guy would explain that these parts were a special type of ceramic and that the newbies' job was to watch the screen, looking for any short, black whiskers on whatever part they were inspecting. New with the company, they were excited to learn this technical process and eager to gain as much knowledge as possible. Being young, they were also naïve.

Once the inspection started, the older guy would say, "Okay, I'm going to insert the probe, and you tell me what you see."

Well, instead of inserting the probe into the turbopump, he lifted up his shirt and began to slowly move it down inside his underwear. Sure enough, a couple of seconds later, a newbie would get excited and yell out, "Yeah, OH YEAH! I see some now, and WOW, they are really long!" When he got to this part, the entire table lost it, and I had to excuse myself.

28

Leaving California and Completing Circles

In January of 2010, soon after I returned from Huntsville, I decided to call an end to our marriage, a difficult decision with huge consequences. Emotions affecting my family members, selling a house I loved, finding a new place to live—the collateral damage from a ruined marriage. It put a strain on us all, and I was the cause. Despite many years of marriage counseling, I simply was no longer happy and felt it wasn't going to get any better. Surviving cancer and the mindset changes that accompany beating that disease had helped me understand that my candle, at 58, was well over halfway consumed, and I didn't want to waste the rest of it being unhappy.

Learning to chill

I started to look for other jobs that I might like, and considered quitting LM after twenty-nine years to start another career, but I didn't find anything. For four months, professionally speaking, it felt like I was in a boat drifting down a river, without a paddle and nothing visible downstream.

Then, one day in May, the Chief Financial Officer from LM-Huntsville, Colleen, called. She informed me that the Targets Division had just been awarded a sole-sourced contract, but that they were struggling with getting it off the ground. Colleen knew me from Airborne Laser days in Sunnyvale and from when I ran the DO-12 redesign. She said that they could use someone like me down there and wanted to know if I was interested in returning to Alabama.

Once again, there I was with a professional predicament, no solution in sight, and out-of-the-blue, an opportunity showed up at my office door. I thought about all the times before when this had happened—my Burbank transfer, the PATS project, the moves from ABL to SBIRS to Concept 9, and the TDY in Huntsville. *Why do I deserve all this luck?* But it couldn't be just luck. Every time I had gambled in Vegas and Lake Tahoe or played the lottery, I lost. I wasn't a particularly lucky person. Maybe it was what the man on the El Paso flight many years earlier had said, quoting his father, "He who works the hardest is the luckiest."

It didn't seem like it was all hard work either. Sure, I worked hard, but my life's journeys felt more like a plan—a script that I was following by unwittingly accepting opportunities as they presented themselves to me. The way that fortuitous professional moves appeared at the right times made me believe that these couldn't be mere coincidences. In the back of my mind I always had that feeling that someone or something was calling the shots from behind an invisible curtain.

The more comfortable I became with this belief, the more relaxed and less stressed I felt. In the past, when I had been faced with making a tough decision, I usually forced one to get it out of the way. Many times, it was the wrong one. Now, I was learning that, in similar situations, I could calmly set that decision aside, knowing that whatever was meant to be would eventually become obvious.

I had been forcing events in my life because I thought I needed to always have control instead of letting some parts of life just happen. I was in the driver's seat every minute—deciding the direction, route, and speed—or at least, I thought I was. But I began to realize that I was fooling myself. When I occasionally moved to the passenger seat and let the answers unfold, as if following that unseen script, life became more enjoyable and less stressful. I was more at peace with myself and, more importantly, with others.

Targets

I convinced my supervisor to let me make a trip to Huntsville to scope out their situation. They were indeed at the beginning of a new program and needed leadership. The Targets business was cyclical, and this new work had hit them at a staffing low point, so they had to ramp up fast.

I reported back to my supervisor in Sunnyvale and discussed the possibility of transferring permanently. Huntsville had plenty of work to keep me busy for the next couple of years. And it seemed like this transfer offered me a clean break personally as well.

With his approval, I worked TDY in Huntsville from May to the beginning of September 2010, when my permanent transfer was approved and I officially moved. Fortunately, our house in Pleasanton sold in August.

I left California after living there twenty-nine years, and I was sad despite the benefits of moving. When I first moved west, I liked it so much that I thought I would spend the rest of my life there. That wasn't to be, but I was anticipating a good life ahead of me in Alabama. Ten years later, I still feel the same way, albeit not without regrets: leaving close friends, saying good-bye to the most beautiful state in the nation, and, most of all, moving so far away from my children and a growing number of grandchildren. It's a situation I still struggle with today.

My assignment on Targets in Huntsville turned out to be a good one, offering an opportunity to learn new aerospace systems. But three months after my transfer was complete, an upper-level management decision was made affecting my position, as had happened back on the Concept 9 program. Lockheed Martin was one of the bidders on a re-compete proposal for the Ground-Based Midcourse Defense (GMD) program. The way it was explained to me, our main Targets competitor had a proprietary lock on a critical component that LM needed in order to offer a credible proposal. Upper management in Huntsville cut a deal with that competitor which called for sharing a large portion of our target program with them. Once the carving-up of the program was complete, I found that I had lost most of my responsibilities and was left with heading up the Carriage Extraction System for the air-launched portion of the program. Hindsight says it was a drug deal gone bad. LM did not win the GMD re-compete contract, but our competitor got a bigger foot in the Targets door and a major chunk of our program.

Despite my reduced responsibilities, I held onto my old position for a few weeks until our program leadership was briefed on a new target that MDA requested, which I'll refer to as Type-X. I lobbied my boss to work on the kick-off effort, and he assigned me to lead the detailed trade study, an effort to determine the cradle-to-grave cost and an estimated schedule. That task lasted for seven months until July of 2011, when MDA issued a proposal for the target. My new title was deputy program manager on the proposal effort, a position that was slated to continue after the contract award.

However, two months after the contract award, upper management split the contract into two major hardware deliverables, front end and booster. My program manager retained his slot, but they eliminated my DPM position, and I was shifted over to manage the booster subcontract. Despite my personal promise long ago to stay away from official management, I had liked the idea of finishing my career with a DPM title, but I was good with either position.

The Type-X Target assignment gave me additional experience and increased responsibilities that included program acquisition and cost estimation, cost account and subcontract management, oversight of component qualifications, and higher-level customer interface.

It also gave me the opportunity to meet Mark Wise, whom we hired as the booster chief engineer. An outstanding professional, he proved to be a valuable member of the team, adept at solving problems both on and off the job. If I ever got stuck finding a solution to a problem—at work or at home—Mark was sure to have the right answer and the right tools. I called him an engineer's engineer, on a par with John Kalisz and Al Gegaregian.

Completing Circles: Judy

Early in this memoir, I talked about life circles, experiences that take us back to another time in our lives. Going back to Pittsburgh for the only high school reunion that I ever attended—a combined fortieth for my class and the previous one—illustrates that concept. It was there that I saw Judy, my girlfriend from the class ahead of me, for the first time since 1976. She had reappeared briefly when I was working at the Sunoco station. It was great getting reacquainted and catching up on both sets of families and mutual friends. As I said before, Judy circled into my life four times, but out only three—that meeting resulted in our happy marriage two years later.

Lots of what-ifs with this one, but whoever was pulling the strings to make it happen, thank you for completing the circle.

Completing Circles: Arnie

Just before the Target program carve-up, my life circled back to help an important friend from my past. I had been on a short vacation on the Outer Banks of North Carolina, and had flown directly to Dayton, Ohio, for an all-day meeting at Wright Patterson Air Force Base. That evening, I was packing to leave Dayton the next morning, when I got a call from Arnie Gunderson, who had retired from Pratt and was now working for a small company in Houston. He was unhappy with his current assignment and asked me if there were any open positions on my program. I instructed him to send his resume to my work email address that evening and I would look into it.

The next morning, I arrived back in Huntsville and was at my office by 9:00. I printed his resume and took it to the appropriate manager for our program. He said that he was impressed with what he saw and was okay bringing him on board, assuming we had an open slot that was a good match for his skills. At 9:30, I walked over to the weekly staffing meeting, arriving at the very moment that they were discussing the position I felt was ideal for Arnie.

Holding his resume up, I said, "I have the right guy for that slot, and I already received approval from George to hire him." The program manager told the HR person to put Arnie's name down and to close the open requisition line item. BANG! He was in. Usually it took at least two weeks to hire someone, but this was accomplished in less than fifteen hours—lightning speed for a hire in any business. I was stunned that it had really happened, proud of myself for making it happen, and enjoying the anticipation of working with a good friend again.

Arnie reported to work, and while he waited for his home to sell in Texas, he rented a room in my house, coming full circle from the chain of events twenty-nine years earlier in Palmdale, when he had found me a job and put me up. Circle complete.

Completing Circles: Therise

While I was on the Type-X program, the leadership representative from each discipline was required to meet our customer counterpart, with the objective of getting to know each other and discussing future coordination. I was assigned to meet with the customer responsible for program security—an odd match given that I was the subcontract cost account manager. Right before the meeting, I learned that her name was Therise. Well, she turned out to be the same Therise from my ATF days in Burbank. I had lost touch with her before transferring to Sunnyvale over twenty-two years earlier, and had no idea where she was living or who she was working for until I saw her sitting in our conference room—in Huntsville, Alabama! A coincidental circle complete.

Completing Circles: Dennis

In July, 2011, Judy and I decided to drive from Huntsville, Alabama, to our former hometown, Leetsdale, for the Independence Day celebration. Four months earlier that year, my friend Dennis Hencher, at fifty-six, had suddenly passed away, leaving a devastated wife and teenage son. Our plan was to visit family and friends, attend a picnic, and watch the local parade from Kevin and Barb Daily's house. Other old friends were traveling from various places with the same plans. Mark Becker and John Marshall, who both appeared in the identical-rugby-shirts story, were coming in from Indiana and Illinois, respectively, along with their spouses.

During the festivities, someone remarked that John, Mark, and I were all wearing the same colors—black short-sleeve shirts and tan cargo shorts—and that no one else at the picnic was wearing that combination. To document our attire selection, John's wife had us pose for a photo. It wasn't until returning home to Alabama and receiving an email with the photo that déjà vu hit me like a ton of bricks. My thoughts immediately went back to the Indy plane trip, with Dennis as pilot, when we all wore the same rugby attire. We had talked about missing Dennis at the get-together. Was it merely a coincidence, or was Dennis having a little fun with us? My money is on Dennis for completing this circle.

Mark, me and John

Completing Circles: Uncle Duane

The thought that Dennis was somehow involved in our fashion choices would never have occurred to me if it weren't for several other unlikely coincidences over the course of my life, some soon after the deaths of loved ones. In 1999, I was working on the SIBRs program in Sunnyvale when something happened that made me stop and take notice of those other coincidences.

I would arrive in the office at 6:30 a.m., much earlier than my peers, to avoid morning rush hour. While I was on my computer one morning, around 7 a.m., a strange feeling crept over me, as if someone were looking down and watching me from over my shoulder. It was a strong feeling, and it lasted long enough for me to turn around and look up, expecting to see someone, but no one was there. No one was anywhere in the area. I even wondered, a little embarrassed, if the company might have installed a camera in the ceiling to keep an eye on me.

After a few moments, the feeling left me and I went back to work.

That afternoon, my mother called to tell me that her brother Duane had passed away that morning. The next day, I flew out to Ohio for the service in Delaware, his hometown. The evening after the service, I asked my cousins, Tracy and Skip, to share some details about their father's last day. When they got to the time he died, approximately 9 a.m. in Ohio, I realized that they were talking about 7 a.m. in Sunnyvale, the same moment I had the feeling of someone watching me in my office.

It was almost as if Uncle Duane had closed his own circle in my life. How could I think otherwise?

Completing Circles: Patti

Once I settled into a new home in Huntsville and got into a weekly routine, I wanted to get back into Jujitsu self-defense training, something that I had taken up in California. After researching the various options for dojos in the area, I chose Quiet Storm Jujitsu. It was owned by Professor Joe Medlen, who was associated with Sho Shin Ryu, the same national organization as my dojo in Livermore. But I also liked the fact that Professor Medlen had a day job as a bail bondsman, which gave him several opportunities to apply what he taught—and it showed!

One evening after practice at the dojo, I started a conversation with another student, Tom, about shooting. I mentioned that I wanted to resume my firearms training, and he told me that he was an NRA Instructor and would be happy to teach me at his range. As he handed me his business card, I saw his name—Tom Gargulinski.

"Are you, by any chance, related to Patty Gargulinski from MDA?" I asked.

"That's my wife," he replied.

"Holy Crap, I know her! We go back a couple of years." I proceeded to tell him the story about my TDY assignment, and the skill his wife had in commanding a conference room.

With 220,000 people living in the Huntsville-Madison area, what were the chances that I would meet Patti's husband at a random dojo? (And why can't I hit those odds at the roulette table?) As time went on, we became good friends. And yes, when I had the occasion to meet his wife again, she remembered both the DO-12 failure and the resulting stern meeting where I first saw her. This completed circle was one for the books!

29

Poof

In October 2014, as we were approaching our first launch, the program manager walked into my office and said that he "didn't have any more work for me." No discussion, no warning—just look for another program. He told me about another Targets position open in Huntsville that they were hoping I would take, but it was a high-pressure job reporting to a manager who was known for his lack of people skills. At that point in my career, I didn't need the hassle of working for another problem-child boss.

My administrative supervisor, an older guy who had been around the block a few times, was pretty cool. He told me, with a wink, that it was either the position I dreaded or a layoff. A layoff meant receiving twenty-six weeks of severance pay plus accrued vacation. After working almost non-stop for forty-seven years, thirty-five of them in aerospace, I was just plain tired and ready to hang it up. It took all of thirty seconds to decide on the layoff which, at age 62, meant early retirement, and I pulled the ripcord.

I thought back to when Lockheed Aircraft in Burbank hired me, that I would work there for five years and move on to another company. Well, that never transpired and I ended up hanging around the Lazy L (an inside nickname for Lockheed Martin) for over thirty-three years.

In retrospect, my professional engineering career at Lockheed Martin felt like the sparklers my Uncle Duane would bring to our Fourth of July family picnics on the farm. When you put a match to a sparkler, it doesn't catch right away. You need to patiently heat its tip until it finally ignites. Once a sparkler catches, it burns so intensely that thousands of sparks come flying off, emitting a bright light.

Prior to starting at Lockheed, I had warmed up slowly by following other paths until I got my engineering degree, seven years later than the norm. But once I did, my career lit up, shining brightly and staying that way until the afternoon the PM walked into my office and extinguished it. POOF! The flurry of sparks simply disappeared, and there was darkness. And I was okay with the poof.

I'm not one for fanfare or finales. Applause, farewell pats on the back, a framed piece of paper, a smiling photo—not necessary for me. In the end, the real value is more than accolades and praise. Those are as temporary as the award plaques that managers hand out. Guess I'm not a stroker, one of the people types that Gene Beauchamp had told me about, years earlier on the F-117 program.

If you step into my home office today, you won't see any certificates on display. They're all in a folder, tucked away somewhere in one of my filing cabinets. You will, however, see pictures of finished products that I worked on, group photos of my teams, and a couple of hardware souvenirs.

My gratification and personal satisfaction come from reflecting on all the products I have helped create—products that, I hope, helped our country, culture, and society. In one of our father-to-son chats, my father told me that we, as lucky citizens of this great nation, are born into debt. Each one of us owes something to all those who came before us and contributed to the greater good that we benefit from today. Not only our founding fathers, but also road and bridge builders, inventors, carpenters, mill workers, plumbers, accountants, and many more. It's our responsibility to repay the debt to them, and to make our own contributions for the benefit of those in the future.

I'm also thankful for all the wonderful professionals and friends that I had the privilege of working with and getting to know on a personal basis, a rich and fulfilling experience.

For me, it was a good ride and, simply put, it was time to go. And I was good with that.

30

Un-Poof

S o, what were some things I realized about retirement? The clock beside my bed was for telling time; it no longer needed to buzz me awake every morning. I got up when I felt like it and went to bed after my favorite TV shows ended.

It took me a couple of weeks to realize how much stress I had been under—a stress that slowly grew and intensified over the years. It brings to mind the story of a frog placed in a pot of water on the stove. The stove is turned on, and at first the water is comfortably warm. Then the temperature gradually increases. So gradually, that the frog, becoming accustomed to the slow rise in temperature, doesn't feel the need to jump out of the water until it's too late.

I was that frog. It was always, "I can take on this challenge. I can handle this slightly bigger workload or extra responsibility." But unlike the frog, I jumped.

Over the next eleven months of my retirement, I checked all the boxes on my to-do list. Additional insulation, check. Radiant heat barrier in the attic, check. Building a 175-foot railroad tie retaining wall, check.

I had a leisure to-do list as well. Complete several firearms training classes, check. Learn how to reload pistol ammunition, check. Travel, domestic and foreign, check, check, and check.

With my usual efficiency, it wasn't long before my lists were complete. I began to feel bored and realized that perhaps retirement at 63 was a bit premature. I still had a considerable amount of energy, although my stamina had somewhat diminished. But I'm told that's something that eventually happens to everyone.

After twelve months, I began to seriously consider going back to work. One benefit was financial; we can all use a little more savings to fund a better retirement. Knowing I didn't want to jump back into that pot of water and take on responsibility for any products, consulting seemed a viable option with less stress. In an advising position, I could help others produce their products and stay cool.

After some serious self-marketing over a four-month period, I landed a two-week job in the spring of 2016 and discovered that I liked it. Then, in May of that year, I got another short-term, five-month job at the Missile Defense Agency as a subject matter expert. The job dealt with Risk Management, and the contract was good until the end of that fiscal year, September 30th. It was a good gig and I got to work with several of my former customers, some I had interfaced with on the Type X program.

Fortunately, at the end of my term, a new contract was awarded for the follow-on to the Type X program. Because of my previous experience at Lockheed Martin, MDA kept me on and I was assigned to the new program.

At the time of this writing, I'm still at MDA and having fun. I don't work to pay the bills. I work because I enjoy it.

When will I finally retire? The day I'm no longer having fun.

EPILOGUE:

Looking Back . . .

. . . at Life

In looking back at the last sixty years or so, my life has been a full one with seldom a dull moment. And, like anyone's life, it wasn't all good. Probably the most painful events were my brother's suicide and my first divorce. Add to that list the times I butted heads with some of my bosses, the emotional impact of my second divorce, the emotional and physical impact of prostate cancer, and many minor struggles not worth mentioning. But when I compare my life to that of others less fortunate, my life was a breeze and I can't complain.

Indulging in one philosophical view of life, to appreciate *good*, one must live with *bad* to understand the contrast. If *bad* didn't exist, the word *good* wouldn't even be in the dictionary.

My career of mechanical engineering, which started eight years later than the norm, fit me like a RECARO driver's seat in a brand-new Shelby Mustang. Other careers could have worked for me, but the one I chose, with some well-timed help, checked all my boxes. When that alarm went off every morning, I got out of bed with an attitude of positive anticipation for the day ahead. Those who wake up dreading the day should find another use for their lives, because they're wasting our most precious gift from God, time.

Time is something we all want more of, but do we, as individuals, value and use that gift as well as we could? I would roughly estimate that less than 5 percent of my time awake was wasted, and I'm happy with that number. In retrospect, however, I would have shifted my priorities and spent more time with family, especially my spouse and children.

. . . at Opportunities

An Army major from one of my recent programs picked up on something when he read excerpts from this book. He thought it interesting that I graduated from a small, low-profile school, and yet was relatively successful. Of course, all engineering schools have basic requirements for accreditation that must be met. But I believe that the school is just one ingredient, and that the two ingredients with the most impact are hard work and a pinch of luck.

On the career side, from forty years working in or around aerospace engineering, I have discovered that, contrary to the binary perception of engineering from the outside world, there are as many varieties of engineers as there are shades of gray. Within the well-known fields of mechanical, chemical, industrial, etc., the variety of subdivisions is overwhelming, especially at larger aerospace companies.

Working as an engineer for Lockheed Martin in the Aeronautics Division, as one example, one may choose or be hired into a number of functional groups—design, production, tooling, ground support, quality, liaison, mass properties, research, materials and processes—or analysis groups such as stress, thermo, aero, dynamics and others.

And breaking it down even further, the Design Group offers different disciplines: structures, hydraulics, powerplants, composites, controls, weapons systems, antennas, and RCS. Within each specific area, team members fall into a hierarchy depending on experience and the size of the group:

entry-level, individual contributor, lead, manager, and so on. A plethora of possibilities!

Coming out of school, I had some sense that these options existed because of my experience at Pratt &Whitney, but I never imagined there would be so many. A graduate fresh out of engineering school and without an internship or experience in industry would need some time to fully grasp the depth and breadth of options available.

I was fortunate when I started at the Skunk Works to have been placed in Liaison Engineering, which exposed me to many of the disciplines listed above. When I moved up to the Design Group, I already knew that it was the right position for me. That's why I'm a huge advocate, especially in large corporations or organizations, for rotation programs that expose new hires to the wide variety of options before them.

. . . at Hard Work and Luck

Throughout this memoir, I've often referred to hard work and luck, thinking back to that conversation with the gentleman on the El Paso plane who shared his father's words about he who works the hardest being the luckiest.

In retrospect, I have found his advice to be true. Seneca, a Roman Philosopher who lived about AD 50, is attributed with saying, "Luck is where the crossroads of preparation and opportunity meet." If you replace "preparation" with "hard work," the message is the same.

But inside my head, I struggle with the undeniable and still unproven influence of a spiritual component. In the engineering world, we deal with facts and science; we seek evidence. We give little credence to feelings or emotions except for the occasional hunch, and then we still look for justification.

Despite what a skeptic might say, and the lack of physical evidence, the spiritual events that I experienced felt totally real to me, and every detail is embossed into my memory. They led to changes in the way I viewed my life and my priorities. However, memories and feelings don't meet the engineer's standard of proof.

This engineer's standard is based on faith. And, so far, I'm comfortable knowing that someday, the curtain shielding the reality will be pulled back.

In closing, work hard. Keep your eyes and ears open. Live a clean and spiritual life. Maintain a positive mental attitude in both good times and bad. Lead from the front. Treat all people with respect, regardless of how objectionable you may find them. Learn to humbly serve as the butt of a good prank, and be creative with your payback.

It's my experience that if you follow this advice, the important things in life will fall into place as they were meant to be.

Best of luck!

HELPFUL STUFF

O ne cannot help but collect many pebbles of knowledge through- out a professional career spanning over forty years. This chapter is my collection of some of those pebbles, in addition to the ones scattered throughout my story. I picked them up by watching and reflect- ing on the actions and behaviors of others, accepting advice from friends and mentors, and making my fair share of blunders and gaffes. The result- ing observations and lessons learned are organized and placed here for the reader's quick reference.

Projects and programs

As highlighted in previous chapters, several times in my career, I have been asked to take over projects or programs that were in trouble, and I was able to successfully run them to the goal line.

Along the way, I created and refined a personal checklist that I used in each of those successes. This list is generic in nature and somewhat priori- tized. Obviously, one size doesn't fit all and no two projects are alike, so mod- ifications will be required based upon the situation. Consider the following list as a boilerplate outline, and then tailor it as required to fit the need.

- Sit down with your immediate manager to understand their perspective on the situation. Most importantly, obtain and understand the expectations and agree on your deliverables

- Familiarize yourself with the program: specifications, required end product/s, and schedule. Determine the feasibility of delivering on time with the existing schedule by investigating and identifying obstacles to closure. Review the current budget. Expect that budget, schedule or both will be problematic. That's why you were called in to help.

- Meet face-to-face with the customer as soon as possible and get to know the personalities and management styles. Determine the customer's needs, wants, and issues

- Review your organization's structure and meet one-on-one with your leads to get their take on the situation. Learn what issues they have. Then have them introduce you to their team members. Obtain and read resumes for everyone on the team to learn their capabilities and weaknesses. You may find hidden talents not tapped in their current roles.

- Assess and prioritize the schedule. Determine the primary and secondary critical paths. Then start working the first landmine before it explodes. Make changes in the schedule where needed; implement drastic ones if necessary. If possible, create a schedule re-plan and link every line item task from top to bottom. In the re-plan, insert schedule margin (for additional detail, see **When** paragraph below).

- Establish a Line of Balance spreadsheet (a list of hardware and subcontract deliverables) with a person identified as responsible for each item.

♦ Establish an Action Item list (AI). Each action item contains a creation date, description, assignee, status, estimated closure date, and a box to show when it closed. Review the status with your team or leads, as frequently as the program or project dictates.

♦ Establish and hold status meetings that include a five-day "look ahead" with items pulled from the project schedule. Include all team members, if possible, for maximum communication and cohesiveness.

Nothing ever goes as planned; each program is unique with the potential for unforeseen showstoppers. You must be flexible and willing to modify your plans as necessary. My boss Bob Hnat from the TAV program talked about the willow tree and the oak. The willow tree's branches bend easily in the wind because they are flexible, while the oak's branches are stiff and unyielding. Which tree has the best chance of surviving a storm?

Whether you're involved in a new, recovery, or resurrection project, three key ingredients are critical for any project to succeed, the **What**, **When**, and **How**. Think of them as the "three-legged stool of success." Remove one leg, and your project will collapse.

The optimal time for implementation of these legs is the beginning of a proposal, if possible. Waiting until after the contract is awarded is a sure way to guarantee budget and schedule problems.

What is a detailed Drawing Tree (DT). Populate it down to the lowest-level-drawing product. The DT creates a visual image for every component that will be built and feeds quality information to the cost and schedule. The DT also provides an effective communications tool for your design team and those on up the chain of command.

When is the Integrated Master Schedule (IMS). My tool of choice has been and still is Microsoft Project. Your schedule must contain as much detail as you know and can capture. If you have identified unknowns, put them in there as well. If you don't know the duration of a task, then mark it "estimated" and lay in your best guess. Again, I like to insert a margin line item at the end of each major section for unknowns, rather than adding fat to each task within those respective sections. With specific margin line items, you can see real time how much margin you're burning. All tasks must have predecessors and successors which correlate and connect the program from start to finish. For an average two-year all-up schedule, you will probably have a minimum of 1000 and as many as 2000 line items, depending on complexity. One of the most important products generated by any scheduling software is the Critical Path. It serves as a key to program risks.

How is a detailed Process Flow Diagram (PFD) that comes after the What and When products are completed. I usually create this document on a J-size drawing because of its complexity. It's a time-phased document, depicting both series and parallel tasks/events described in images and words. All the major- and mid-level processes, such as testing, transportation, integration and delivery are included. During its generation, you must have the capability and discipline to mentally picture every process for every part, test, or assembly that it will need to convey. Generating the PFD has many benefits: 1) highlights holes missed in planning 2) reveals both complexity as well as ease of various segments and processes 3) shows areas that need to be enhanced with additional tasks 4) serves as a great communication tool for all members of the team and for the customer. The more complicated the program, the more reason to generate one.

Despite pressure from management to hit the ground running, resist slamming it into drive and stomping on the accelerator until you've taken the time to plan. Look at it as though you were making a cross-country road trip. Would you just jump in the car and take off? Of course not. You would plan a route, decide on scenic versus speed, check the weather, reserve hotels—or at least take some of those steps or more to make sure your trip wasn't a bust.

Using these three tools, you'll be much better prepared when the shit hits the fan. And it will hit at some point, coming from any number of directions and caused by an unplanned event, or an obstacle, or tasks simply taking longer than expected. But with a sound plan, you'll be prepared to take the hit and quickly frame your recovery.

If you're assigned to a development program, first it should be structured as a "Crawl, Walk, Run" process.

Crawl: Break down the assembly or vehicle into constituent components and subassemblies. Structures or components that have been qual-tested can go straight to integration. The new designs and unqualified components should get functionally tested or qualified at the lowest level.

Walk: After successful testing of the individual components, integrate them into the next higher assembly for expanded verification testing.

Run: Continue this process until the last test, which is the big one with all components and subassemblies fully integrated.

Using this low-risk approach, if a failure does occur, it will be easier to find the root cause.

Finally, regardless of which problem or design is the toughest, tackle that one first and save the easy ones for last. Hard ones usually take more time, and you don't want to find yourself, in the home stretch, wandering around a dark alley with a dim flashlight. This practice helps avoid those last-minute technical issues, when management tends to breathe down your neck, trying to "help."

Effective management

Another area I worked to strengthen involved management skills. I never reached perfection and, most likely, you won't either. But I found that if I followed the points below, I operated as a more effective manager and I think I engendered more loyalty from my reports. (Of course, this is how I saw myself. I'm sure there are several bosses and subordinates out there that would say, "Oh really?")

Ask and listen: You don't want to be the last one to hear about a critical situation, or a "Taj Mahal Manager," sitting in your cushy chair expecting your staff to come to you. Get out there on a frequent basis, walk the floors and stop in the offices, and visit your suppliers when you think it would be helpful. Get to know your reports and service workers; listen to them share stories about their interests. The more approachable you are, the more willing others will be to keep you informed.

Get a sense of your program's biometrics. You must be able to *feel* the pulse of your program. In a general sense, programs or projects are a type of living organism.

When an issue arises, ask questions without expressing any emotion other than empathy. Listen carefully, continue to ask questions until you have a full grasp of the issue, and don't interrupt. NEVER lose your cool, show physical or verbal signs that might be interpreted as disgust, and never, ever blame others.

Assess: Ask your team about options available for fixing issues. Usually, the obvious one will stand out above the others.

Guide, mentor, and assist: If possible, let your team determine the best solution, or make it a joint decision. They're more likely to take ownership as stakeholders than as directed subordinates.

Direct: Only when all else fails.

If criticism is warranted, do it in private, never in public. Never express your personal opinions about other team members, subordinates, or superiors to anyone at work. Don't bad mouth other organizations, customers or vendors in a public forum.

Be cautious of your body language. I've been told that about 80 percent of face-to-face communication is nonverbal. Work out any issues you may have in a private setting using non-defensive language. Always discuss issues from a position that focuses the goal line. This is all easy to say, tough to do.

After I retired, I reflected back on the managers and supervisors I had worked for over the years to identify the ones I admired the most and tried to emulate—my A-list. All managers bring their assets and liabilities to the job. I chose the ones who had more of the former than the latter. Of the fifty-seven that I was able to remember, only six, about 10 percent, were what I would consider top-notch.

So how does this metric translate to advice? If it were representative of every industry and not based on one person's experience, expect to have nine average-to-crappy bosses for every outstanding leader. And when you do find a good one, assume that they'll be moving on soon, because top-notch managers are always in demand. Do a good job for them, and chances are they'll pull you along on their upward climb. Outstanding leaders surround themselves with outstanding colleagues and subordinates.

These pebbles have worked for me throughout my career. Keep the ones that apply to your project, ignore those that don't, and modify as necessary. I hope you find this list helpful.

PROGRAMS REFERENCED IN CHRONOLOGICAL ORDER

J-58 Gas Turbine	Engine-Engr. Aid	P & W, W. Palm Bch, FL
L-1011 Aircraft	Designer	Lockheed Burbank, CA
F-117 Aircraft	Liaison Engineer	Lockheed Burbank, CA
F-117 Aircraft	Designer	Lockheed Burbank, CA
E-Program	Designer	Lockheed Burbank, CA
YF-22 Aircraft, Pole Model	Project Lead	Lockheed Burbank, CA
TAV Program	Design Lead	Lockheed Sunnyvale, CA
SCAMP	Design Lead	Lockheed Sunnyvale, CA
ACES Program	Design Lead	Lockheed Sunnyvale, CA
FBM Snubber FRB	Project Lead	Lockheed Sunnyvale, CA
JDAM	Design Lead	Lockheed Sunnyvale, CA
D-5 Missile	Designer	Lockheed Sunnyvale, CA
PATS Antenna	Project Lead	Lockheed Sunnyvale, CA
Airborne Laser (ABL)	Design Lead	Lockheed Sunnyvale, CA

SBIRS	Design & Lead	Lockheed Martin Sunnyvale, CA
Container Experiment	Project Lead	Lockheed Martin Sunnyvale, CA
Project 9	Cost Acct. Manager	Lockheed Martin Sunnyvale, CA
Project 9	P. L. & Subcontracts	Lockheed Martin Sunnyvale, CA
P-Program	Lead & Subcontracts	Lockheed Martin Sunnyvale, CA
DO-12	Project Lead	Lockheed Martin Huntsville, AL
Orion Capsule	Design Lead	Lockheed Martin Sunnyvale, CA
EMRBM	Project Lead	Lockheed Martin Huntsville, AL
Type-X Program	Subcontracts CAM	Lockheed Martin Huntsville, AL
Various Programs	SME	MDA Huntsville, AL

BIBLIOGRAPHY AND RECOMMENDED READING-SHORT LIST

Clarence L. "Kelly" Johnson and Maggie Smith, *Kelly: More than My Share of it All* (Washington, D.C.: Smithsonian Institution Press, 1985).

Ben R. Rich and Leo Janos, *Skunk Works: A Personal Memoir of My Years at Lockheed* (New York: Little, Brown & Co, 1984).

J. P. Womack, D. T. Jones and D. Roos, *The Machine that Changed the World* (New York: Simon & Schuster, 1990).

Edward Lovick, Jr. (2010) *Radar Man, A Personal History of Stealth*

Richard J. Hernstein, Charles Murray. (1994) *The Bell Curve*

Richard P. Feynman. (1988) *What Do You Care What Other People Think?*

Musashi, *The Book of Five Rings*

Sun Tzu, *The Art of War*

Nassim Nicholas Taleb. (2007) *The Black Swan*

James Burke. (1978) *Connections*

Dale Carnegie (1936) *How to Win Friends & Influence People*

M Scott Peck ((1985) *The Road Less Traveled*